THE HOME-BORNEO HEAD-HUNTERS

ITS FESTIVALS AND FOLK-LORE

William Henry Furness, 3rd, M. D.

THE
HOME-LIFE
OF
BORNEO HEAD-HUNTERS

ITS FESTIVALS AND FOLK-LORE

BY

WILLIAM HENRY FURNESS, 3rd, M. D.; F. R. G. S.
MEMBER OF THE AMERICAN PHILOSOPHICAL SOCIETY; OF THE AMERICAN ORIENTAL SOCIETY;
DE LA SOCIÉTÉ DE GÉOGRAPHIE; FELLOW OF THE ANTHROPOLOGICAL INSTITUTE OF GREAT BRITAIN AND IRELAND

This book was originally published in 1902 and is in the public domain

CONTENTS

Preface 2
Home-Life 6
Ceremonies at the Naming of a Chief's Son 24
Early Training of a Head-Hunter 67
A War Expedition 86
'Jawa' or Peace-Making 128
Personal Embellishment 183
Permantong, or Lali – A Bornean Species of Taboo 206
The Punans 220
Tuba-Fishing 247
Index 254

Preface

While to scenery, it is distance,—and photography,—which lends enchantment, it is, on the contrary, propinquity which, in my experience, lends to the Borneo Head-Hunters and to their Home-life, a charm which cannot be wholly dispelled even by the skulls hanging from the rafters of their houses. After living among them, for months at a time, an insight is gained into their individualities and peculiarities which a casual sojourn can never disclose. Some, of course, are ill-tempered, crotchety, selfish; others, again, are mild, gentle, generous. The youths have their languishing loves, which they are eager to confide to sympathetic ears. The maidens are coy, or demure, or bashful, when their lovers are near, and delight in teasing and tormenting. The Bornean mothers and fathers think their babies the prettiest that ever were born; and the young boys are as boyish as school-boys here at home, and are quite as up to all mischief.

It is so much easier to descend than it is to rise in what we call civilization, that, before a month is passed in a Kayan or a Kenyah house, the host and hostess, who, on first sight, seemed to be uncouth savages, frightfully mutilated as to eyes, ears, and teeth, are regarded as kind-hearted, devoted friends. It becomes well-nigh impossible to realise that they cannot add the simplest of sums without the aid of fingers and toes; and that Cæsar, Shakespeare, and Washington are to them meaningless, unpronounceable words.

Their honesty, (in a twelve months' residence the only thing stolen from me was a tooth-powder bottle,) their simple, child-like nature, their keen interest in the pursuit of the moment, and their vivacious excitability, place them in advance of any 'savages' with whom I have ever, in my many wanderings, come in contact.

The greater part of my time in Borneo was spent among the Kayans and Kenyahs of the Baram district of Sarawak; consequently, in the following pages I have barely mentioned the Dayaks, (or Ibans, as they call themselves,) or any of the coast tribes, of whose home-life I saw comparatively little; so much has been already written about these tribes that I am jealous for my friends of the far interior.

I have refrained from giving dates, or details, as to the height of the thermometer, or as to my personal comfort or health, or as to the number of men who carried my luggage, or what I had for breakfast, or dinner,—items extremely important at the time, but of no permanent or public interest whatsoever.

I have attempted to portray the impressions made on a mind which I endeavoured to keep wholly unprejudiced, and even free from all tendency to despise as gross superstition that which by the natives is deemed holy and religious. I do not wish to forget that I was received as an honoured guest in Kayan Long-houses; it is a sorry payment to vilify my hosts. Rather let me throw what charm I may over the daily round of the natives' dateless life.

To His Highness Rajah Brooke, I owe sincere thanks, not alone for his kind hospitality, but for facilities in freely visiting all parts of his admirably governed territory, and for his liberal permission to collect Ethnological and Natural History material.

It is with pleasure that I acknowledge my indebtedness to the Rajah's Resident, Dr. Charles Hose, for valuable information on innumerable points, for a genial hospitality of many weeks, and for the opportunities to visit the people of his District, 'my people,' as he likes to call them, whose manners and customs he knows so thoroughly, and whose interests he guards with so much vigilance and efficiency.

W. H. F. 3rd.

July, 1902.

THE TATTOOING OF A KAYAN MARRIED WOMAN

ABAN AVIT'S HOUSE, ON THE TINJAR

THE CLUSTER OF STAKES AND POLES IN THE FOREGROUND IS A CHARM TO DRIVE AWAY THE EVIL SPIRITS OF ILLNESS. IN THE LEFT CORNER OF THE PICTURE, THE TALLER POLE, DECORATED WITH STRIPS OF PALM LEAVES, IS THE RECORD OF A SUCCESSFUL HEAD-HUNT. THE PHOTOGRAPH SHOWS ABOUT TWO-THIRDS OF THE LENGTH OF THE HOUSE.

Home-Life

The houses in which the Borneo people live are the outcome of a life of constant apprehension of attacks from head-hunters. In union alone is strength. Surrounded by a dense jungle which affords, night and day, up to the very steps to their homes, a protecting cover for enemies, the Borneans live, as it were, in fighting trim, with their backs to a hollow square. A village of scattered houses would mean the utmost danger to those on the outskirts; consequently, houses which would ordinarily form a village have been crowded together until one roof covers them all. The rivers and streams are the only thoroughfares in the island, and village houses are always built close to the river-banks, so that boats can be quickly reached; this entails another necessity in the construction of the houses. The torrents during the rainy season, which, on the western half of the island, lasts from October till February, swell the rivers with such suddenness and to such an extent that in a single night the water will overflow banks thirty feet high, and convert the jungle round about into a soggy swamp; unless the houses were built of stone they would be inevitably swept away by the rush of water; wherefore the natives build on high piles and live above the moisture and decay of the steaming ground.

Beneath the houses is the storage-place for canoes that are leaky and old, or only half finished and in process of being sprung and spread out into proper shape before being fitted up with gunwales and thwarts. It is generally a very disorderly and noisome place, where all the refuse from the house is thrown, and where pigs wallow, and chickens scratch for grains of rice that fall from the husking mortars in the veranda overhead. Between the houses and the river's bank, — a distance of a hundred yards, more or less, — the jungle is cleared away, and in its place are clumps of cocoanut, or Areca palms, and, here and there, small storehouses, built on piles, for rice. In front of the houses of the Kayans there are sure to be one or two forges, where the village blacksmiths, makers of spear-heads, swords, hoes, and axes, hold an honorable position. In the shade of the palms the boat-builders' sheds protect from the scorching heat of the sun the great logs that are being scooped out to form canoes; the ground is covered with chips, from which arises a sour, sappy odor that is almost pungent and is suggestive of all varieties of fever, but is really quite harmless. In the open spaces tall reedy grass grows, and after hard rains a misstep, from the logs forming a pathway, means to sink into black, oozy mud up to the knees.

Just on the bank of the river there are usually four or five posts, about eight feet high, roughly carved at the top to represent a man's head; these have been put up after successful head-hunting raids, and on them are tied various fragments of the enemy, — a rib, or an arm, or a leg bone; these offerings drive away the evil Spirits who might wish to harass the inmates of the house, and they also serve as a warning to enemies who may be planning an attack. Such remnants of the enemy are held by no means in the same veneration with which the heads, hung up in the house, are regarded; after the bits of flesh and bone are tied to the posts they are left to the wind and rain, the pigs and chickens.

POSTS ERECTED IN FRONT OF A HOUSE AFTER A HEAD-HUNT

ON THESE POSTS ARE HUNG SMALL FRAGMENTS OF THE ENEMY. THE CARVED FACES RECORD THE NUMBER OF HEADS TAKEN.

Not a few of the Kayan and Kenyah houses have been enlarged and built out at both ends until they shelter from six hundred to a thousand persons, and are possibly a quarter of a mile long; this statement seems to verge on a 'traveller's tale,' but it must be remembered that these houses are really villages of a single street, the veranda being a public thoroughfare, unobstructed throughout its whole length, in front of the private family rooms. From the ground to the veranda a notched log serves as steps, and it takes no little practice to enable a clumsy, leather-shod foreigner to make a dignified entrance into a Borneo house. The notches in the log are worn very smooth by the constant tread of bare feet, and, as there is no door-mat below for muddy feet, the shallow notches are often coated with a thin and treacherous layer of slime; foreigners generally enter a Kayan house on all fours, giving to the natives an astounding idea of occidental manners. To the natives, however, these steps present no difficulties,—no matter how steep or slimy the log, they seem to get a firm hold on the edge of the notches with their prehensile toes, and, even with heavy loads on their backs, walk up as freely as if on level ground. The piles on which the large houses rest are fifteen or twenty feet high, and often two and a half feet in diameter at the base; in some few cases they are carved with grotesque figures of human heads, or conventionalised representations of monkeys, crocodiles, and snakes.

In the days before the humanising influence of Rajah Brooke's government had spread to the Kayans, and Kenyahs, and tribes living in the central highlands, it was a preliminary custom, in building a house, to thrust into the first excavation wherein the heavy, up-river, corner post was to rest, a young slave girl alive, and the mighty post was then planted on her body, crushing out her life as a propitiatory offering to the demons that they should not molest the dwelling. Happily, this custom has been abolished, and in houses now built, instead of a girl, a pig or a fowl has been substituted. I regret to add that in the house of Tama Bulan, wherein we lived for some time, the earlier custom had been followed.

The roofs of the houses are partly thatched and partly shingled. The shingles are hewn out of 'Billian,' a species of iron-wood which stands for years, without decay, the alternate change from damp to dry heat;

each one has a square hole at its upper end, through which passes the strip of rattan wherewith it is tied to the frame of the roof. The thatching is of palm leaves doubled over a stick five feet long and then bound on the roof, overlapping like shingles; several layers of these palm-leaf tiles make a perfectly tight roof, and one that may be quickly repaired. In building a Borneo house not a nail is used and but very few pegs; all beams and cross-ties are either roughly mortised and bound together, or else merely tied one on top of the other with rattan or with long strips of fibrous bark; even the planks of the floor or walls are not pegged, but are tied to one another and laced to the joists.

In selecting the site for a house, before so much as a twig of the jungle is cleared away, there are always extreme and prolonged pains taken to discover, through 'Omen birds,' the temper of the evil Spirits of that locality,—to a Kayan there are no such things as beneficent Spirits. Until this temper is definitely discovered the whole household is under a 'permantong,' or taboo, and may not leave its quarters, whatever these quarters may be, be they the old house or a temporary shelter.

This taboo lasts many days,—ten days perhaps,—during which certain old men who know the habits of omen birds and omen animals make frequent trips into the surrounding jungle to observe whether the red hawk fly, or whether the little honey-sucker bird, (called the 'Isit,') chirp to them, on the right or on the left of their path. Finally, they must catch a glimpse of the barking deer, and then the welfare of the house is assured. As soon as one of these favorable omens is seen the hunters build a fire,—a signal to the birds and animals, conveying thanks for favors received. When the last of these omens has been seen, then, and not until then, is the permantong over and the clearing for the house begun, and all hands turn in to help.

The veranda, or main street, of these houses is where all public life goes on; here, in the smoky atmosphere that pervades the place, councils of war and peace are held, feasts spread, and a large part of the daily work performed. It is seldom a very bright or cheery place; the eaves come down so low that the sunlight penetrates only at sunrise and sunset, and the sooty smoke from the fires turns all the woodwork to a sombre, mahogany hue. The floor is usually of broad, hewn planks, loosely laid upon the joists, with little care whether they fit close or warp and bend up out of shape, leaving wide cracks through which a small child might fall; they show plainly the cuts of the adze, but they soon become polished by the leathery soles of bare feet shuffling over them from dawn till dark. At intervals of perhaps fifty feet are fireplaces,—merely shallow boxes about five feet square by six inches deep, filled with flat stones imbedded in clay; herein are built the fires that give light at night and add to sociability at all times; no council or friendly talk is complete without the crackle of a fire to enliven it and to keep away evil Spirits. Of course, no chimney carries off the smoke, which must disperse as best it can among the cob-webby beams overhead, after giving a fresh coat of soot to the row or bunch of trophy-skulls that hangs in the place of honor opposite to the door of the chief's room. The odor of burning resinous wood, mingled with other ingredients, saturates the veranda, and in after-life the smell of musty garret, cedar-wood chests, and brush-wood burning in the autumn instantly recalls the veranda of a Borneo long-house. It must be confessed that occasionally there mingles with this aromatic odor a tang of wet dog, wallowing pig, and ancient fish, but then, after all, these are not peculiar to Borneo.

THE VERANDA OF ABUN'S HOUSE AT LONG-LAMA ON THE BARAM.

THE ROW OF SKULLS HANGS FROM A BEAM SUSPENDED OPPOSITE TO THE DOOR INTO THE CHIEF'S ROOM; BENEATH THE SKULLS IS A CLAY AND STONE HEARTH

WHEREON A FIRE IS LIGHTED EVERY EVENING, NOT ONLY TO GIVE LIGHT, BUT ALSO "TO DIFFUSE A PLEASANT WARMTH ABOUT THE SKULLS." THE WALL OF PLANKS, EXTENDING DOWN THE RIGHT SIDE OF THE PHOTOGRAPH DIVIDES THE FAMILY ROOMS FROM THE PUBLIC VERANDA. THE BOYS ON THE RIGHT ARE SEATED UPON ONE OF THE LARGE MORTARS WHEREIN THE RICE IS HUSKED. ON THE LEFT IS THE USUAL CROWD OF LOUNGERS SEATED UPON THE LOW PLATFORM WHICH EXTENDS ALMOST THE WHOLE LENGTH OF THE HOUSE BELOW THE EAVES.

There is no ceiling to a Borneo long-house; above the plank walls that divide the private rooms from the veranda, and from one another, the space is open to the ridge-pole. Across the rafters are placed, higgledy-piggledy, spare boards, supplies of dried rattan, and long rolls of bamboo matting; here and there, hang rice baskets, hampers, wicker fish-traps of all sizes; and sometimes every available space is hung with bunches of bananas, which must be gathered green and ripened in the house, to keep them from the depredations of monkeys and fruit-bats. At intervals along the roof are trap-doors of palm-leaf thatch, which can be lifted and supported on a pole to admit more light and air. For the accompanying photograph as many of these trap-doors as possible had been raised in order to get enough light, and just over the row of skulls several shingles had been taken off. In the photograph this row of forty or fifty skulls hanging from a beam begins with one that looks like a gourd, on the left.]

Along the whole length of the veranda at its outer edge, under the eaves, is a railing, or fence, of poles and boards tied to the upright supports of the roof; when parents in the household are unusually careful of their children, this fence extends from the floor to the eaves, which are here only about four feet above the floor, but usually this safeguard is only two poles about six inches apart, and serves as a rest for the backs of men when they sit on the wide platforms, which are raised about a foot above the floor and extend nearly all along this lightest and airiest part of the house. These platforms are of much smoother planks than the floor, and are often of single huge slabs of wood from the buttress-like roots of the 'Tapang' tree. To make these lounging-places still more luxurious, mats of fine rattan or bamboo strips are spread upon them, and then a Bornean desires no more comfortable place whereon to sit by day or to recline by night, unless, perchance, it be a dry sandy river-bank, above the rapids, where are no crocodiles, mosquitoes, nor pestiferous black-flies, and where grow gigantic Caladiums, whereof a single leaf is large enough to cover his entire body and afford him a protection from the rain, as impervious as a rubber blanket. These low platforms, especially in front of the chief's door, which in the photograph is directly opposite the row of skulls just mentioned,] are the places where men congregate after nightfall to gossip and smoke round the fire, which is here needed to dispel darkness, dampness, and evil Spirits. Diversion is often created by one of their number, who, more self-sacrificing than the rest, goes through the violent antics of a war-dance, or sings long, rambling songs about the valorous deeds of Tokong, who originated head-hunting, or of some other warrior who gained the blissful regions of 'Apo Legan' by the slaughter of his enemies. Whatever the theme,— and the themes are generally legends or familiar stories,—the details are supplied by the imagination of the singer, who composes them on the spur of the moment, while the chorus is singing the last two or three words of the verse, followed by 'Ara Wi Wi, Ará!' a meaningless refrain, like our own 'Tooral, looral,' although I am afraid that in a former publication I unwittingly gave the impression that its translation was 'Sleep dear little one, sleep.'[1]

To these songs an accompaniment is often played upon an instrument, known among certain Kayans and Kenyahs as a *Kaluri* or *Kaleeri* or *Kaludi*. It is probably of Chinese origin; substantially the same instrument is used in China and in the countries bordering thereon to the northward and westward. I saw almost an exact counterpart of the Borneo Kaluri played by the Naga tribes inhabiting the hills near the Burmese border. It consists of a bottle-shaped gourd with six hollow reed pipes set into the body of it; a finger-hole is cut in each pipe at such a place that the fingers of both hands while holding the instrument can cover all the holes. The middle reed is the longest, and is therefore the bass; it has no finger-hole, but its tone is subdued by a movable cap at the end; the neck of the gourd forms the mouth-piece. The music of a Kaluri somewhat resembles that of organ pipes, perhaps slightly nasal in timbre, but having an impressive charm withal when heard amid native surroundings, in the dim, smoky atmosphere of a Borneo long-house

---

[1] See *Folk-lore in Borneo*, p. 29.

at night, when light from the flickering fire accentuates the harsh lines in the faces of the natives grouped about the performer, and where eyes, robbed of the softening effect of lashes and eyebrows, glitter fiercely, and where brass studs glisten in pointed and blackened teeth, and where carnivorous ferocity and alertness is imparted to the men's faces by the upturned tiger-cat's teeth in their ears,—all these so intensify the relentless, recurring, savagely persistent minor key of the Kaluri that dim questionings are stirred whether or not, after all, bloodshed be not the noblest aim in life and the blackened and battered skulls overhead be not glory's highest prize. Music hath charms to soothe,—Kaluri music hath charms to *make*,—a savage breast.

JUNGLE IN THE LOW COUNTRY NEAR THE BARAM FORT

THE LARGE LOG IN THE FOREGROUND HAD BEEN ROUGHLY HEWN FOR MAKING A CANOE, BUT ON ACCOUNT OF A WARNING FROM AN OMEN-BIRD WAS ABANDONED.

In the verandas of the Kayan houses there are always large wooden mortars wherein rice is hulled; from morning until night there is always to be heard, somewhere in the length of the house, the rhythmical thumping that betokens that young girls are at their everlasting task of threshing, hulling, and winnowing the rice for the daily repast. The rice mortars are cut from large logs of wood, and are somewhat prismatic in shape, usually five or six feet in length by two or three feet wide on the upper surface; they rest upon a base not more than a foot wide, [as in the photograph, where, on the right, some boys are sitting on the edge of a mortar,] but are made firm by stout poles that are set into them and extend through the flooring to the ground below, and also by strong braces that are pegged to the house beams above. The upper, broad surface of these mortars is slightly concave, and is divided into two or more sections, each with a round pit six inches deep in the centre. In husking the rice, these pits are filled with the grains, and then two, or sometimes four, girls, standing upon the broad top, pound the rice in the pit with wooden pestles five or six feet long, which they hold at the middle with both hands. The motion that they adopt is exceedingly graceful; they stand with the heels together, and lift the pole or pestle perpendicularly above their heads as high as they can reach, then, bending the body at the hips and swinging the arms down, they jam the pestle into the rice pit; as they raise the pestle again for another stroke they put one foot forward to push back into the pit the grains that may have jumped out on the flat surface of the mortar. When thus pounding, the young girls keep perfect time with one another, the poles never clash, and each girl brushes back, first with one foot, then with the other, the grains she jostles out, so that when they pound fast the motion becomes almost a dance. Not infrequently the pestles are ornamented at their upper end with several sliding rings or a sliding block that jingles when the pestle strikes; this rhythm and this jingle impart some alleviation to the tedious task. When the husks are all beaten off, the chaff is winnowed out by tossing the grains and catching them again and again upon a flat basket. The task of hulling rice falls exclusively to the women and girls; they begin it when they are so small that they can barely lift the pestle, and, once started in proficiency, the task becomes an element of their life, and their winnowing-baskets are hung as symbols of industry on their graves.

In the accompanying photograph of a veranda, the coffin-shaped box hanging on the wall on the right is a case wherein war-coats are kept, so that the goat-skin and feathers whereof they are made cannot be eaten by hungry dogs. The photograph does not give an absolutely correct idea of the daily appearance of a veranda; there is only one dog to be seen,—there should be at least a dozen. The exposure had to last so long that, lest the dogs should jar the camera, we had them all driven down the notched log to the ground, and then the log was turned wrong side up, so that they could not return. (We tried this method of getting rid of the dogs once at night when they were particularly troublesome and quarrelsome, and seemed to prefer our bodies to any other couch, but the crafty curs knew an adequate revenge; as soon as they found themselves locked out they made night hideous with concerted and disconcerting baying at the moon, until we were glad to readmit them. Our leather shoes we always had to tie high up on the rafters at night, or they would have been eaten up, all but the soles and heels.)

This photograph was taken from a point just opposite the chief's door, about half way down the length of the veranda.

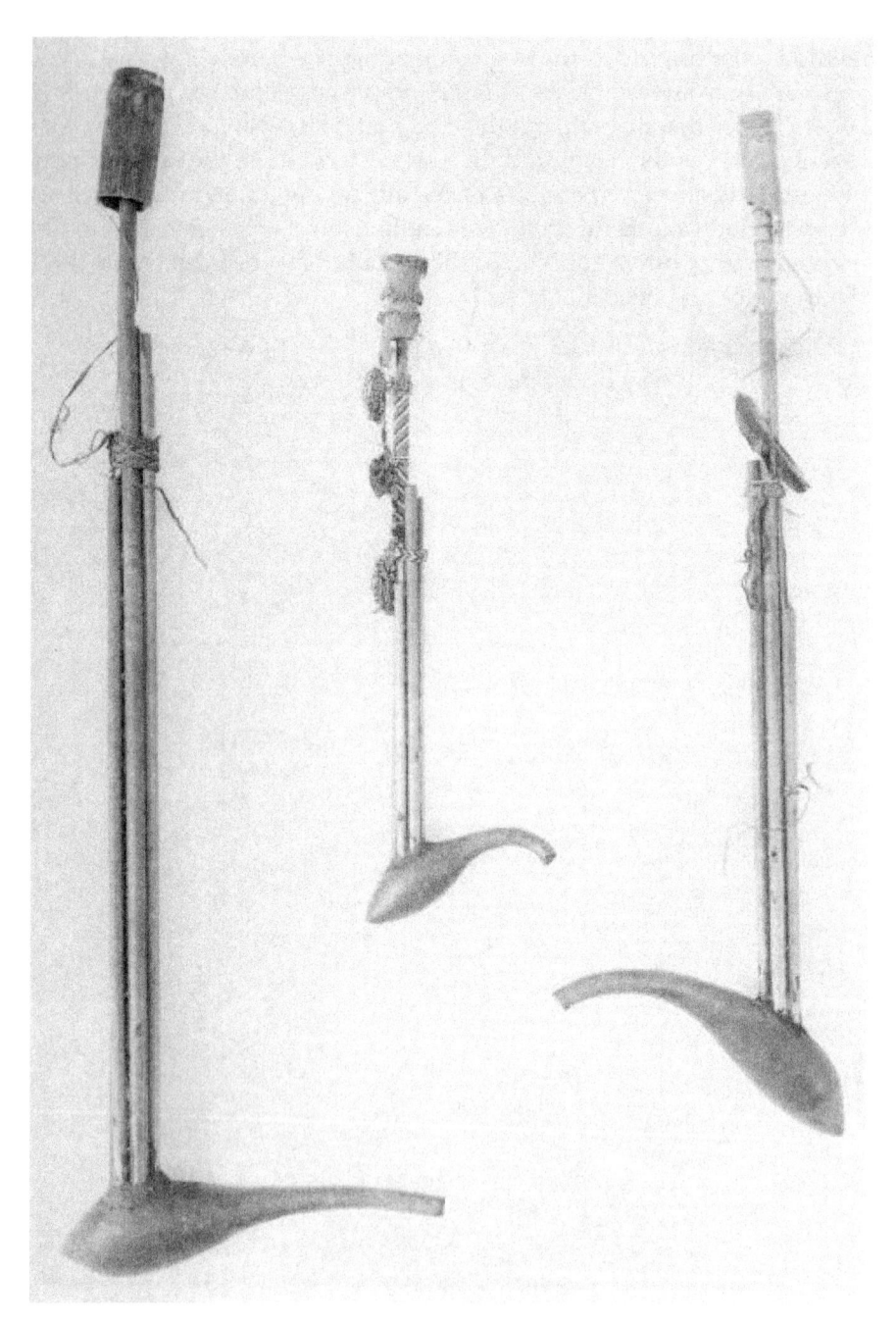

KALURI — MUSICAL INSTRUMENTS.

The family rooms, even those of the chief, are often dark and disordered little compartments, and in them it is usual for anything but quiet to reign; the smallest of the infants sprawl on the floor, the fowls, that have flown up to steal the rice drying on the platforms at the back of the house, squawk and cackle, and the old women who are relegated to culinary sinecures, such as rice-boiling, add a mild confusion by whacking the dogs that wander in and prowl about the cooking-pots. The space under the eaves, unlike that of the veranda, is boarded up from floor to roof with rough hewn planks; the only light is admitted through small windows in the planks or through trap-doors in the roof. Of course, there is never a pane of glass in the windows, and I doubt that the natives of the interior, or even of the coast towns, ever saw a glazed window.

In spite of the darkness of these rooms, there is, nevertheless, more industry in them than is ever found in the veranda; the women are really the workers of the community, and seem never to sit absolutely idle gossiping, as do the men; when the harvesting is finished and there is no more work out of doors, they employ their time in making mats and baskets of rattan strips, in stringing beads into ornaments for war-coats, in weaving cloth for feast-day garments, and in fashioning large, round, flat hats for the next season's work in the rice-fields. During the rainy season, the husbands and lovers seem to have little to do but sit in the veranda, lounging against the railing at the open space under the eaves, whence they can observe the river and its incidents, and watch the smoke from their long cigarettes curl and drift among the fronds of tall cocoanut palms that sway and rustle on a level with their faces. These are the days when war expeditions are planned and resolutions made to add fresh heads to the row already hanging in front of the chief's door, and thereby remove any taboo enforced by the death of relatives. The men seldom linger in the family rooms during the day, and the women, except when busy hulling the rice in the big wooden mortars, spend no time in the veranda.

The doorway from the veranda into the family room opens into a very dark and narrow passage, with the partition wall of the next room on one side and a rack for fire-wood and long bamboo water-bottles on the other. Possibly it is to announce the coming of a guest that the flooring of these little entries is always laid down in such a wobbly fashion, and of logs and billets of wood so rickety, that it is impossible to walk upon it without stumbling or an unseemly clatter; whatever be the reason, such is the fact, and I never stepped over the high threshold into the dark of one of these passages without expecting to trample on babies or to fall through on the wallowing pigs below.

    The end of the passage opens directly into the middle of the room, where the floor is better laid and made more comfortable by the addition of mats. The whole room is perhaps twenty-five feet square, but this space is diminished by two or three little sleeping-closets for the parents or for the grown daughters. In the right-hand corner, near an opening under the eaves, the floor is raised a few inches, where the sons or the male slaves sleep at night, and where the women work at their bead-stringing or mat-making during the day; it is the lightest and pleasantest place in the room. Against the partition that divides the veranda from the room is the fireplace, which is merely a hearth of clay and large flat stones, as in the veranda, except that in the centre are three stones whereon the cooking pots rest; above is a rack, just beyond the reach of the flames, where firewood is kept dry, ready for immediate use, and where scraps of pork may be preserved by the smoke. Here and there, on the walls, on hooks made of deer horn or of the twisted branch of a tree, hang all sorts of implements for farming, fishing, and hunting, little hoes for weeding the rice-fields, home-made axes called 'biliong,' scoop-nets for catching fish when the streams are poisoned with Tuba root, paddles, spears, large round sun-hats, basket-like holders for the few but valuable china plates used only on feast-days, and sometimes, as a mural decoration, the warrior's coat and shield are displayed; these personal adornments, however, are usually kept in the little sleeping-closets, or else in a wooden case attached to the wall of the veranda just outside the room.

A FAMILY-ROOM, OR LAMIN, IN ABUN'S HOUSE ON THE BARAM.

BEYOND THE MAN SLEEPING ON THE FLOOR, IS THE FIRE-PLACE; ABOVE IT, A RACK WHEREON WOOD IS KEPT DRY, READY FOR USE. ON THE LEFT OF THE FIRE-PLACE IS A DOORWAY OPENING INTO ONE OF THE SMALL SLEEPING-CLOSETS FOR THE MARRIED PEOPLE OR FOR THE UNMARRIED GIRLS. LEANING AGAINST THE WALL IS A BAMBOO WATER PITCHER WITH A COVER OF PALM-LEAF MATTING; ABOVE, HANGS A BASKETWORK CASE FOR HOLDING CHINA PLATES. ON THE WALLS OF THE ALCOVE ARE HANGING SEVERAL LARGE, FLAT, PALM-LEAF HATS, A SCOOP-NET, AND A FLAT SIEVE OF SPLIT RATTAN. THIS ALCOVE, WITH ITS SLIGHTLY RAISED FLOOR, IS THE SLEEPING-PLACE FOR THE UNMARRIED MEN OF THE FAMILY, OR FOR THE MALE SLAVES.

These sleeping-closets, partitioned off for married couples or for unmarried girls and widows to sleep in, are as dark and stuffy as closely fitting planks can make them, and the bed is merely two or three broad and smooth planks whereon a fine rattan matting is spread; sometimes a roll of matting or a bundle of old cloth serves as a pillow, but more often there is nothing but the flat boards. On one occasion, I was ushered into the bedroom of a Chief's daughter who was ill with the grippe and had asked for medicine; it was almost pathetic to note the attempt that this poor 'first lady' had made to adorn her little boudoir. By the light of a sputtering lump of damar gum, burning in an earthen dish and disseminating mainly an aromatic smell and dense smoke, and only incidentally a flickering light, I could see that there had been fastened on the walls bright pieces of gay-colored cloth, and over in one corner, in a sort of pyramid, were her 'ladyship's' best bead-work baskets; even ill as she was she called my attention to them. She was tossing in fever on the most uncomfortable bundles of coarse cotton calico, (sadly in need of washing,) which she had crumpled in folds to counteract the unevennesses of her bed of planks. Grippe is intolerable enough when the patient is surrounded with every comfort, on a soft clean bed and in an airy room, but the lowest depth of discomfort is reached when to the fever are added a sweltering tropical heat in a dark closet, the air dense with damar smoke and soot, a bed of hard boards, and never a drop of ice-water. Yet in the midst of all these, the girl, fortunate in her ignorance, was dignified and uncomplaining.

On all ordinary occasions, the family eat together, usually only twice a day, morning and evening, in the family room. In the centre of the room is placed a large wooden dish piled high with boiled rice, and then, as a plate for each member of the family, is set a piece of fresh banana leaf, whereon are a little salt and a small quantity of powdered dried fish, highly odorous; this is the usual bill of fare, but it may be supplemented with a sort of mush or stew of fern-frond sprouts and rice, or with boiled Caladium roots and roasted wild yams. When there is a feast and guests from neighboring houses come to dine, the meals are spread in the veranda and the menu is enlarged with pork and chicken, cooked in joints of bamboo, which have been stoppered at both ends with green leaves, and put in the fire until they are burnt through, when the cooking is done to a turn.

All hands are plunged into the common dish of plain boiled rice, and it is 'excellent form' to cram and jam the mouth as full as it will hold. It is, however, remarkable how deftly even little children can so manipulate the boiled rice before conveying it to their mouths, that hardly a grain is spilt; it always filled me with shame when dining *en famille* with the Kayans or Kenyahs to note what a mess of scattered rice I left on the mat at my place, while their places were clean as when they sat down; to be sure, I did not follow my hosts' example in carefully gathering up and devouring all that had fallen on the unswept floor. Whenever I apologized for my clumsiness, their courtesy was always perfect; the fault was never attributed to me, but rather to their poor food and the manner in which it was served.

The long intervals between their meals and the unsubstantial quality of their food give them such an appetite and force them to eat so voraciously that the usual welcome by a Kayan host to his guests is, 'Eat slowly,' and this admonition is unfailingly given. They seem to regard their family meals as strictly private, and would always announce to us that they were going to eat,—possibly to give us warning not to visit them at that time, and they were also quite as punctilious to leave us the moment that our food was served.

When any member of a family is ill and calls in the services of an exorciser, or, as they call it, a 'Dayong,' the room is placed under a taboo, or permantong, and only members of the family may enter, and even they are under certain restrictions, for instance, to refrain from singing or playing musical instruments, and they are debarred from eating meat. The sign of a taboo is a bunch of green leaves or a flat basket used in winnowing rice tied to the door-post. If, by accident, a man should violate this taboo, he must pay a fine to the owners of the tabooed room; this fine is usually a few cheap beads or a china plate. They seem to regard this custom with such reverence that we availed ourselves of its privileges whenever we wished for privacy, and although the natives laughed at our adoption of their customs, they left us nevertheless strictly alone when we tied a basket or a bunch of leaves in front of our little apartment in the veranda.

VERANDA OF A NEWLY BUILT IBAN HOUSE ON THE BAKONG RIVER, A TRIBUTARY OF THE BARAM.

THE SKULLS ARE HANGING NEAR THE VERY END OF THE VERANDA IN A CLOSE CLUSTER, AND NOT SUSPENDED ALONG A BEAM. THE FLOORING IS OF STRIPS OF THE STALK OF THE NIBONG PALM, INTERLACED AND TIED TO THE BEAMS. THE LOW, SQUARE BOX IN THE FOREGROUND IS A HEARTH, LINED WITH CLAY AND FLAT STONES. BESIDE IT ON THE FLOOR, AND ALSO HANGING FROM A RAFTER IN THE UPPER LEFT-HAND CORNER, ARE WATER GOURDS. IN FRONT OF THE DOOR, LEADING INTO ONE OF THE FAMILY-ROOMS, A WOODEN RICE MORTAR IS TURNED UPSIDE DOWN. ON THE DOOR IS HUNG A FLAT BASKET, TO INDICATE THAT THE ROOM IS TABOOED ON ACCOUNT OF ILLNESS. BEYOND THE RANGE OF THE PHOTOGRAPH ON THE LEFT, AND EXTENDING OUT INTO THE OPEN AIR IS A WIDE PLATFORM OF SPLIT BAMBOO, WHEREON THE RICE BEFORE IT IS HUSKED IS SPREAD OUT ON MATS TO DRY.

Possibly, this description of Home-Life in a Borneo household would be incomplete without a detailed account of its ordinary daily routine, which, as I saw it during several weeks in Tama Bulan's house, is somewhat as follows:—[2]

The crow of a cock breaks the silence of the night; then a dog rouses up, yawns and stretches, and shakes off the ashes of the fireplace where it has been sleeping, and begins the daily round of quarrels with its companions. Then daylight gradually creeps in and a door slams with a bang at the far end of the house, where the poorer and hard-working people live; a woman with a bundle of bamboo water-vessels slung on her back hurries along to the stairway down to the river. She looks just the same as when she went to sleep. Her dress is the same and her hair is in a disordered tangle, and as she walks her feet come down heavily on the warped planks and make them rattle, no doubt to wake the lazy men, who sleep on and let the women make the fire and get the water while they snooze. Soon she comes back, her hair dripping and glossy, and little drops of water still clinging to her skin. By this time there is quite a procession of women going down to bathe and get the cooking water from the river, and there is a slamming of doors and a few wails from the children. Then the men who have been sleeping on the raised platform along the open space below the eaves, unroll themselves from their shroud-like coverings of cotton cloth, once white, and a little hum of conversation springs up, possibly a comparison of dreams, the interpretation of which, as in all uneducated classes, has a great bearing on their daily life. The mother who comes out with her babies in her arms, or sitting astride of her hips, knows nothing of our custom of caressing with a kiss, but in her maternal bursts of affection she buries her face in the neck of the child and draws in a long breath through her nostrils; in fact, she smells it. In their language the verbs *to smell* and *to kiss* are the same. Then down she goes to the river and takes the morning bath with her child in her arms, sometimes holding it by the hands and letting it kick out its legs like a frog,—the first lessons in swimming. One by one the men straggle off to bathe in the river, and never missed the opportunity of telling us that they were going to bathe, and when they returned they were also most punctilious in telling us that they *had* bathed. With all this bathing, however, they are not a clean people. Soap is unknown to them, and they never use hot water, consequently their skins have not the soft, velvety appearance that constant bathing usually produces.

---

[2] The substance of the following paragraphs appeared in a Paper which I read before the American Philosophical Society, 1896.

(We once gave some of the girls cakes of Pears' soap, but they ate them.)

After bathing there is a lull in the activity of the house, while the married women and young girls cook the morning meal of boiled rice and dried salted fish.

Breakfast over there are always parties of men and women setting out for the clearings where the rice is planted, and armed with a billiong (an adze-like axe, which they use) and their parang, and their spear, the men go down and get the boats ready, and the women follow after with the paddles, and hampers to bring back bananas or bunches of tender, young fern-fronds, which they make into a stew. Then the house settles down to the ordinary tasks of making large flat hats of palm leaves, drying and flattening banana leaves for cigarette wrappers, or of pounding the husks off the rice by the women, and sharpening spears or decorating parangs by the men industriously inclined; but the latter are rare. They usually spend their time in gossip with their companions or merely sit and blink, soothed by long draughts of smoke drawn deep into their lungs from the strong Java tobacco cigarettes, which they roll for themselves. Men, women, and children all smoke.

Morning wears into afternoon, and then the hours are given up to recreation by those who had not gone in the forenoon to the rice-fields. Occasionally, we sat on the river-bank and watched from a high bluff the young boys or the young girls playing in the water. Here let me say that we never saw the faintest conscious immodesty in either the one or the other. We used to sit lost in admiration at the skill of the girls in swimming. It was a sort of game of tag that they were always playing, only, instead of one chasing all, all chased one, and this one would get off some little distance from the rest and then suddenly disappear under water. Then the chase begins. All swim as fast as they can to the spot where she had vanished, some swimming with a rapid overhand stroke, while others swam entirely under the water. Then, possibly still in front of them, possibly far behind, up bobbed the girl who was '*it*,' shaking the water from her eyes and giving a shout of derision at her pursuers. Down she went again and the chase was renewed, all under water, so long, sometimes, that the surface of the river became perfectly smooth, and no one would have imagined that in another moment it would be again bubbling up and dashed into spray by a crowd of laughing, shouting, black-haired, merry girls. Back and forth, up and down, they splashed from one side of the river to the other, until one of the men called to them from the house to stop their sport lest they rouse a sleeping crocodile. This put an end to the fun. Another thing, which was quite new to us, was the way in which they could play a sort of tune by splashing their hands in the water and flapping their arms to their sides. They stood in a group, and by sinking their hands, the back downward, in the water and then clapping them above the water and slapping their elbows to their sides, they produced a series of different sounds, like that of a large stone dropping into a deep pool, with a rhythm that was perfect and very pleasing.

Afternoon deepens into dusk, and the workers from the fields come home and trudge wearily up the bank and disappear through the little doorways. Small flickering lamps are lit here and there, and the fire on the hearth disseminates a cheery glow and warms up the row of human skulls hanging in front of the Chief's door. The veranda gradually becomes deserted, even by the dogs, while the families are eating their evening meals in their private rooms. The noisy flapping of wings and cackling of chickens seeking their roosts for the night and the low, contented grunts of pigs beneath the house betoken that the day's foraging is over.

After the evening meal the men once more lounge out in the veranda and, grouped about the low, smouldering fires, smoke their long cigarettes and gossip, or listen to the drone of the Kaluri played by one of the youths. By eight or nine o'clock they are all once more wrapped in their coverings of cotton cloth, and, stretched in a row beneath the eaves, lulled by 'lisp of leaves or ripple of rain.'

Ceremonies at the Naming of a Chief's Son

One day, during my second visit to Borneo, I was sitting in the veranda of a native's house on the Tinjar River, chatting and gossiping with my host and his household, when I noticed in the group a man whose face was very familiar to me and closely associated with some incident or other in the year before; I looked at him for a minute, and then asked if he were not the man who had so effectively helped us when we were unable to find men to paddle our canoe down the river from the house of deceitful old Laki La. He modestly replied that he was one of the men; whereupon I reiterated my gratitude to him; but, unfortunately, his name, once so familiar to me, had quite escaped my memory, and, apologizing for my forgetfulness, I asked him what it was. His countenance fell; he looked much embarrassed for a moment, and then nudging the man sitting next to him looked from him to me. His neighbor took the hint, and at once told me the name, which was one I had never before heard; I concluded, therefore, that either he or I had mistaken the incident. A little while afterward I happened to meet the man again when he was alone, and being so sure in my recollection of his face, asked him if that were really his name which had been told to me; he assured me that it was, but even then I doubted, and insisted that it was not the name by which I had known him a year ago. 'You are quite right, Tuan,' he replied, 'but since you were here I have been exceedingly sick—so sick that the evil Spirits were trying to make my soul wander away from my body [and here his voice dropped to a whisper]; so I changed my name; now they will not know where to find me.' He looked furtively on all sides, as if afraid that the trick would be overheard by the Spirits; it was only after much persuasion and repeated assurances that the Spirits could never harm him through a white man that I induced him to tell me his former name, which he did in a timid whisper close to my ear. This incident, trifling in itself, is valuable, I think, in that it adds another to the list of instances recorded in Dr. J. G. Frazer's valuable *The Golden*

Bough (vol. i., pp. 404-420), where the utterance of a personal name is fraught with an unknown and deadly peril. To speculate on the source of this mysterious dread is tempting enough,—especially since in theorizing about the beliefs prevalent in the youth of the world there is no one who can contradict. As to its antiquity there can be no doubt; and that it is well nigh universal, the records of folk-lore are full of proof. It is sufficient here and now to note its existence among the Kayans and Kenyahs in the interior of Borneo, where, moreover, this unwillingness to utter the name of a person extends to inanimate objects. When they have planned a Tuba fishing, nothing will induce them to utter the word for fish. A Kayan, Kenyah, or Punan never thinks of saying that he is going to search for camphor, but that he is going to look for the 'thing that smells,' and even this he says in a whisper, for fear the camphor crystals deep in their secret, native home might hear and elude him after he had all the trouble of chopping down the tree.

TAMA BULAN, THE MOST INTELLIGENT CHIEF IN THE BARAM DISTRICT.

HE IS OF THE KENYAH TRIBE, AND LIVES ON THE PATA RIVER, ABOUT TWO HUNDRED MILES FROM THE COAST. THE NAME TAMA BULAN MEANS 'FATHER OF MOON,' AND WAS ASSUMED AFTER THE BIRTH OF HIS FIRST CHILD, A DAUGHTER, NAMED 'BULAN.' HIS PREVIOUS NAME WAS WANG.

These superstitions connected with the utterance of a name are deeply rooted among the Borneans, but the interdiction on the speaking of names of relatives is not so extended as it is among some other primitive people, notably the Kaffir women of South Africa, who may not speak a word, or even a word containing a syllable, resembling their husband's name or the names of any of his male relatives, but must use paraphrases which do not contain the interdicted syllables.[3] Among the Kayans and Kenyahs, as far as I know, the restriction on the utterance of names of relatives extends only to the fathers-in-law of a married couple, whose names must not be mentioned by either the husband or the wife. Again, it is most ill-omened for a son to mention his dead father's name; and, of course, neither man nor woman dare pronounce their own name; this is a downright courting of all conceivable disasters and diseases. It is quite possible that this unwillingness to mention their own name leads them to adopt a substitution, which for every-day use sufficiently designates them. Thus, when a child is born the parents substitute for their own names the name of the child prefixed by 'Tama,'—*father of*,—or 'Tina,'—*mother of*,—a highly ingenious device; the combination thus formed is really no name at all; it is merely a designation. On the same principle, when wife or husband dies the survivor is designated as 'Aban,'—*widower*,—or 'Bállo,'—*widow*,—of such a one. The simple-hearted folk evidently believe the Spirits to be the very strictest of constructionists, and that they pay no attention to anything but the name itself, pure and uncombined; to a substitution they pay no heed.

One might suppose that under such circumstances it would be rather more convenient, certainly far less hazardous, to have no name at all. But without a name there would be no existence,—how could a nameless thing be admitted to 'Apo Legan,' or Heaven? The receiving of a name is really the starting-point of life; and the bestowal of a name by the parents is probably the most serious of parental duties,

---

[3] J. G. Frazer, *The Golden Bough*, p. 413.

and to be performed with ceremonies proportioned to their rank. So essential is the ceremony of naming that in the enumeration of a family an unnamed child is not counted; and should a child die before the ceremony of naming, a Kayan or Kenyah mother would mourn for it no more deeply than had it been stillborn. This is true even when an unnamed child lives to be nearly a year old.

Children of the labouring classes are named at the completion of what the father considers a successful harvest of rice; and the day is set for the ceremony when the phase of the moon is deemed auspicious; the rest of the household, with the exception of the few friends who assist, is undisturbed. When, however, the son of a Chief is to be named, and thereby admitted into the circle of kindred or into humanity, the occasion is made a holiday, and a feast-day for the whole community, and friendly households far and near for miles around are summoned to attend. It was on such an occasion as this, that we, Dr. Hiller and myself, had the rare fortune to be the visitors of Tama Bulan, the most influential Chief in the Baram District of Sarawak.

We had but recently come to Borneo when we first met Tama Bulan at the Baram Fort, whither he had come to attend a peacemaking and ratification of friendship with certain Ibans who had recently moved into the district, and also to barter at the Bazaar the rattans, raw gutta-percha, and camphor that his people had collected. We were much impressed with the sedate dignity of this inland Chief and the quiet demeanor of his people, and greatly desired to become more thoroughly acquainted with them. As he was sitting cross-legged on the veranda of Dr. Hose's bungalow and discussing the affairs of the up-river people, he mentioned with pride that as soon as he reached home there were to be great feastings and ceremonies over the naming of his only son. Here was the chance of a life-time could we but induce him to let us be present during these ceremonies. We were totally unacquainted with Tama Bulan's language, — the Kenyah, — or even with Malay, the Lingua Franca throughout Borneo and the greater part of the adjacent islands, — but what of that? Sign language is all sufficient at a pinch, and, furthermore, a vocabulary of a hundred and fifty to two hundred words is soon acquired, and, in simple Polynesian dialects, will prove adequate for all ordinary purposes. I doubt if any Caucasian has ever witnessed these ceremonies as observed by the Kenyahs; at any rate, as far as I know, they have never been recorded; accordingly, we strenuously urged Dr. Hose to obtain for us an invitation. When he, finally, with much tact, told the Kenyah

Chief how anxious we were to return with him and pay him a visit in his home, the proposal was listened to with unusual gravity. Tama Bulan's keen black eyes studied us very carefully from head to foot; evidently he was weighing the chances of possible accidents either to us or to his people. At last he broke silence, and, having in mind the dangerous rapids in the river, his first question was, 'Can the Tuans [*gentlemen*] swim?' When assured that we were adepts in that art, he deliberated again for a while, and then asked, 'How can we get along without talking? the Tuans cannot speak my language, nor can I speak theirs.' This objection was put aside by Dr. Hose, who flatteringly rejoined, 'Ah, Tama Bulan does not know the power of the white man as well as I thought he did. The Tuans are so clever that in two days they will be able to speak your language as well as you do yourself; everything is easy to a white man.' Whereat Tama Bulan smiled broadly, and, after another searching gaze, consented to let us return with him, — provided the government would not hold him responsible for any accidents. And so it was agreed, and the matter settled. But for some time my conscience did not acquit me of the conviction that we had forced ourselves unwarrantably on an unwilling host; however, I solaced myself with the cheering reflection that we could amply recompense him at the close of our visit.

Tama Bulan is a Chief of the Kenyah tribe, and his home is between three and four hundred miles in the interior of the island, on the Pata River, a tributary of the Baram. His house is one of the largest and best built in that large district, and is, moreover, conducted on rigid principles of Kenyah morality. Of course, in such a community theft is unknown, where every one knows every article of property belonging to the others. Thieving being thus eliminated, one of the strictest rules in Tama Bulan's house is that no woman, young or old, shall frequent the veranda after nightfall; young girls must remain in their family apartments, and if they have sweethearts they must entertain these sweethearts there, and not sit sentimentally with them in convenient dark corners, whereof there is no lack in a veranda. Another of Tama Bulan's rules is wisely sanitary, namely, that no rice may be hulled in the veranda; the dust arising from the chaff is not only irritating to the nostrils, but is also apt to produce an itching rash on the skins of young children and infants. To each family is apportioned a small shed at the back of the house for the threshing and hulling of the rice; and where, moreover, the workers are to a certain degree secluded, and not liable to distraction and idleness as they would be in a veranda.

Tama Bulan himself is one of the best types of a Bornean Chief. Although only about five or six years ago he was a passionate head-hunter (and is still, I believe, in his heart of heart, having been carefully and religiously brought up by his parents), he is now a genuinely loyal and highly valuable subject to Rajah Brooke, and has been made a member of the 'Council Negri,' a legislative body composed of the Rajah, of the English Resident Officers of the first class, of several of the most influential Malays in Kuching, the capital of Sarawak, and of three or four of the most trustworthy and intelligent of the native Chiefs. This Council Negri, one of the admirable devices of that wise legislator, Rajah Brooke, meets once a year to discuss what might be termed national affairs, and to lay before the Rajah all complaints or suggestions.

THE HANDLE OF A PARANG, OR SHORT SWORD, CARVED OUT OF DEER'S HORN, AND DECORATED WITH TUFTS OF HUMAN HAIR AND WHITE GOAT'S HAIR. THE DESIGN IS CALLED "KOHONG KALUNAN" – A MAN'S HEAD, BECAUSE IT IS COMPOSED OF SEVERAL GROTESQUE FACES.

Our host, with whom we became eventually intimately acquainted, and of whom I became very fond, (his staunch friendship on one occasion saved our lives,) was a man of about forty-five, well built, but not muscular in appearance, about five feet six inches tall, his face broad, cheek bones somewhat high, eyes wide apart, lips thin, and mouth large but well shaped; his smile is ready, kind, and benignant, and his laugh reveals two rows of polished, regular, and highly blackened teeth. In his general expression there is not the least suggestion of what we are pleased to term a savage; his demeanor was quiet, unobtrusive, and dignified, and his voice soft and subdued. In obedience to fashion (to whose behests every son of Adam is a slave) his ear-lobes are pierced, and by means of heavy copper rings, inserted in early infancy, are so elongated that they almost touch his shoulder. The upper part of each ear is also perforated, so as to permit the insertion of a tiger-cat's tooth; this ornament is, however, inserted only for full dress; in every-day life a plug of wood about half an inch in diameter is substituted. These 'looped and windowed' ears serve, in the lack of clothing, as pockets, and are extremely convenient receptacles of cigarettes, or even of boxes of matches. His head is shaved in a straight line extending horizontally from one temple to another, but his straight, black hair is allowed to grow long at the back. I describe Tama Bulan thus somewhat at length because he is a typical and pure-blooded Kenyah.

The skin of the Kenyahs and Kayans is not yellow, but somewhat darker than a Chinaman's; they have none of the characteristics of the thick-lipped African negro, nor have they the bushy, krinkly hair of the Papuans; nor the almond eyes, or the stretched inner canthus of the Mongolians.

On ordinary occasions, they wear nothing but a loin-cloth, made either of bark fibre of native manufacture, or of red, white, or black cotton cloth, bought from Chinese traders in the Bazaar (the Malay name for a trading-post). On their heads they wear a close-fitting, pointed cap made of thin strips of rattan, (or 'rotan' as they call it,) or of bamboo woven into a pretty chequered pattern of black and yellow; when exposed to the sun they often exchange this skull cap for a broad, flat disc made of palm leaves and tied to the head.

In order that we might not burden Tama Bulan and his canoes with our heavy luggage of several boxes of tinned provisions, cooking utensils, and not a few articles for judicious presents, such as tobacco, bolts of cheap cotton cloth, and a quantity of steel bars, wherefrom the natives forge parangs and spear-heads, Dr. Hose kindly lent his large dug-out, which afforded comfortable quarters for ourselves and also (a pleasant arrangement) for our host, the Chief. The dug-out was about sixty feet long and five feet wide amidship, made of a single log, but deepened considerably by the addition of planks bound along the sides with rattan and caulked, thus giving about six inches of additional freeboard. The party consisted of eight canoes, bearing Tama Bulan's followers, and as they swung into view after their start from the Bazaar, a short distance below Dr. Hose's bungalow, which stands on a high and steep bluff, they shouted to us and loudly rapped their paddles on the sides of the canoes, by way of urging us to hurry down to the bank, so great was their impatience to be fairly started on the homeward voyage. We had divided the central third of the canoe into two compartments, separated from each other by our luggage, sleeping mats, mosquito curtains, etc.; in the forward division we took up our quarters, reserving the aft division for Tama Bulan, who seemed to fill and overflow it with his shields, parangs, large sun-hats, bundles and baskets packed with cheap cloths, Malay sarongs, heavy copper ear-rings, pressed glass bowls, and beads of every description,—all commissions executed for his household and received in exchange for jungle products. Where, or how he managed to sleep I cannot imagine,—but he was the Chief, and uneasy lies the head that wears a crown. As for us, we were really comfortable with rubber blankets and thick rugs spread over the flooring of bamboo strips which rested on the thwarts amidship, except that after awhile, as sitting cross-legged became misery, we longed for a chance to dangle our legs. Overhead was a roof of 'kajangs'—a thin thatch of palm leaves—to protect us from the sun and rain. As soon as the canoe was all packed, and our Chinese cook and two Malay servants were properly ensconced in other canoes, and it took a deal of excited shouting and innumerable shiftings before this was accomplished to the satisfaction of the crew of each canoe, the word was given, and with a few powerful strokes from the paddles which sent the spray dashing and the water eddying all about us, we were round the turn of the river and had bid adieu to even such comfort and civilization as the Baram Bazaar affords, and had fairly started on this journey to the far interior of Borneo, with its untold possibilities, at the mercy of unknown natives, of whose very language we knew not a word.

THE CHINESE BAZAAR AT CLAUDETOWN – BARAM FORT.

IT CONSISTS OF A ROW OF SEPARATE SHOPS, WITH A WIDE VERANDA IN FRONT. TO TEMPT THE NATIVES, THERE IS THEREIN DISPLAYED EVERY VARIETY OF MERCHANDISE, FROM GLASS BEADS TO SEWING MACHINES, FROM SILK SCARFS TO CALICO, FROM ARRACK TO WHITE-SEAL CHAMPAGNE, FROM CHINESE CONFECTIONS TO PATENT MEDICINES.

MEXICAN DOLLARS ARE THE MEDIUM OF EXCHANGE, BUT A LARGE PART OF THE TRADING IS IN THE JUNGLE PRODUCTS COLLECTED BY THE NATIVES, SUCH AS RATTANS, GUTTA-PERCHA, CAMPHOR CRYSTALS, TAPIOCA, SAGO, RHINOCEROS HORN, EDIBLE BIRDS'-NESTS, ETC.

IN THE PHOTOGRAPH, WHICH WAS TAKEN DURING THE RAINY SEASON, WHEN STEAMERS CANNOT CROSS THE BARAM BAR, THE OPEN SPACE IN FRONT OF THE ROW OF SHOPS IS PILED UP WITH RATTANS AWAITING SHIPMENT. THE GROUP OF IBANS CLAD IN MALAY SARONGS ARE ADJUSTING THE GAFFS ON A FIGHTING-COCK PREPARATORY TO ENGAGING IN ONE OF THEIR FAVOURITE SPORTS.

Until the central high-lands of Borneo are reached, the river scenery is utterly uninteresting and monotonous; near the coast, where the river water is still brackish, the banks are lined with the feathery Nipa palm with fronds like stiff ferns, often forty feet high. These palms have no stalk, but start in a cluster close to the ground or just at the surface of the water, and grow so close together as to make an almost impenetrable wall. At first they appear beyond measure beautiful, with their polished, glancing leaves, quivering and wavering with every breath of air; and the gleam of the dark maroon mid-rib of the leaves swaying slowly with the motion adds a flickering light to the deep shadows, suggestive of mystery through the illimitable aisles beneath the over-arching fronds. But a closer acquaintance reveals the realm of crocodiles and snakes, not to mention the unromantic mosquito, diminutive in size but mighty to annoy. [Once on a time, in the salad days of my Borneo life, I tried to take a photograph in the depth of a Nipa swamp, but indeed, the torment of the myriads of rapacious and voracious mosquitoes which attacked me while making the necessary exposure was absolutely intolerable. When I threw the focussing cloth over my head I entrapped unwittingly so many mosquitoes that I could hardly see to focus; in one minute they had stung me on the lips, cheeks, eyelids, within the nostrils, and on the ears. I am not a coward, but I really could not face, literally, the overwhelming onslaught for the two minutes which, on account of the dim light, were necessary for the exposure; the poor wretch of an Iban who was with me, clad only in his loin-cloth, actually cried and moaned with the suffering; my negative turned out to have been under-exposed because both of us had been over-exposed.] After twenty or thirty miles of this unbroken wall of Nipa palms the charm diminishes, until at last all beauty is lost in satiety and the sight becomes infinitely tedious. It is, by the way, from these Nipa palms thus growing in brackish water that the natives obtain salt; the ashes of the stalks, leaves, and roots are soaked in water, which, when the water is evaporated, yields a very dirty looking salt, much preferred, however, by the natives to that which can be bought in the Bazaar. Where the Nipa palms end wild sugar-cane begins, and its gray-green, grassy stalks become quite as monotonous as the Nipa; it is not until the low muddy banks of the river change, first to sandy and then to pebbly beaches, that the real beauty of the river begins.

Notwithstanding the exciting novelty of our situation I cannot say that that first day passed quickly, or that it was full of interest; a day is a long time when it is spent hour after hour in gliding along a wall of unvarying green. Tama Bulan's last purchase at the Bazaar was a Chinese tea 'cosy'—a little cylindrical basket lined with felt, holding a small teapot closely fitted and keeping the tea hot for a long time. Every five minutes, as it seemed, we heard the click of the hasp; then the creak of the cover as the teapot was lifted out; then a loud and prolonged sucking sound as Tama Bulan luxuriously drained with infinite gusto a diminutive cup of tea. I am quite sure that the teapot was so often replenished from the river that it yielded, finally, nothing but tepid and muddy water,—but ah! the charm of drinking from a china teapot and quaffing with an ecstatic gurgle! The old Chief often peered through a little crevice in the pile of luggage between us, and then he would chuckle and give vent to a flow of words which bubbled out so fluently between his broad smile and his blackened teeth that they seemed to stumble over themselves and end off in fit of coughing. We smiled, nodded, mumbled, and pretended to understand it all,—even the cough.

Toward dusk of the first day we halted at a sloping sand-bank, enclosed on three sides by a dense hedge of wild sugar-cane, full of mysterious rustlings and sighings, and stretching far over the low ground to the beginning of the jungle. The other boats of our party were already tied up to the shore, and the brown-skinned men in their scarlet waist-cloths were bustling about collecting fire-wood and building cranes whereon to hang their little kettles of rice. A row of fires was soon started, and the short twilight of the tropics deepened into dark; the dancing fires cast giant shadows on the gray-green leaves of the wild sugar-cane, and lit up the intent faces of the natives and their glistening eyes and brass-studded teeth as they squatted about the fires or stirred the bubbling pots. When the meal was ended and they were smoking long cigarettes of Java tobacco rolled in the dried leaf of the wild banana, the moon rose and the embers of the fires were scattered. To become more at home with our hosts and fellow travellers we entered into their games and contests in broad jumping, high jumping, and tugs of war. Alas for me, I was indiscreet enough to turn a handspring for them, and also walk on my hands, feats that apparently were perfectly new to them; ever after I was introduced by Tama Bulan to his friends with the laudatory remark that I could walk on my hands and turn over; whereupon, be it on muddy bank or hard floor, I was incontinently obliged to repeat the performance.

SCENE ON THE BARAM

A RAFT BRINGING RATTANS TO THE BAZAAR.

When the Chief retired to his boat it was the signal for the general breaking up of the pastime. Grass mats were brought from the boats and spread on the sand, whereon the men threw themselves, and, in the soft light of the tropical moon, we were all soon lulled to sleep by the constant drone and chirp of nocturnal insects.

Early the next morning we awoke and saw, by the light of the setting moon, the men shaking out their mats and making preparations for starting off. We were soon under way once more, and between waking and sleeping we were conscious of the rhythmical click of the paddles and of an occasional command of 'Mishai! Mishai!' from Tama Bulan to the rowers to wield their paddles stronger and faster.

It is not worth while to give in detail all the long fifteen days of our journey up the river, or of our visits to the various houses on our way; as may be readily inferred, there were many hours, monotonous, weary, and at times perplexing; three men died of the grippe, — which seems to have penetrated this most remote corner of the world, and was at that time fairly epidemic on the Baram. Unfortunately for us, these deaths were attributed to our presence; a council was held, and we were, in consequence, requested to return; but we protested our innocence, asseverated our friendship, and having already come so far begged to be allowed to go on, and finally allayed their fears and gained their consent. We distributed tobacco and medicine freely, and held numerous clinics in our boat and on the river-banks, for the treatment of a troublesome inflammation of the eyes, probably due to the depilation of eyelashes, added to constant bathing in the muddy, turbid river. At one time the rains descended and the floods came, and for five mortal days we were tied up to the bank of the river, unable to advance on account of the irresistible current and of the immense logs and trees that were constantly brought down by the stream. During this enforced inactivity we became better and better acquainted with our companions; we learned their names and a generous smattering of their language,—an easy task; we powdered many and many a wound and abrasion with iodoform, whereof the color and smell delighted them, and brought us greatly into favor. From the boys who accompanied the party, and who acted as general 'slaveys,' we picked up most of our familiarity with the language; they were always ready to talk unconstrainedly with us, and we amused ourselves while amusing them. One little fellow in particular we never grew tired of watching; his actions were as quick and inquisitive as those of a monkey, with the added revelation of a shrewd intelligence. I blush to confess that we taught him the bad manners of putting his thumb to his nose and wiggling his fingers whenever his elders told him to do anything for them; the outraged indignation with which this perfectly novel and insulting gesture was received, and the sly winks little Adom gave us over his shoulder, at every repetition, were truly delightful. One day we painted him from head to foot, with water colors, in stripes of blue, green, yellow, and black, to his joyous delight; and although he was greeted with outbursts of laughter by the whole party, he was, nevertheless, exceedingly reluctant to wash off his decoration. Lishun was another of our particular 'pals,' and a sturdier, braver little fellow it would be hard to find; he was certainly not over eight or nine years old, but on many occasions he saved our canoe from being swept back round a sharp turn of the river where the current ran at headlong speed. Just as the men were losing all hold with their poles and the bow of the canoe was inevitably swinging out toward the middle of the river, Lishun, with a rattan rope attached to the bow, in one hand, would plunge into the swirl of water, and, disappearing for a breathless moment, would emerge among the roots and branches on the river-bank, with a shout of laughter from pure enjoyment, and there make fast his rope, while the polers with a fresh hold brought the bow of the canoe to the right direction. Why his little limbs were not torn to pieces and his body battered against the rocks in that seething, whirling water is to be explained, I suppose, only by the fact that water was almost as much his element as the earth or air. Then there were Terluat, a solemn little fellow, who preferred listening to talking; Apoi, a fat and greasy lumpkin with an inane giggle if you did but look at him; Deng, about sixteen years old, as clean-limbed and symmetrical an example of adolescence as can be imagined; and Gau, an ugly little monkey-faced boy, but as bright as a new penny and an expert in cat's-cradle. Blari, Tama Bulan's nephew, and Tama Talun, the Chief's right-hand man and a kind of 'master of ceremonies,' were our particular friends among the men, apart from the Chief, Tama Bulan, himself.

SOME OF OUR KENYAH COMPANIONS DURING OUR VISIT TO TAMA BULAN'S HOUSE.

THE WELL-BUILT MAN IN THE CENTRE IS BLARI; THE BOY ON THE RIGHT IS LISHUN, SQUATTING CLOSE BY HIM IS DENG, AND STANDING BETWEEN HIM AND BLARI IS DENG'S ELDER BROTHER. THE NAMES OF THE THREE OTHERS I DO NOT RECALL.

During the weary days of waiting for the floods to subside, we used the youngsters to teach us their language, and never missed the opportunity of having them in our boat, where we could make the idle moments pass in showing them a collection of illustrated papers that we had brought with us. One evening, after they had been giving us a concert of their own music, we tried what effect some of our songs would have on them. Somewhat to my surprise, such melodies as 'The Suwanee River' and 'The Old Kentucky Home' possessed not the smallest charm for them; they evidently thought our style of singing exceedingly amusing,—perhaps it was; and they made no attempt to restrain their laughter. Afterward we heard them trying to imitate it by merely a continuous rise and fall of voice in a high key. One song, however, did appeal to them as more like their own; this was 'Three Old Crows Sat on a Stone' with the refrain of 'Jimmy Magee Magaw;' frequent repetitions were called for; and finally they caught the air and adapted words of their own to it, with a refrain of 'Balli Boin Akán,' a phrase wherewith the Dayongs, or priests, address pigs that are about to be sacrificed.

At the end of five days, during which the freshet acquired daily and nightly new strength from heavy thunder-showers, the Omen Birds, the guides and guardians of these people, were harangued and alternately cajoled and threatened. At one time a fruitless attempt was made to deceive them. The whole party disembarked, and, donning their spears and parangs, made a wide circuit in the jungle, so as to make the birds believe that the canoes were not going home, but were on an ordinary hunting expedition. Once Tama Bulan, while sitting in our canoe, shook his fist at a bird perched on a bough near by, and upbraided it for not causing the rain to cease. When he observed our interest in his proceedings his face broke into an embarrassed smile, and he poked me in the ribs, and said, chuckling, 'Tuan does not believe in the birds, does he? He thinks Tama Bulan is crazy.' I assured him that when in Borneo the white man was as much under the protection of the birds as were the natives themselves, which was equivocal, but gratifying to his belief. On another occasion both Dr. Hiller and myself were sprinkled with water from a stick cut into shavings at one end and held on the blade of a parang. Had the skies immediately cleared, it would have afforded such irrefragable proof of our league with evil Spirits that I know not what would have been our fate. But at last the waters fell, and, finally, we reached the mouth of the Pata River, the large tributary whereon Tama Bulan lives; and then after three days of hard boating over rapids which necessitated our disembarking twice and carrying our boat and all our baggage overland for a short distance, we arrived within one turn of the river from Tama Bulan's house. Here a halt for final purification was made.

An arch of boughs about five feet high was erected on the beach, and beneath it a fire was kindled, and then Tama Bulan, holding a young chicken, which he waved and brushed over every portion of the arch, invoked all evil Spirits which had been accompanying us, and forbade them to follow us further through the fire. The fowl was then killed, its blood smeared all over the archway and sprinkled in the fire; then, led by Tama Bulan, the whole party filed under the arch, and as they stepped over the fire each one spat in it vociferously and immediately took his place in the boats.[4] A half hour more brought us to the huge log which serves as a landing along the shore below the house of Tama Bulan.

BULAN, THE DAUGHTER OF TAMA BULAN.

(From a photograph taken, and kindly loaned, by Professor A. C. Haddon, F. R. S.)

Tama Bulan did all in his power to show us that we were welcome, and assigned to us an immense slab of Tapang wood about eight feet square and suspended about three feet above the floor by beams from the roof; hereon we could spread our mats at night and keep our possessions out of the reach of the hungry mongrel dogs that

---

[4] For instances elsewhere of the observance of similar purification, see *The Golden Bough*, Frazer, vol. iii., p. 398 *et seq.*

pervaded the veranda. As soon as we were thus properly shelved, and had our things stowed away comfortably, our host came and requested us to visit him in his private apartment and meet his family. With much pride he conducted us into the presence of his daughter, Bulan, who had gathered about her a bevy of her intimate girl friends, all busily engaged in making cigarettes; she received us with quiet dignity, but, owing to our lack of proficiency in Malay, I must acknowledge that the conversation could not be termed particularly brilliant. However, we did our best to be entertaining; Dr. Hiller and myself displayed the elaborate Japanese tattooing on our arms, and I sprung by hand, at her father's instigation, into Bulan's good graces. She was about seventeen or eighteen years old, with a strong resemblance to her father, and mild, gentle eyes which she slowly opened and shut with demure solemnity; her teeth were, of course, blackened; her hair was parted in the middle, and brought down low in glossy black waves over her forehead and held in place by a fillet of plaited rattan; her eyebrows and eyelashes had been either shaved or depilated. The one ineradicable blemish in her beauty is her left ear; over-ambitious parents had suspended therein too heavy weights when she was young, and one beautiful ear-lobe had given away; to be sure, it had been patched and reunited, but the patch was undeniable, and an ugly lump the result. Alas! even three hundred miles in the heart of Borneo *il faut souffrir pour être belle*. I showed her some of the pictures of American men and women in the Magazines we had with us; she was much amused at the small waists of the women, which I was obliged to tell her were effected by steel bands laced tightly about them. This was incomprehensible to her, and the torture which she inferred excited her sympathy. In every picture where neither beard nor moustache marked the sex I had to tell her which were men and which were women; she could see no difference in the faces, and the dress and coiffure had no meaning to her.

We were next shown the little son and heir who was to be the centre of the coming festivities; he was the whitest Bornean baby that I ever saw, his skin was what might be called a dark-cream color. Infant as he was,—not yet a year old,—he evinced the utmost terror at the sight of us, and emitted such bawls that he had to be carried away quickly. His ears, even at that early age, had been slit, and were already quite elongated with large bunches of pewter rings, which were, in fact, his sole article of dress. It always seemed strange to see babies in arms carried about without a rag of clothing on them; long clothes are so indissolubly associated in our minds with infancy that there seemed to be something monstrous and discordant in a tender little baby continually stark naked. This baby, in spite of its bad temper, was, however, the idol of the household; nephews, nieces, friends, and slaves of its parents were all proud to be allowed to carry it about the veranda, in its sling hung with charms.

While we were away on a five days' visit to another Chief on the Apoh River, Tama Bulan most hospitably caused to be constructed for us in the veranda, nearly opposite his apartment, a little room partitioned off by matting and a wall of bamboo rods, wherein, as he explained, we should be free from the annoyance of children and dogs; but even while he was speaking a row of little, beady eyes peering at us through the cracks between the bamboos made me sympathize with the feelings of the *freaks* at a circus when the small boy lifts the flaps of the tent.

On the day of our arrival, the only indication of the approaching festivities were hundreds of bunches of bananas, suspended everywhere from the roof; but when we returned from the Apoh River, preparations were already in full swing for the Naming, and we contributed freely from our store of tobacco for the manufacture of cigarettes. Bulan's room was the centre of this industry, and the workers, all women and girls, occupied every inch of the floor, squatting in groups round baskets piled high with the stringy weed. While some prepared the dried banana leaves, others rolled the cigarettes; some rolled them on their thighs, others on polished boards held in their laps. It was a merry gathering, with a constant buzz of gossip, and now and then loud bursts of innocent laughter that bespake the vacant mind. The holiday had already begun, and during the days devoted to the ceremonies there is no work in the rice-fields, consequently the house was full of young people who would be, at other times, hard at work out of doors. The small boy was, of course, ubiquitous, — as, on similar busy occasions, he is in civilized countries; and little Adom seemed to be everywhere at every instant, upsetting baskets of tobacco, purloining rolls of banana leaf, dropping chips and rubbish from rafters above on the heads of the workers beneath, and at every turn in everybody's way; nevertheless he was treated with uniform forbearance, and only occasional playful sallies from the girls kept him from downright hindering them in their work. Kindliness and hilarity ruled the hour.

GROUP OF BOYS

THE FOURTH ON THE LEFT IN THE FRONT ROW IS LAWI, AN ADOPTED SON OF ABAN LIAH, AND A PRESUMPTIVE CHIEF. THE OTHERS WERE ALREADY HIS DEVOTED FOLLOWERS.

As fast as the cigarettes were made they were strung on a thread and hung, a dangling fringe, on a framework of rattans about six feet long, representing a horn-bill with his wings outspread. The head was carved of wood and painted, so that it had a most life-like appearance, and in addition it was ornamented with several strips of bead-work cloth draped around it and enveloping the neck; its tail was composed of real feathers with the broad black band. The cigarettes were hung almost as closely as feathers all over the body, wings, and tail,— indeed, there must have been a thousand affixed to it. When the last cigarette was hung in place, and it took far into the night before the whole was finished, the huge bird was suspended from a rafter beyond the reach of pilfering hands, until the proper time for distribution.

In deciding the exact date for the important ceremony of naming the son of a Chief, the phase of the moon is of vital importance. According to the Kenyah calendar, the moon passes through twelve phases, whereof only two or three are really auspicious; and when some are in the ascendant they prognosticate even downright ill luck to all who are then named. These phases are as follows ('bulan,' meaning *moon*): (1) 'Bulan musit,' *the birth of the moon*; (2) 'Bulan anak,' *the moon has a child*; (3) 'Bulan dyipu boin,' *the pig's tooth moon*; (4) 'Bulan bakwong,' *the bird's-bill moon*; (5) 'Bulan petak,' *moon of sickness*; (6) 'Bulan batak-palan,' *the fish moon*, moderately good, but not auspicious for building houses; (7) 'Bulan salap jiit' and (8) 'Bulan salap bioh,' *the big* and *the little belly-moons*; both good moons; the 'Salap bioh' is the best for naming children. (9) 'Bulan loong-payong jiit,' *moon of the small payong fruit*; (10) 'Bulan loong-payong bioh,' *moon of the big payong fruit*; these two phases are auspicious for almost any undertaking. (11) 'Bulan blasong jiit,' *moon of the small pearl shell* (the shell often attached to the front of a war-coat); this is also an auspicious phase. (12) 'Bulan blasong bioh,' *moon of the big pearl shell*,— *i.e.*, full moon; this is considered not a very favorable phase. A child born under it goes to extremes. It is either very intelligent or else an idiot. Fighting and trouble are most apt to occur during the full moon.

The usual age at which a child is named is at about the end of the first year or at the beginning of the second. Up to this time all the children, especially those of a Chief, are under a 'lali,' a word signifying a *restriction*, and used in the same sense as taboo. As long as this lali is in force the child must not be bathed in the river, but in the private apartment of its parents; it must not be carried even down the ladder from the house to the ground; even to mention its future name is so ill-omened as to be prohibitory; it is known only by the indefinite appellation 'Angat' if a boy, and 'Endun' if a girl,—Angat means literally *a little worm*; what Endun means, if it have a separate meaning, I do not know. On the present occasion, the moon was in the phase of Salap bioh, the big-bellied moon,—that is, gibbous.

Numerous guests now began to arrive to participate in the ceremonies; they came so quietly, and so little commotion followed their arrival, that we were hardly aware of their presence until we noticed the large groups outside of Tama Bulan's door.

On the morning of the appointed day, alternate blows on two large gongs gave notice that the ceremony was about to begin. We filed into the Chief's room with the others, and, passing through the narrow and dark little entry with its very ramshackle floor, we found the family and the guests sitting cross-legged about a large mat in the middle of the room. In the centre of this mat was a heap about a foot high of white husked rice; at one side of this heap sat the proud mother, holding the pale little son and heir. When we were all seated, the gongs redoubled and trebled their din, to drown all sounds of evil portent while the rites take place.

It is the first duty of the Dayong, or priestess, (on this occasion Tama Bulan's first wife, the mother of Bulan,) to drive away all evil Spirits which may be perchance still lurking near the child. Old age is seldom, if ever, beautiful in Borneo, and as old Tina Bulan stood up to officiate, with her straggly hanks of swarthy hair, her blackened snags of teeth, her shrivelled, bony arms and corded neck, she looked the supreme incarnation of a witch, straight from the 'pit of Acheron.' But ugliness, as well as beauty, is only skin deep; and we learned to know this Tina Bulan as a dear old soul, as kind and good-natured as mortal can be.

She held by its legs a young chicken, which, with excited gesticulations, she waved above and about the little stark-naked, bawling baby, struggling in its mother's lap, and as she waved she dipped water from a bowl, and, sprinkling it upon the fowl, exhorted it, as follows:

'Misau balli yap!
Balli Isit! balli Sakit!
Misau balli Mibang nelatang,
Balli nupi jiat, iya malat!
Ja! dua! talu! pat!
Pat porat petat, peti pasi balli jiat!'

Which, somewhat freely translated, means, 'Drive away, O hallowed fowl, and hallowed Isit [omen bird], all sickness and evil Spirits that surround us! Render harmless all bad dreams! One! two! three! four! Away, all evil demons, here, there, and everywhere!'

As she counted ja! dua! talu! pat! she waved her hands violently and threateningly, as if fairly pushing the evil Spirits from her. Trembling with excitement, she then dropped cross-legged close to the heap of snow-white rice, and with a bamboo joint measured out eight portions; out of these, she made a separate pile at one side. Eight measures of rice are the portion for the child of a Chief, half that number suffices ordinary children. The rice, thus measured, is for the god, Penylong, the guardian of all souls, and for his wife, Perbungan; the spiritual essence alone of the grains goes to the gods; the ceremony over, the rice may be eaten by mortals. In the middle of this lesser pile of rice she planted a small sprig of a tree, called the *tree of life*, 'Kayu urip;' with this symbol in front of her, she carefully picked out from the pile eight full, well-shaped grains; wrapping them in a strip of bark-fibre, and holding the strip close above the child's head, she tied a knot in it enclosing and holding fast the grains. (This strip thus knotted is called 'Tebuku urip.') Eight times was this repeated, and all the while the brazen gongs kept up their hideous, deafening din; now and then, when the wearied performers stopped for a moment to change hands, the vigorous and well-sustained bawling of the noble infant filled the gap. Once I caught sight of little Adom sliding stealthily down from his perch on the rack for bamboo water-bottles, whence he had been enjoying his wonted bird's eye view of the whole performance, and, seizing the arm of a tired gong-beater, his little dust-begrimed face all contorted with earnestness, helped him to beat louder.

Every time that Tina Bulan enclosed in a knot the eight grains of rice, she murmured: 'May your soul live long, and, by the omens of this knotted cord of life, may you live to a venerable old age!'[5]

If each grain of rice mean a year of life, the reckoning does not fall far short of the Biblical three score and ten.

When the ceremony was completed of the Tebuku urip (where 'urip' means *of life*), the 'Kayu urip' (*the tree of life*) was placed in a joint of bamboo, wherein also the tebuku itself was stored. The bamboo joint is assigned only to a man-child; out of bamboo are made tobacco-

---

[5] I asked to have these words repeated to me after the ceremony; they are as follows: 'Nilang megang beleuer, tebuku urip lakip makun alun!' This 'tebuku' (knotted cord) illustrates a custom among the Kayans and Kenyahs which, I think, is noteworthy. When they wish to make a record of days or of things, they do so by tying knots either in a thin strip of rattan or in a cord of bark-fibre; this strip is called a 'tebuku.' It was a source to me of never-failing wonder to note how accurately and for what a length of time the maker of the strip can remember what every knot represents. I have seen a 'tebuku tali' ('tali' here means *strip*) wherein there were possibly three hundred knots, recording every article seized in a raid on a long-house; every knot or group of knots represented an article or collection of articles, and the itemized list was read off months and months afterward by the man who tied the knots, and, for aught I know, he could have remembered them for years. Of course, none could read it but the man who made it.

boxes, and quivers for the poisoned darts of the blow-pipe. Such things are carried only by men, never by women.

KENYAH WOMEN IN ORDINARY COSTUME.

THE RINGS STRETCHING THE EAR-LOBES ARE OF COPPER, CAST BY CHINAMEN AT THE BAZAAR. THE GIRDLES OF BEADS ROUND THE HIPS ARE MADE IN GERMANY AND IMPORTED BY CHINESE TRADERS.

At the naming of a girl, the Kayu urip and the Tebuku are placed in a small basket, like those wherein rice is carried; this symbolises women's work in the rice-fields.

These symbols are hung up in the child's room, over the sleeping-place, and are ever after venerated.

The moment that Tina Bulan had placed the Kayu urip and the Tebuku in the bamboo joint the gongs ceased, and I think a sigh of relief swept over the whole assembly. Thus far no sound of evil omen had been heard; indeed, any malevolent lizard or rancorous frog, in order to make his fateful croak audible above the indescribable din of those fearsome gongs, would have to employ a siren whistle with megaphone attachment.

The little baby was now danced and jiggled and carried about in its sling to stop its wailing. Several young girls and old women handed round on flat baskets, heaps of little packages of salt and ginger-root wrapped in pieces of green banana leaf; these, together with two or three bananas, they distributed to each guest.

Tama Talun, who sat beside me on the floor throughout the ceremony, and with genuine courtesy explained from time to time what was going on, told me that the salt, the ginger, and the sweet banana indicated what it was hoped would be the future disposition of the child, namely, he should be duly calm, hot, and gentle, never sluggish nor apathetic. Of course, I opened my package, ate a pinch of salt, nibbled the ginger-root, and wished the while good luck to the babe; then cheerfully pledged him in a cup of arrack, which was also passed to each guest. This apparently completed the ceremonies of the first day for Tama Bulan, Junior (I cannot call him by his real name; what that was, as yet not a soul but his father and mother knew). The women all arose and began to file out of the room; wishing not to miss anything, I too rose up, and was slowly making my way among them to the door when I became aware of an unusual amount of giggling around me, nay, of several explosions of laughter from the men in the room behind me. I turned about and saw all their faces on a broad grin. What ridiculous breach of etiquette had I committed? I paused, and good-natured Tama Talun came to my rescue, shouting out over the heads of the rest, 'Go on, Tuan, it's all right; they are only foolishly laughing because the Tuan seems to think he is a woman. We men have to stay behind until all the women get into the next room.' With the exception of Dr. Hiller, I was the only one in that dusky assemblage that could blush; my cheeks and forehead at once fulfilled their duty, and I gently edged out of the crowd.

It is usual, on the naming-day of a Chief's son, to bestow names on all the babies of a befitting age in the house; advantage must be taken of the same auspicious day. Therefore as soon as the ceremony was thus far completed in Tama Bulan's room, there was a second wild uproar of gongs a little further down the veranda, and to this room the guests all repaired. There, the same ceremonies were repeated, except, as I mentioned before, only four measures of rice were apportioned for the humbler folk; but, nevertheless, eight grains were tied up in each knot of the Tebuku.

Thus it went on throughout that whole day; the guests wandering from room to room, tasting pinches of salt, nibbling ginger, sipping arrack, and stuffing themselves with bananas; between whiles cooling off by bathing in the river.

The rites of the first day are but preliminary to the more august ceremonies of the second day, which are conducted in public outside the Chief's room, in the veranda, opposite to his door, where all the household and guests can assemble to welcome the youngster as soon as his name is proclaimed.

When the morning meal was over, the strong young men of the household, provided with rattan ropes, descended to the muddy wallows among the massive upright posts that support the house, and began at once to give chase to the pigs. These knowing, omen-yielding animals perform a highly important part in the rites, but they pay the dear forfeit of their lives for the privilege; they seemed verily to suspect, on the present occasion, the fate in store for them, and, at an early hour, had ungraciously betaken themselves to the woods. An hour passed, then another, and then another, — and no hunter with his pig had returned. Tama Bulan gradually became greatly worried, and kept reiterating that no one could estimate how evil would be the omen if the large pig which he had destined for this ceremony could not be found. At last, however, cheering shouts were heard from the neighboring jungle, and, soon after, one by one, the pigs, six or seven in number, with *the*pig to the fore, were brought up to the veranda, slung on poles, with their four feet tied together; here they were plumped down in a row close to the place where the rites were to be held.

On the hearth, below the row of human skulls hanging opposite the Chief's door, there must now be started New Fire,—that is, fire produced by the fire-saw, the most primitive method of obtaining it, and, possibly, because it is the most primitive, it is obligatory at all august ceremonies. According to tradition among the Kayans and Kenyahs, one of the early inhabitants of the earth, named Laki Oi, the Prometheus of Kayan mythology, taught the people this method, and called it 'Musa;' he also invented the fire-drill, which he called 'Nalika.' The Musa consists of a piece of soft fibrous wood, which is held down by the feet, firmly on the ground, and rests upon a bundle of fine slivers of dry wood; underneath it, is passed a strip of dry but flexible bamboo, which is sawed back and forth until the friction starts a spark in the fine dust which has been thereby rubbed up; the spark is fostered and soon blown into a flame in the bundle of slivers. When the materials are in proper condition, fire can be produced in much less than a minute. Should all the fires in a house go out, or when fire is to be started for the first time in a new house, the Musa is the only method whereby fire may be kindled,—no flint and steel, nor fire-drill, nor fire-syringe, nor matches, (common enough, thanks to the Chinese bazaar,) can be used; it must be the Musa, and the Musa alone. At the naming of a child, the piece of soft wood is carved into a grotesque head at one end. The image thus made is called 'Laki Pesong,' the god of the Musa.

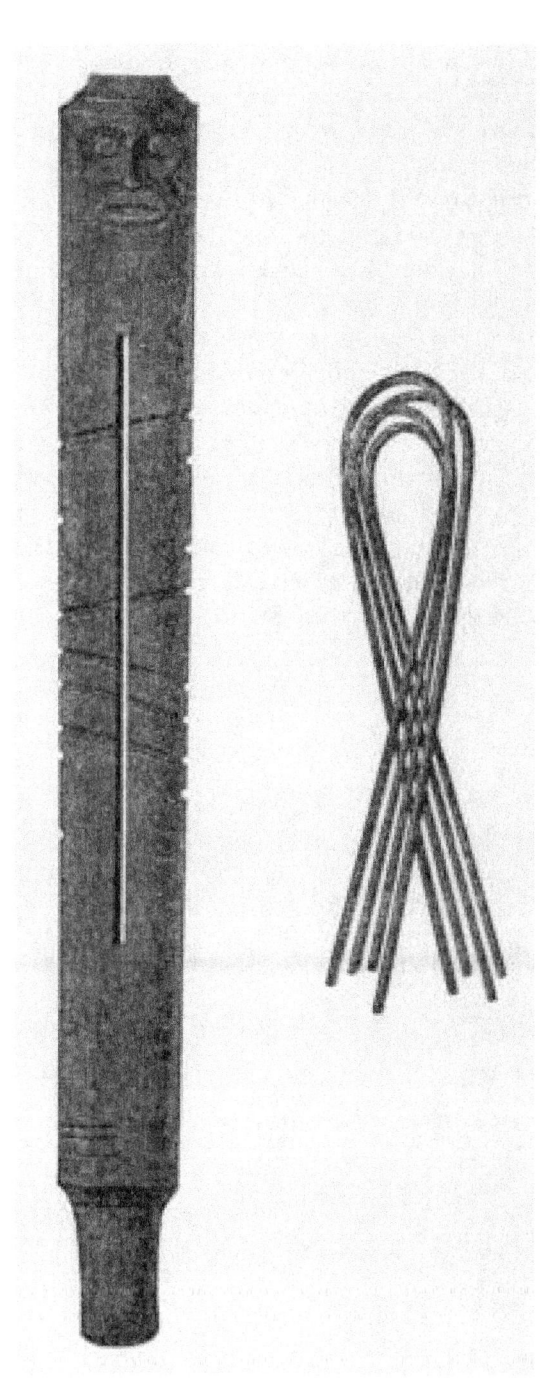

The Stick, 'Laki Pesong,' and Strips of bamboo used in making
New Fire. One-quarter of the natural size.

But to return to Tama Bulan's house. As soon as New Fire had been kindled, the gongs, as on the day before, began their deafening clangour; the parents, looking very grave, slowly emerged from their 'Lamin,' or *private room*. The mother carried the baby, who, for a wonder, was not crying,—but I could see by his expression that he was well primed for a vigorous bawl on the slightest provocation. Solemnly they marched and took their places on the large mat close to the hearth. Some strong youths now seized the big black pig, Tama Bulan's prime selection, and partly lifting it, and partly swinging it about by the ears and tail, not without squealings which would have been ear-piercing but for the gongs, they hauled it up close beside the Chief. Across the swine's body and over its neck were wreathed the mother's most prized and costly strings of beads; according to Kenyah computation, the value of these beads amounted to the price of several slaves, or probably to the cost of two whole houses. I suppose that this was not merely for the sake of decorating the victim, but was designed to flatter and cajole it into having a beautiful liver, overspread with bright omens for her boy.

MAKING FIRE WITH A 'FIRE-DRILL.'

THE PIECE OF WOOD WHICH IS HELD UPON THE GROUND MUST BE SOFT, FIBROUS, AND DRY; THE STICK WHICH IS DRILLED INTO IT IS HARD. FIRE CAN BE THUS STARTED IN ABOUT FORTY SECONDS. THIS METHOD OF

PRODUCING FIRE IS NOT HELD TO BE SACRED, AS IS THAT OF CREATING FIRE WITH THE 'MUSA' OR FIRE-SAW.

The relatives and the guests disposed themselves in a large circle around the solemn parents, the infant, and the pig; directly in front, and facing them, the Dayong sat cross-legged, a very tall and skinny old man, whose lower jaw was furnished with but one tooth, which, when he omitted to suck it in, stuck out at right angles. He did not wear, as far as I could see, any peculiar costume or badge of office; he was clad in nothing but an ordinary loin-cloth.

When the assemblage had settled themselves in their places, some sitting on the floor, others standing on the large rice mortars so that they could look into the centre of the circle, the old Dayong arose, and grasping in his right hand a parang and a stick, the latter cut into a brush of splinters at one end, with his left hand he sprinkled water upon them from a bowl held by an assistant. The dripping stick and the parang he waved over the child's head and muttered words, which Tama Talun, again my kind interpreter, said expressed the desire that the life of the child might be as 'laram,' *cool*, as the water he was sprinkling over it.[6]

To insure protection to the child against evil Spirits, a young chicken was waved above and around it, as on the previous day; and then at once the chicken's head was chopped off and some of its blood smeared on the baby's hand. This indignity supplied the provocation, which, from the first, I had anticipated, and instantly stirred up all the depravity of the infant, who had been thus far just as quiet as a lamb; the gongs now stopped their din, but the bonnie babe proved an excellent substitute, and awoke every echo in the smoky rafters overhead. He kicked, and roared, and wriggled in his mother's lap, bent himself backward, and beat with his little fists at the fluttering chicken every time it was waved near his face; I was really afraid he would burst a blood-vessel so scarlet did his little body become with the exertion of expelling those piercing shrieks; not a tear issued from

---

[6] The words 'laram,' *cool*, and 'manin,' *hot*, are used idiomatically; if a man is told to do anything, he need not instantly obey, as long as the command is, as he says, still 'manin;' if a man lay down a tool for which another has been waiting, the tool must not be instantly picked up, it is still 'manin.' A heavy, or, perhaps, an unjust fine, is termed 'manin.' The sense in which the old Dayong here used the word 'laram' is, I think, quiet and firm, like Tama Bulan, not hot-headed and inconstant.

his eyes, and the bunches of pewter rings in his stringy little ears kept flapping against his cheeks as he shook his head and thrashed about in violent contortions. He never once stopped bawling throughout all the rest of the ceremony.

All evil Spirits having been now effectually dispelled, the Dayong squatted down by the pig, and taking from the fire a small stick of wood with a glowing end he touched it to the pig's side, by way of calling the poor beast's attention to what he was about to say. When the pig's struggles had calmed down, the old man laid his hands on its side and soothingly addressed it as 'Balli Boin Akán, Balli Boin Akán,' and begged it to intercede with Penylong and Perbungan, and to tell unerringly whether or not the name now about to be given to the child had been auspiciously chosen. The name had never yet been divulged; even the old Dayong knew not what it was. It was an absolute secret between Tama Bulan and the mother of the child. Some days before, not knowing that the name was thus sacredly secret, I had asked what it was to be, but Tama Bulan courteously told me that it was utterly impossible for him to reveal it. All through this ceremony, Tama Bulan sat cross-legged beside his wife quietly, every feature wearing a very serious expression, keenly watching the Dayong.

Most of the time, the mother sat with her legs straight out in front of her, and with her squirming baby wriggling on her knees from side to side; she kept her eyes cast down, watching the child, but never attempting to stop its bawling, to which, indeed, no one seemed to pay the slightest attention.

Little Adom had a view better, of course, than any body except the principals; there he was lying flat on his face on a beam directly above the naming-party, his legs and arms dangling down on either side. When I caught sight of him his little, black eyes danced with mischief, and from his lofty perch he defied us with that impudent gesture which, in an unhappy hour, I had taught him: putting his thumb to his nose, twirling his fingers, and winking and blinking his eyes and lolling his tongue out like a veritable little goblin. All the solemnity in the world could never impress him.

When the Dayong had finished his address to the pig, italicising important words by prods in the ribs with a bony thumb, he took up a strip of bamboo, such as is used for the fire-saw, and, bending it into a loop so that the two ends just touched, he set fire to it at the bend and allowed it to burn through. The burning of this loop was watched with breathless interest by Tama Bulan, as well as by a group of old crones who had now gathered close about the Dayong. When the loop snapped asunder and the flame went out, the Dayong put the two strips side by side and so rested the unburnt ends on his thumb-nail as to make them exactly even, and then closely scrutinized the burnt ends. He said not a word, but ominously shook his head, assumed a troubled expression, and even forgot to suck in his solitary tooth. The two strips were taken from him by one of the old women and subjected to the same measurement and scrutiny, except that she kept up a constant argument, and a shaking of her head; finally, she fumbled over the burnt ends and knocked off a little particle of ash just ready to fall; then she held them up before the Dayong, and the tone of what she uttered was decidedly more reassuring. He measured them again very closely, and seemed to be better pleased. Tama Bulan could restrain himself no longer, but got up hastily to examine the strips for himself; he also rubbed with his finger one of the charred ends, and then adjusted the sound ends on his thumb-nail, but he shook his head, and said, somewhat despairingly, 'I'm afraid one is much too long.' Hereupon, the ever kind Tama Talun explained to us that by these strips it is decided whether or not the undivulged name which had been chosen is a good one; if the two pieces are of exactly the same length, the omen is unfavorable; if they are very unequal in length, the name is likewise ill-chosen. There should be just the tiniest, slightest difference in the length of the strips; then it is absolutely certain that the name is well-chosen. (Ah! what a shrewd, clever head devised this augury! how easy by this rule of thumb-nail to make the difference slight, and how hard to make the strips exactly even or greatly uneven!) So it happened that, after the strips had passed over the thumb-nails of half a dozen of the wisest crones and toothless old men, they were returned to the Dayong, who was now fully convinced that his first measurements had been entirely wrong, and he now emphatically declared that the omens were most auspicious. Throughout this momentous discussion the object of it all kept up an unintermitting bawl; if the evil Spirits have ears, never during this hour would they have molested him; there was no need of gongs with that baby to the fore.

The charred ends of the bamboo strips were then dipped in a cocoanut shell of water held by one of the old women standing near; the ash and water were mixed by the Dayong into a paste between his thumb and finger and smeared on the baby's forehead and in its hair. At the instant of doing this he leaned forward and asked Tama Bulan what name he had selected. Tama Bulan whispered mysteriously very

57

low close to the Dayong's ear. The Dayong then reached for the cocoanut shell of water held by the old woman, and most carefully and solemnly advanced it toward the child; the shell was nervously followed every inch of the way by four or five pairs of brown claw-like, old hands with anxious zeal, lest a drop of its precious contents should be spilled; in spite of the risk it ran from this excess of zeal, it got to its destination safely, and the very instant that the water was poured over the head of the baby the Dayong said aloud, impressively, 'Be thy name Lijow!' The name, for the first time thus uttered aloud, was murmured throughout the large assemblage, and the happiness of the selection commended with 'nods and becks and wreathed smiles;' it was the name of one of Tama Bulan's ancestors, and means *Tiger*. (It is unlucky to name a child after a living person,—it is apt to make the child stupid; and it is fatal to select the name of one who has recently died,—speedy death follows.)

The cocoanut shell was now refilled with home-made arrack, whereof a drop was placed on little Lijow's lips from the finger of the Dayong; then the mother, henceforth Tina Lijow, took a sip from it, and Tama Bulan drained it to the dregs, whereof I imagine there were plenty, due to the Dayong's grimy finger. Then the Dayong poured out a measure for himself, and then we, as guests of importance, were courteously served, and after us followed all the rest of the guests in turn. Again, as on the first day, packages of salt, ginger-root, and bananas were passed around, and The Ceremony was over. Everything had gone off to perfection, not an evil omen had marred its smooth success,—thanks to the gongs and the strength of dear little Lijow's lungs; if his voice keeps its promise until manhood, he will make himself heard throughout Sarawak.

It now only remained to wrap up the precious strips of bamboo in a piece of banana leaf and place them in the bamboo joint along with the symbols of the first day's rites. After this was properly accomplished, the 'Balli Boin,' that sacred pig, was killed, and his considerate liver politely proclaimed in its every tint that Lijow's life would be all that the heart of a devoted Kenyah parent could desire.

Tama Bulan, with a beaming face, said to us, 'Don't forget to tell Tuan Hote [Hose] that I have called my boy Lijow; he wanted to know what the name was to be, but I couldn't tell him then.'

The naming of little Lijow having been thus most successfully finished, the Chief's family party moved out of the circle gathered about the hearth, and another family party took its place in front of the

Dayong; their Balli Boin was hoisted and pulled into position, and the same ceremonies with the taking of omens were punctiliously repeated. Of course, for these people of lesser rank, there was not felt the same widespread interest as for the Chief's son, and, therefore, the assemblage gradually dwindled; the cool river offered more attractions than the hot, breezeless veranda, with its din of gongs and of squalling babies and of squealing pigs, and its loud-voiced Dayong with an unruly, projecting tooth. I think there were in all six babies named on that day, and by the time the last had been proclaimed a member of the clan the afternoon was well advanced.

Many a jar of arrack had been broached during the ceremonies, consequently all the members of the household and their guests were decidedly fain to sing and dance. The raised portion of the flooring extending along the greater part of the veranda under the eaves was lined with men waiting in turn for the cups of arrack that were freely passed from lip to lip. Tama Bulan beamed upon his whole large household, and with his own hands dipped out the mild drink from the large jars with a ladle made from a seed of the Billian tree (ironwood). The minor notes of Kaluris now resounded, and here and there on the floor of huge, broad planks, for which Tama Bulan's house is famous, the horny feet of dancers thumped and shuffled and scraped as one after another essayed to outdo all predecessors in the wild movements of a war-dance. They leaped in the air, waving their parang and shield; they stamped in time to the music; they whirled and twisted, sometimes falling on one knee, slashing at imaginary foes; the long feathers of the Argus pheasant waved from their war-caps, and the black and white feathers of the horn-bill rattled on their war-coats and glittered in the crimson level rays of the sun that swept in under the eaves of the house. Now was the time to bring forth the great horn-bill with its plumage of cigarettes; it was tenderly moved to a beam within easy reach, and its bristling feathers, which had cost so much fair labor, were greedily snatched off, and in a trice the atmosphere of the veranda, thick with tobacco-smoke, became even to the long rays of the setting sun almost impenetrable.

While this smoking was literally in full blast, the women retired to their rooms and arrayed themselves in every bit and shred that they possessed of gaudy bead-work, for their necks, their ears, and their waists; they donned their brightest fillets for the hair, and they tied round their waists their skirts of black cloth with patches of bright calico stitched down the side. Down to their waists, except for these bead necklaces, they were, as usual, bare.

The withdrawal of the women was a signal to the men to range themselves in two long rows facing each other; thus they sat on the floor, puffing hard at their cigarettes and chuckling with one another in anticipation of the ordeal they were about to undergo. From one of the rooms the women issued in single file; she who headed the procession carried a large bowl, the next carried a cocoanut-shell spoon, the third bore a large flat dish piled high with cubes of raw fat pork, behind her, fourth in the line, followed Bulan, the daughter of the house, who carried nothing; but everyone could see, by the twinkle of her eye, that she meant mischief; this same order:—bowl-bearer, spoon-bearer, pork-bearer, helper, was preserved in a regular series all down the whole line of sixty or more women.

Sedately and slowly and silently they marched the whole length of the veranda close to the wall of the apartments, and then turned in between the lines of squatting men. When the first man was reached, the procession halted, and from the bowl held by the first woman, the spoon-bearer dipped a spoonful of a muddy-looking liquid and poured it into the man's gaping mouth. As it touched his tongue, his face was a study in contortions; when the spoon was withdrawn he tried first to smile, then his eyes were lost in wrinkles, his mouth puckered up, he looked seasick, and then with a shudder that shook his frame, gulped down his dose; the spoon-bearer passed on, then the bearer of the pork cubes halted in front of him, and Bulan, taking from the dish one of those nauseating gray, greasy, tepid cubes of raw fat, popped it dexterously into his mouth and then wiped her greasy fingers across his upturned face. Again shuddering tremors shook his frame, but—he bolted it! then gazed about him with a sickly smile. Down both lines there burst forth peals on peals of laughter; the men shouted and stamped their feet with merriment over the victim's misery, unmindful that his fate would soon be theirs. The women tried hard to maintain their gravity, but the varied and ludicrous sufferings of their lords and masters were often too much for their dignity, and they unreservedly joined in the mirth; to those against whom they had any private grudge they administered an extra dose, or stirred up the dregs of the drink, or bestowed a particularly flabby and repulsive piece of pork. As we sat about half way down the line, we had quite a while to await our turn, and to speculate on the ingredients of the awful drink,—it was almost adequately nauseating that we should have to take it out of that family, that tribal spoon. My turn came at last. Well, it was a ghastly dose and no mistake. It was lukewarm, it was fiery hot with peppers, it was salt, it was pungent, it was sweet, it was flat, it was sour, and it tasted strongly of brass bowl. All this was administered from a spoon that without washing or wiping had been already in the mouths of thirty or forty black-toothed predecessors. Our uncontrollable and immeasurable disgust created infinite amusement and prolonged laughter, and when Bulan, full of mischievous merriment, followed with the pork cubes, knowing that she had the Tuans at her mercy, she did not leave the fraction of an inch of our faces that was not bedaubed with grease. And then how she laughed! As though one such dose was not enough, there was the prospect before us of having it, Heaven save the mark! again and again administered down to the very last woman of that long, interminable procession; first a spoonful of that appalling, unnameable liquid! then a mouthful of raw pork! The devoted Tama Bulan and Tama Talun came at length to our rescue, and told us that after the first two or three doses there would be no offence if we just dipped our finger in the drink and touched it to our tongue, and if we merely took the pork between our lips; sometimes this evasion was successful, but now and then the drink was forced upon us, and we got a worse smearing from greasy fingers. Shrewd old Laki La, profiting by experience at other similar feasts, held a tumbler under his chin, and as fast as the drink and pork were deposited in his mouth they were re-deposited in the tumbler. Tama Usong, to whose house on the Apoh River we had paid a visit only a little while before, sat next to me, and I asked him how he was getting along, and if his stomach was not nearly full. 'Oh, no, indeed, Tuan,' said he, laughing; 'I long ago put my stomach out here,' and he pointed behind him to a row, a foot long, of cubes of pork which he had surreptitiously deposited on the railing of the veranda. It was a hideous nightmare! But at last the little girls brought up the end of the procession, and then the greater part of the assembly dashed for the river to wash off a little of the fat with which their faces were fairly dripping.

Tama Talun explained to us that this was a survival of old times, when warriors returned from a head-hunt, and sat thus and were obliged to take in their mouths a small piece of their enemy's flesh, served to them just as the fat pork is served now-a-days. They were not to swallow the human flesh, but merely hold it between their lips to show contempt for the enemy, and also thereby to absorb his valour. Dr. Hose, when told of this interpretation, asserted that the object of this ceremony is to impress evil Spirits, who, when they see so many men with faces smeared with food, will be led to think that a very great feast had taken place in honor of the newly named children, and that, therefore, these children must be most important people, and to harm them would stir the anger of a vast multitude. Dr. Hose's knowledge of the Kenyahs extends over so many years that it is venturesome to dissent from him; nevertheless, our interpretation was received directly from an unusually intelligent native, while the ceremony was going on before us, and was, moreover, given voluntarily without any questions on our part. Dr. Hose rejects this interpretation, because of his conviction that cannibalism, in any form whatsoever, never existed in Borneo.

MUJAN, ONE OF THE BELLES OF TAMA BULAN'S HOUSEHOLD.

(From a photograph taken, and kindly loaned, by Professor A. C. Haddon, F. R. S.)

By the time we had returned to our places in the veranda, after having washed off in the river the abhorred grease from our faces, the women had doffed their uncomfortable burdens of finery and were squatting among the men, in a close group round Tama Bulan, who was cutting the rattan bindings of several more large jars of arrack. The Chief was the first to quaff the beverage, and as he lifted the cup to his lips the whole assemblage began to intone a continuous 'oo-oo-oo-oo,' in harmony but with a deep bass predominant, and kept up this resonant accompaniment until the last drop was drained. After

Tama Bulan, the guests were served in turn, and as each one lifted the cup to his lips (and it must be drained to the last drop at one draught) this 'oo-oo'-ing rose and fell like a bewildering, deafening humming in the ears; it was to me a noteworthy experience; unquestionably it marvellously accelerates the action of the alcohol in the arrack. When the cup had been passed round several times to each man and woman, and the oo-oo-ing was becoming somewhat discordant and boisterous, the door of one of the rooms was flung open and the genuine feast was brought in, piled high in three small canoes borne on the shoulders of men staggering under the weight. One-half of each canoe was heaped with little packages of boiled rice wrapped in green banana leaves and tied with pieces of grass; the other half fairly bristled, like a fretful porcupine, with bamboo skewers whereon were several bits of boiled pork. (It will, perhaps, be noted that a feast does not consist in variety or quality, but in quantity.) Here and there among the guests were placed bowls of salted fish pulverised, and to each guest were given a packet of rice and a stickful of meat, while Tama Bulan shouted the hospitable injunction, 'Kuman plahei plahei' — *Eat slowly, slowly!* There was no stint; everyone was freely at liberty to have as many portions of rice and of meat as he could eat, and was welcome to help himself to all he wished of the dried fish.

In my packet of rice there was a little discoloration at one end, that looked like iron rust, but Ma Obat, a one-eyed and villainous-looking old fellow, who sat beside me, seeing that I scrutinized the spot rather carefully, politely took the lump of rice out of my hand, and with a thumb-nail that looked, I must say, like a coal-heaver's shovel, scraped away the dubious portion and then handed the lump back to me. The discolored grains were gone, but, woe's me, they were replaced by several grimy finger-marks. For the sake of his triumphant and kindly beaming smile I could not refuse to eat it, and so with eyes fixed on the rafters overhead, — it was bolted!

This feast marked the conclusion of the ceremonies, and we stuffed and smoked, and then as darkness was beginning to fall, Dr. Hiller and I, with several of the young men, strolled down the veranda to pay respectful visits in the family rooms. In Mujan's room, I am sorry to say, we found both Mujan and her elder sister in a state of — well, intoxication; the arrack and the oo-oo-ing had been too much for them. Ordinarily, they were quiet, demure girls, the belles of the veranda, and industrious workers at rice-pounding. But such lapses are, according to Kenyah morality, by no means unpardonable, nay, at such a high tide and festival as the present, were to be rather applauded as a great and ladylike compliment to the host. Mujan and her sister were sitting with their backs against the partition; the head of the elder reclined on the shoulder of the younger, and, though awake, she gave, from time to time, a sighing snore. Mujan, the younger, was trying to entertain a group of visitors, and her fingers were crumpling cigarette wrappers and tobacco in a futile attempt to make some cigarettes for her friends. All she could murmur to us was,'Aku mabok, Tuan, Aku mabok'—*I'm drunk, sirs, I'm drunk*. We stayed only a few minutes, joking with her about her state, and then went with the others to visit Sara, another fashionable belle, who, however, in our eyes, was far from personally attractive; she had lost four of her upper front teeth; their loss made her conversation anything but easy to understand. When we arrived, Sara had retired to her modicum of a sleeping-room, but she was persuaded to emerge, and then she announced that the arrack had given her a severe headache. Deng's elder brother,—I forget his name,—at once volunteered to apply cups to her temple, and she acquiesced. She provided the cupping instrument, which consisted of a small cylinder of bamboo, sealed at one end with a lump of wax. The operator, with a small knife, scratched four or five little wounds on her temple, and then making a small hole through the lump of wax on the bamboo cylinder he applied the open end to the wound and proceeded to suck the air out of the cylinder with his lips. When the air was sufficiently exhausted he closed the hole in the wax with his teeth, and the bamboo remained adhering to her temple, like a horn. She smiled, chatted, and never once winced throughout the whole operation, and after about half an ounce of blood had been drawn pronounced herself much better.

SARA, ANOTHER BELLE OF TAMA BULAN'S HOUSEHOLD.

SHE WAS UNATTRACTIVE IN APPEARANCE, BUT HER VIVACIOUS CONVERSATION RENDERED HER VERY POPULAR

(From a photograph taken, and kindly loaned, by Professor A. C. Haddon, F. R. S.)

Just at this minute, Tama Bulan hurried into the room, and, asking us to come out, excitedly told us that a woman, named Lueng, whose child had been one of those to receive a name that day, was very ill and had fallen down in her room suddenly, and could not be wakened; had we ever heard of such a thing, he asked, in our country, or had we by chance any medicine for her. We went at once with him and found the woman in a state of profound collapse; she had been suffering from a severe attack of grippe, and the excitement of the day had been too great for her; we could get no further history than this, and from the cackling old women who were busy about her and from her husband and her brother we could get no coherent answers to our questions. We did the best we could with our limited resources; we stimulated her heart with hypodermics of strychnia; we had her laid flat instead of propped up, as she had been by the old women; at length she revived sufficiently to ask for water. When we bade them to give it to her they positively refused, saying we wanted to poison her;

by administering a hypodermic injection we had indiscreetly overstepped the bounds of Kenyah submission to the white man's medicine. Instead of water, the old women insisted on pouring down the patient's throat a thick, warm paste of rice and water, at which, of course, she gagged and choked. We saw that our efforts were of no avail, and were therefore compelled to resign her to her friends and the Dayongs. One very officious old woman seemed to think that the sovereign remedy for such ills was to reach and scratch the patient's back-bone by kneading the finger-tips deep down into the abdomen. Indeed, at one time, I thought she would actually push her fingers through the skin and tear the vitals from the unconscious woman. We told Tama Bulan that we could do nothing further, and that the woman would probably die; whereupon, knowing the temper of his people, he urged us to leave her to the Dayongs and to come away. Shortly after, as we were sitting in the fading twilight in the little apartment which Tama Bulan had caused to be put up for us, we saw them bring the limp body out of the room and place it on a mat in the veranda, only a few feet away from our door. The husband and the brother were frantic with grief and anxiety, and continually bent over her and shouted her name; then they took a blow-pipe and, putting one end close to her ear, they shouted her name again, hoping to call back her soul that was wandering off. They told her that her little child was crying for her and wanted to be fed. I crept into the group, once, and listened for her heart-beats, but they had stopped for ever. Tama Bulan asked me, aside, 'Is she alive, Tuan?' and when I told him she was dead, he whispered, 'Don't tell them; let them discover it themselves.'

A female Dayong was then summoned to find out whither the soul had gone, and to lure it back to the body; to this end she made several successive demands of valuable beads from the husband, as a fee, and the agonised, headlong haste with which he ran to get them from time to time, was truly pathetic.

I have said elsewhere that I could detect among this people no signs of genuine, unselfish affection. Perhaps this should be qualified by saying that at the solemn hour of death, or of its threatened approach, they manifest an emotion in which there certainly seems to be an element of affection, but even then alarm or terror seems to predominate.

A flickering damar lamp was placed on the floor near the body, and within the circle of its light the old hag of a Dayong, chanting in a monotonous minor key, strutted backward and forward with a shield in one hand and a parang in the other, and many strings of beads about her neck and waist. Twice she paused to ask for a young chicken, and when it was handed to her, she seized its head in her mouth and bit it off, sucked a mouthful of blood from the neck and spat it on the floor, closely scrutinising how it had splattered. Throughout this scene the grief-stricken, wailing reiteration of the dead woman's name echoed through the veranda, now but dimly lit with damar lamps; every sound of mirth and gaiety was hushed; the only noise, except the wailings and the Dayong, came from the dogs and the pigs beneath the house, where they snarled and fought over the remnants of the feast that had fallen through the floor.

When the female Dayong had done her utmost to recall the soul, and had failed, our good, faithful friend, Tama Talun, volunteered to try his power. He demanded no costly beads, merely a parang, and in the same manner as his predecessor he walked backward and forward in the circle of light. We could not understand a word of what he was saying, but every now and then he threw down his parang so that its point stuck in the floor, where it remained swaying from side to side. As it swayed he walked slowly, about ten paces from it, and then gave a hop in the air and a shrill shout. Then slowly he walked back to the parang, pulled it up, and continued his chanting and walking.

While this was going on, the group suddenly realised that the woman was veritably dead, beyond all hope. With a scream the husband and the brother snatched up the body and rushed into the family room with it; some of the group followed, and some crept silently away into the dark corners of the veranda.

Before long, Tama Bulan came to tell us that the people were in a highly excited state, and, most unfortunately, they held us responsible for the woman's tragic and sudden death, and that we had better remain in our little room and not venture out into the veranda.

It was not the most pleasant situation imaginable. We were well aware of the excitable nature and the undisciplined minds of the people among whom we were; we knew that they passed in an instant from extreme friendliness to a Berserker rage; and we were but two against three hundred; our means of defence consisted of only two revolvers. Grave as we knew the danger must be, we very fortunately did not know until some time afterward, from Tama Bulan, how extreme it was, and how difficult it had been for him to save our lives.

After Tama Bulan had left us, we heard a pounding and chopping against the partition wall of the room to which the body had been carried; several boards were removed, and an opening made from it into the veranda; through this opening the corpse was borne; it must not pass through a doorway used by the living. The poor, inanimate body was decked out in all the gay garments so recently worn at the feast, and, with a cigarette between the fingers, it was laid partly recumbent on a bier that had been quickly constructed, and draped with white cloth. On the bier beside the corpse an old woman seated herself (all this we could observe through the crevices of our room) and at once began a wail for the dead. This lugubrious wailing was kept up, to my certain knowledge, without intermission for two nights and a day. Of course, there were constant relief parties.

During these two nights and a day we remained close prisoners in our little room. Throughout the first long night Tama Bulan proved himself inflexibly our staunch friend; he insisted over and over again on our innocence, and pleaded for us with the adherents of Lueng's husband and brother, who were clamouring for our heads as offerings to the dead woman and as decorations for their homes. This thirst for our blood lasted during our imprisonment, and was throughout restricted to the husband and brother of Lueng and to their immediate friends. They were all guests, who had come to the Naming.

When the wailing had been adequately performed the corpse was placed in a coffin hewn from a large log and the cover sealed down with raw gutta percha.

Our most friendly relations with Tama Bulan's household had not for a moment been broken. Nevertheless, the next day Tama Bulan came to us and said that, in view of all the circumstances, he thought it best that our visit should come to an end; and, inasmuch as Laki La and his followers were going down the river, we had better take advantage of the chance and accompany them. Of course, we acquiesced. The object for which we had come was accomplished. We had seen that which no white man had ever before reported, namely, the noteworthy ceremonies of a Naming, and we had passed six delightful weeks in the far interior of Borneo, in intimate, friendly intercourse with men, whom *nous autres* are pleased to term savages. So we fell to work, packed up our things, distributed among our especial friends all that was left of our stores of cloth and tobacco, made Tama Bulan's eyes sparkle with delight over our present of silver dollars, bade good-bye to his daughter Bulan, and his two wives, not forgetting a chuck under the chin to little Lijow, and hastened down to the boat. Our final parting with dear old Tama Bulan was almost watery; and, as we swept out into the current, with our pith helmets we waved a prolonged farewell to the row of flapping palm-leaf hats which lined the long veranda.

Old Laki La was as affable as possible while he sat in our canoe, and we even volunteered to draw for him the solitary tooth remaining in his lower jaw. He waggled it with his tongue pensively for a moment, and then remarked that as he should not live much longer anyhow, he thought that it had better die with him. We considered him a most pleasant old fellow, until we reached his very large house on the Pata, not far below Tama Bulan's; but as soon as we touched his landing-place we were undeceived; he disembarked without so much as turning round to say good-bye, and behind him trooped all our paddlers, whom we had expected to take us down at least as far as Tama Lohong's house on the Baram.

Here was a serious difficulty, and Laki La would pay absolutely no attention to any appeal to him for men.

It was on this occasion that the man I mentioned in the first paragraph of this chapter came forward most kindly, and offered to get together some men to take us as far as Tama Lohong's, and all the way down to the Fort, if necessary; and so it fell out. It made me blush to think of the ingratitude I showed in forgetting his name, and I am still blushing; for even now, cudgel my brains as I will, I cannot recall it.

Early Training of a Head-Hunter

One evening, an hour before sunset, at the time when in every direction, the angular outlines of the huge fruit-bats, with bodies as large as a cat, are silhouetted against the sky, as they make an unswerving and majestic flight toward their nocturnal feeding-grounds, we halted our dug-out canoes at the muddy sloping bank in front of the house of Aban Avit, an influential Chief on the Tinjar River.

We were uninvited, and, as far as we knew, unexpected, but the host, upon whom we were thus unceremoniously forcing ourselves, advanced to meet us, as we ascended the unsteady, plank walk, raised on piles, leading to his house, and, with a warmth unusual among an undemonstrative people, welcomed us with a smile that revealed every one of his thirty-two coal-black teeth. We were, to be sure, old friends, having stopped at his house on our way up-river; but, as he had afterward heard that we were going to make the ascent of Mount Dulit, where all varieties of evil Spirits and dragons have their haunts, he said he had really never expected to see us again; and had we not returned just when we did, he, good soul, had planned to go with a party of his bravest men in search of us; but here we were again safe and sound, none the worse for the dreadful journey, and not one of us marked with the scar of 'Gum Toh,' *a ghost's-clutch,*—a cutaneous tumor, to which these dark-skinned people are subject, well known to us as a *Keloid of Addison*, but which the Borneans aver is due to the clutch of a ghost's hand. As soon as we were within the veranda of the house, Aban Avit insisted that his own private room should be resigned to us; accordingly, his manifold possessions were moved to one side, and clean rattan mats spread upon the floor; his fireplace, heaped with dry wood, was put at the disposal of our Chinese cook, and several long bamboo water-jars were brought from the river so that there should be no delay in the preparation of our evening meal. Ah, the hospitality of a head-hunter!

ABAN AVIT, A BERAWAN CHIEF OF THE TINJAR RIVER.

When all our numerous boxes and bundles had been brought up from the boats, we wandered inquisitively about the long-house, asking endless questions of our host and of his brother; and, as they both spoke Malay fluently, our conversation drifted into all sorts of channels. Aban Avit is a widower, as the *Aban* in his name declares, and Avit was the name of his wife. The Kayans, and allied tribes, adopt names to suit the varying events of their lives. Thus, a widower always takes his dead wife's name prefixed by Aban; a father bears the name of his first-born child prefixed by Tama, or Ma, meaning *father*, as long as the child lives; should the child die, Tama is changed to *Oyang*. For instance, Tama Bulan means the *father of Bulan*. Oyang Batu means he who is *bereft of his son Batu*. Bulan is a girl's name, meaning *Moon*; Batu is a boy's name, and means *Stone*, equivalent to our *Peter*. If Bulan, the daughter of Tama Bulan, should have a son named Madang, Tama Bulan, whose original name was Wang, would then adopt the grandfather's title of *Laki*, and be known as Laki Madang.

Our host [whose photograph is given on the opposite page] was one of the best types of the inland tribes.

Throughout his house, on partition walls and on rafters, there was scroll-work in black and white paint, the black lines evidently made with a finger and the dots of white with a thumb. On the wall of his private room, just above his sleeping-place, were two much conventionalised and interlaced figures with arms and legs like long tendrils. These figures, Aban Avit explained, represented 'Wawa' monkeys (the *Gibbon Ape*), animals held sacred by his family for certainly three generations, and never killed by any member of the household; he regarded them as his best of friends, and that day was sure to be lucky when they crossed his path in the jungle, or when their musical, almost bird-like, call was heard near the house.

This hereditary veneration of an animal suggests a trace of totemism, otherwise rare in Borneo. Aban Avit, in telling us about his veneration for the Wawa, cast down his eyes and spoke in a voice so low we could hardly hear him, as if the very breathing of a name so sacred were profanation. He told us the painting was the work of his own hands.

From this private apartment, which even at high noon was dark, but as soon as the sun had set was verily as dark as the proverbial pocket, we made our way to the veranda, where daylight still lingered; here again we noticed our host's love of decoration; the rack whereon visitors as soon as they enter the veranda, hang their parangs, instead of being a customary row of pegs or merely crotched sticks, was a board, whereof the lower edge, as it hung horizontally from the rafters, about half way up the slant of the roof, had been carved by the Chief himself into graceful double-headed hooks and loops, so that the belts attached to the parangs could be easily hung on them and the weapons would be out of the way, yet conveniently at hand. It is an unequivocal insult for a guest to enter a friendly veranda with his parang about his waist; etiquette demands that it be unfastened before stepping into the house; it should be then laid aside or hung on the rack while the owner is engaged in friendly gossip. The house was new at the time of our visit, in fact, it was not yet wholly finished; at the up-river end, five or six huge piles had been planted for its further extension; these posts, about fifteen feet out of the ground and eighteen inches in diameter, were likewise carved, but with grotesque devil-faces, from whose grinning mouths tusks like the wild boar's protruded, below them snakes, and spiral curves representing the recurved protuberance on the beak and head of the Horn-bill, — the war-bird of all the Kayan and Kenyah tribes. Here and there, of course, conventionalised figures of the Wawa were to be detected. It seems an inviolable rule with all Bornean decoration that the representation of any living thing must be hinted at so grotesquely, that it takes a subtle imagination to discern what it really represents; possibly, this is due to the idea, so widely scattered throughout the far East, that to make a life-like image of any animal involves a risk of danger to the maker, — a danger which may be vague or otherwise as chance may interpret it, — and of which we see an intimation, possibly, in the second commandment of the Decalogue.

When twilight suddenly deepened into night and blazing brands were brought to replenish the fire on the hearth opposite the Chief's door, we squatted round about it, not for warmth, but for the cheer of its flicker, and because, — well, does a pipe ever taste as good as when lit by an ember?

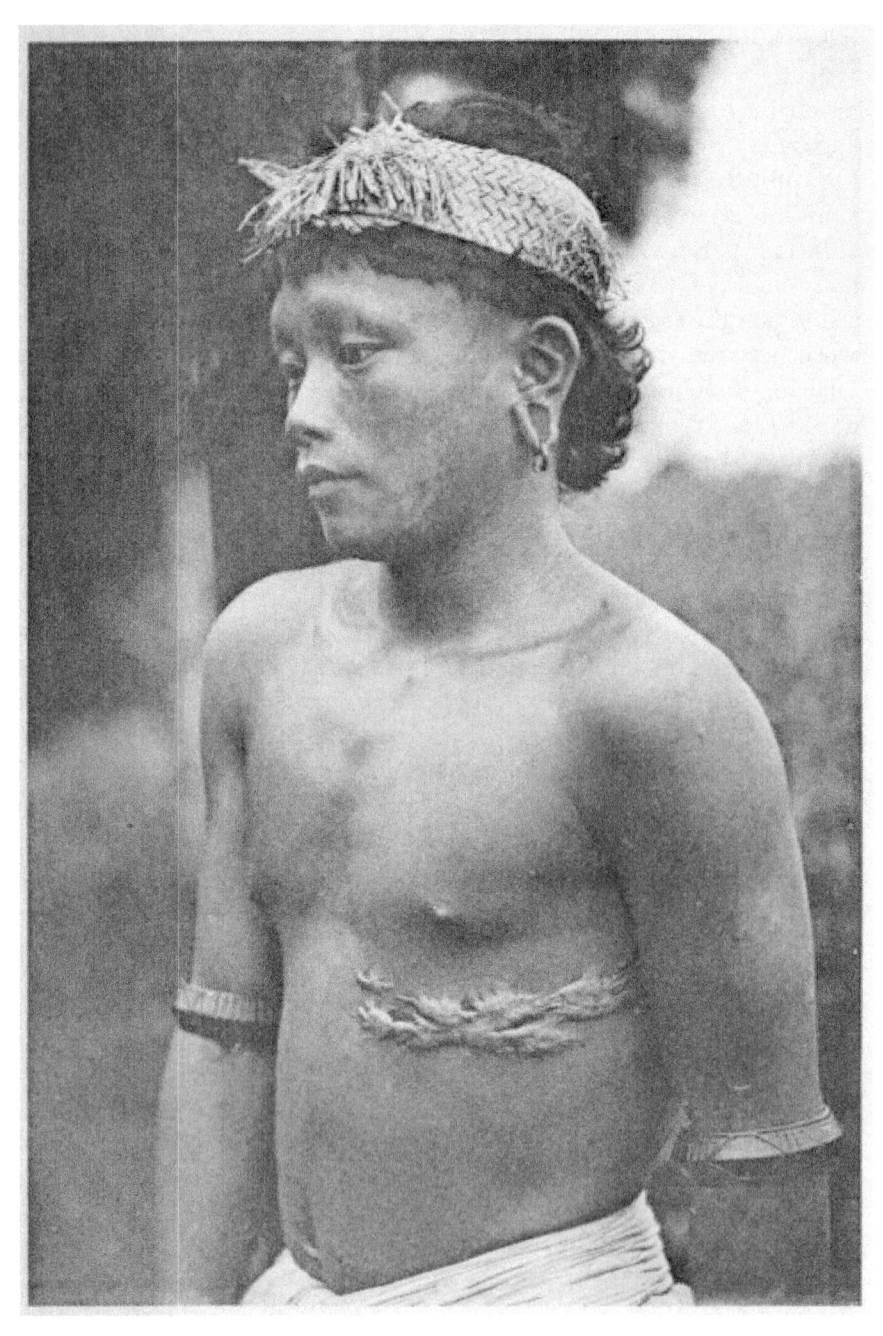

A KAYAN YOUTH, SHOWING THE RAISED SCAR, CALLED BY THE NATIVES 'GUM TOH' OR GHOST'S CLUTCH.

IT IS BELIEVED BY THE KAYANS THAT SUCH A SCAR OR WELT IS CAUSED BY THE FINGERS OF AN EVIL SPIRIT; SHOULD THE VICTIM BE SEIZED ROUND THE NECK HE NEVER CHOKES TO DEATH, BUT AWAKES. THEY MAINTAIN THAT THESE SCARS FORM IN A SINGLE NIGHT; BUT THIS IS EXTREMELY DOUBTFUL. RAISED SCARS OVER ALL OLD WOUNDS ARE EXCEEDINGLY COMMON AMONG THESE DARK-SKINNED RACES.

Aban Avit sat beside us, and while we were filling our pipes he produced from the bamboo box, hanging at his side, some tobacco and some of that beautifully delicate dried leaf of the wild banana cut from the heart of the plant, before the leaf is unfurled; in unskilled hands it tears like wet tissue-paper, but in Aban Avit's a tapering, symmetrical cigarette, eight inches long, was skilfully rolled on his thigh. A circle of small boys squatted around us, their bright, little eyes watching our every movement as intently as we stare at the actions of some strange animal in a Zoölogical Garden. If we struck a match, or sneezed, or buttoned our coats, or wiped our faces with a handkerchief, dilated eyes and open mouths attended the action with wrapt interest. A few men sat near their Chief, and now and then murmured comments to one another in their native tongue, which we did not fully understand, but could guess from the direction of their eyes, that we were the subject of their conversation. The evening duties of the household were not, however, interrupted on our account; men with bundles of dried fire-wood on their shoulders, women staggering under a load of bamboo joints filled with water, and stacked in hampers on their backs, were constantly passing by us, treading heavily, and making the loose boards of the floor clatter and rattle as they plodded their weary way to their apartments. For a time there was almost a constant succession of canoes coming to the landing-place, bringing back the workers from the rice-clearings. The women all bending under full hampers, some with fresh, uncurled fern-fronds, and the sprouts of a variety of large Canna, which they stew with rice to add variety to their diet; some with bundles of the young banana leaf, whereof to make cigarette-wrappers, and others with wild tapioca and wild yams. Each one carried her own light paddle in one hand, and a large round and flat sun-hat in the other. None of them glanced to right or left, but made her way direct to her family room, and like a ghost faded into the darkness through the small doorway. After them followed the men, dangling their parangs in one hand and trailing their blow-pipes and spears in the other. They, too, looked fixedly ahead, until they had hung up their parang and stuck their spear perpendicularly into a rafter so that the shaft should be kept straight; this done, they joined the group round the fire, or went down to the river to bathe. At the far end of the house some young fellows were playing mournful tunes on a Kaluri, and its organ-like notes were wafted fitfully down to us; now and then a baby's wail chimed in, and then was quieted by the mother's crooning lullaby. Beneath the house, the contented grunting of pigs and the clucking of chickens denoted that these omen-givers had returned from their foraging in the jungle, and had sought the shelter of home for the night.

VERANDA OF ABAN AVIT'S HOUSE.

THE COLLECTION OF TROPHY-HEADS IS HUNG, AS USUAL, ABOVE THE HEARTH IN FRONT OF THE CHIEF'S ROOM. ON THE LEFT, NEAR THE EDGE OF THE PHOTOGRAPH, IS THE WOMAN WHO HAD BEEN ABDUCTED FROM HER HOME ON THE BARAM RIVER, AND WAS AT THIS TIME BEING RETURNED TO HER FAMILY BY LAKI JOK ORANG, A CHIEF OF THE REJANG RIVER (see p. 136). THE MAN RESTING HIS FEET AGAINST THE SIDE OF THE HEARTH IS THE BROTHER OF ABAN AVIT. IN THE UPPER LEFT-HAND CORNER IS THE RACK WHEREON THE PARANGS OF VISITORS MUST BE HUNG.

Thus we sat as twilight faded in Aban Avit's veranda, — in the home of these people, whereof every detail made up their familiar, commonplace life, the only life from cradle to grave that they had ever known or would know, while we by their side were aliens from a world twelve thousand miles away, from a country that they had never heard of, and of a race which many of them had never seen before. We were in the very heart of the Bornean jungle, guests, in the house of a barbarous 'savage' and bloodthirsty 'head-hunter,' — but, these terms, when applied at that moment to our host, what misnomers! Could contrast be more emphatic than the perfect peacefulness of our surroundings, and the thought that a man as benignant and hospitable as Aban Avit should cherish as his highest aim in life to add every year to that cluster of human heads hanging from the rafters just above us, and gently swaying in the heat ascending from the flames? Is it conceivable that this gentle-hearted man, and his circle of good-humored friends, could take pride and pleasure in recognising and rehearsing the slashes and gashes borne by each head? The long gash there, on the left side of that skull, showing through the piece of old casting-net, was made by Tama Lohong's parang, the very one with carved wooden handle that he carries to this day. The owner of the next skull was fishing when he fell a victim to a stealthy thrust from Apoi's spear. This small one is that of a young girl who tried to escape from the rear of a house when they burned out those Madangs, way over near the Rejang River. Thus they can enumerate them all, chief and slave, man, woman, girl, and boy. It all seemed so at variance with Aban Avit's genial, courteous hospitality, that I wondered if it were possible to look at these skulls through his eyes, and to sympathise with his thrill of pride and exultation in them. I waited until Aban Avit had his cigarette fairly rolled and lit, and then, trying not to appear in the least antagonistic, lest I should fail to elicit his genuine feelings, I asked, 'O Sabilah, [Blood-brother] why is it that all you people of Kalamantan kill each other and hang up these heads? In the land I come from such a thing is never known; I fear that it would be ill-spoken of there, indeed perhaps, thought quite horrible. What does Aban Avit think of it?' He turned to me in utter, absolute surprise, at first with eyes half-closed, as doubting that he heard aright, and letting the smoke curl slowly out of his mouth for a moment, he then replied, with unwonted vehemence: — 'No, Tuan! No! the custom is not horrible. It is an ancient custom, a good, beneficent custom, bequeathed to us by our fathers and our fathers' fathers; it brings us blessings, plentiful harvests, and keeps off sickness, and pains. Those who were once our enemies, hereby become our guardians, our friends, our benefactors.' 'But,' I interrupted, 'how does Aban Avit know that these dried heads do all this? Don't you make it an excuse just because you like to shed blood and to kill?' 'Ah, Tuan, you white men had no great Chief, like Tokong, to show you what was right; haven't you ever heard the story of Tokong and his people? He was Rajah of the Sibops and the father of all the Kayans, and lived long, long, long ago.' I was not acquainted with the story of Tokong, so I begged him to relate it; then, squatting on the floor with his forearms lightly resting on his knees, and his hands dangling in front of him, he meditatively relit his cigarette, and, gazing lovingly up at the cluster of skulls, began:—

'It was in the old, old days, long before the Government came here, (by the Government, I mean our Tuan Rajah Brooke,) it happened that on a time the descendant of the heaven-born Katirah Murai, Tokong, and his men of the Sibop tribe were on an expedition down-river to punish a household of thieves who had stolen their crop of rice the year before, and had chased Tokong's women and children from the jungle-clearings. It was the time of year when the fields had just been planted, and before the rice had sprouted; so Tokong took out his warriors to teach these thieves that this year there should be no more stealing. When they had gone down-river to the great bamboo clump where they had to cross through the jungle, they drew their canoes up to the bank, and, with Tokong leading, started on their stealthy march. When the eye of day looked straight down at them over their heads, they rested on the bank of a small stream which ran round that great rock, (perhaps, Tuan, you have seen it,) — we call it "Batu Kusieng," — near the head-waters of the Belaga and Tinjar Rivers. They had cooked, and eaten, and had drawn out the pegs of wood whereon their rice-pots rested, and Rajah Tokong was slipping his head through his war-coat and girding on his parang, when he heard, coming from under the great rock, a squeaking, croaking voice, uttering, "Wong kokók teta Batók."[7] He paused, and, turning round to listen to the voice, saw a large frog with its young ones about it sitting just under the edge of the rock. "Greetings to you, Kop," [Frog] said the Rajah. "What is the meaning of your croaking?" and Kop replied, "Alas, what fools you Sibops are! You go out to battle and kill men, but you take back with you to ornament your shields only their hair; whereas, did you but know it, if you took the whole head you would

---

[7] Aban Avit did not translate this, and I believe it is ancient Kayan, retained for its onomatopoetic sound.

have blessings beyond words. Insooth, you heavy-livered people know not how to take a head. Look here, and I'll show you." Thus spoke Kop, and straightway seized one of his little ones, and with one stroke of his parang cut off its head. Tokong was exceedingly angry at the impudence and the cruelty of the frog, and, paying no further attention to it, ordered his men to advance at once. But some of the older men among them could not help thinking that perhaps Kop spoke the truth, and that night, while they sat round the fire, holding a council of war over the attack on the enemy's house, close at hand, they urged Tokong to allow them to follow the frog's advice. At first, Tokong, still very angry because Kop had called the Sibops "fools" and "heavy-livered," refused; but finally, seeing that many of his best men were in favor of it, he granted their request. Next morning, when the sky began to turn gray and the birds in the trees were just waking up, the Sibops noiselessly carried armfuls of bark and grass, and placed them beneath the thieves' house, and set fire to them, and the flames ran quickly everywhere. Out rushed the men and women, some jumping into the flames, others trying to slide down the house-posts; but all were met with slashes and stabs from the swords and spears of Tokong's men. Many were killed that day, and the heads of three were cut off and carried away by Tokong's party, who retreated at once, and, almost before they knew it, were at the landing-place on the river. To their great amazement, they found their boats all ready and launched! No sooner were they seated than the boats began to move off, of their own accord, right up-stream in the direction of home. It was a miracle! The current of the stream changed and ran up hill, as it does at flood-tide at the mouth of a river. They almost immediately reached the landing-place close to their house, and were overjoyed to see that the crops planted only fifteen days before had not only sprouted, but had grown, had ripened, and were almost ready for the harvest. In great astonishment they hurried through the clearings, and up to their house. There, they found still greater wonders! those who were ill when the party set out were now well, the lame walked and the blind saw! Rajah Tokong and all his people were convinced on the spot that it was because they had followed Kop's advice, and they vowed a vow that ever afterward the heads of their enemies should be cut off and hung up in their houses. This is the story of Rajah Tokong, Tuan. We all follow his good example. These heads above us have brought me all the blessings I have ever had; I would not have them taken from my home for all the silver in the country.'

SKULL OF A CHIEF OF THE KELABIT TRIBE.

IT IS DRAPED WITH STRIPS OF PALM LEAVES, POSSIBLY TO REPRESENT HAIR, AND ORNAMENTED WITH WOODEN

EARS, EAR-PENDANTS, AND A LONG WOODEN NOSE. SUCH ORNAMENTATION OF SKULLS IS NOT USUAL, AT LEAST IN THE BARAM DISTRICT.

He turned to appeal to his people sitting near, and they, as many as understood Malay, nodded their heads, glancing from him to us, and murmuring 'Betúl, betúl!' ['Tis true, 'tis true] He paused to get an ember out of the glowing heap of ashes to light his cigarette again, which had become much crumpled during the narration of Rajah Tokong's first head-hunt, and after he had it once more in shape, I asked him if he would not regard it as somewhat of an inconvenience if his own head were to be cut off, just to bring blessings to an enemy's house. 'Tuan,' he replied, 'I do not want to become dead any more than I want to move from where I am; if my head were cut off, my second self would go to Bulun Matai, [the Fields of the Dead,] where beyond a doubt I should be happy; the Dayongs tell us, and surely they know, that those who have been brave and have taken heads, as I have, will be respected in that other world and will have plenty of riches. When I die my friends will beat the gongs loud and shout out my name, so that those who are already in Bulun Matai, will know that I am coming, and meet me when I cross over the stream on Bintang Sikópa [the great log.] I shall be glad enough to see them. But I don't want to go to-day, nor to-morrow.' His faith seemed immovable, but I could not resist the temptation of suggesting a doubt, so I asked him what if the Dayongs were wrong, and there were no Bulun Matai, and that when he stopped breathing he really died and knew no more. He answered me almost with scorn for such a doubt. 'Tuan, nothing really dies, it changes from one thing to another. The Dayongs must be right, for they have been to the Fields of the Dead and come back to tell us all about it.' 'Don't you feel sorry,' I asked, 'for those that you kill? It hurts badly to be cut by a parang; you don't like it, and those whom you cut down dislike it as much as you do; they are no more anxious to go to Apo Leggan or Long Julán [Regions in Bulun Matai] than you are.' 'Ah, Tuan,' he replied, with the suggestion of a patronizing chuckle in his voice, 'you feel just as I did, when I was a little boy and had never seen blood. But I outgrew such feelings, as every one should. My father, a very great warrior, and known and feared by the people of many, many rivers, wanted his sons to be as brave and fearless as he was himself. So one day he dragged out into the jungle old Bállo Lahíng, [widow of Lahíng,] and tied her fast to a tree by rattans on her wrists and ankles. She was a slave-woman, captured when she was a young girl, by his grandfather over in the

Batang Kayan country, and, at the time I speak of, she was very old, and weak, and very thin, and couldn't do any work because she was nearly blind. My father told my brother yonder and me, and one or two other boys, all of us, little fellows then, (I remember, my ears were still sore from having these holes for tiger-cat's teeth cut in them,) well,—he told us we must go out with spears and learn to stick them in something alive, and not to be afraid to see blood, nor to hear screams,—then I felt just as you do. Besides, I was really very fond of old Bállo Lahíng; she it was who tied on my first chawat [waist-cloth] for me, I remembered it well, for she laughed a great deal at me, and then I saw how few teeth she had, and she often used to sing me to sleep with that song about "Tama Poyong with a twisted leg." I couldn't bear the thought of hurting her, and sending her away off to Long Julán, so I flatly refused to take a spear with me. But my father said I must; there was no harm in it; that it was right, and I must take one; he pulled me by the arm, and I had to follow. Then I was afraid she might see me, so I sneaked round behind the tree and just pricked her with the point of the iron, then she guessed what my father had tied her there for, and screamed as loud as she could, "Oh, don't! Oh, don't! Oh, don't!" over and over again, and very fast; I pricked her a little harder the next time to hear what she would say, but she only kept on shrieking the same words. Then one of the other boys, smaller even than I, ran his spear right through her thigh, like this, and the old people laughed and said that was good; and the blood ran down all over the wrinkles on her knees; and then I wanted to make it run just in the same way, so I pushed and pushed my spear hard into her; and after that, I never thought whether it was Bállo Lahíng or not, I just watched the blood; and we all ran round her piercing her here and piercing there until she sank right down on the ground with her hands in the rattan loops above her head, which tumbled over to one side, and no more blood came out of her. Then my father praised us all loudly, and me in particular, and said we had been good boys and had done well! How could I feel at all sorry then for the old thing? I thought only that I had obeyed my father and that I was a great warrior and could wear horn-bill's feathers, and tiger-cat's teeth. That's the way to become a Man; a baby is afraid of blood, Tuan. My father was right. No man can be brave who doesn't love to see his spear draw blood.'

I responded with many nods, drew furiously at my pipe, and fell silent. Aban Avit believed that he had made a convert.

ONE OF THE BELLES OF ABAN AVIT'S HOUSE.

ACCORDING TO THE FEMININE FASHIONS OF THE BERAWANS, THE EAR-LOBES ARE NOT ELONGATED WITH

WEIGHTS, BUT ARE STRETCHED AROUND DISCS OF WOOD OR LARGE MUSHROOM-SHAPED PLUGS OF SILVER-WORK, IMPORTED BY MALAY TRADERS FROM BRUNEI, THE METROPOLIS OF NORTHERN BORNEO. FAINT LINES OF TATTOOING MAY BE SEEN ON THE ARMS BELOW THE ELBOW AND ON THE INSTEP OF THE RIGHT FOOT. THE YOUNG WOMAN WAS EXCEEDINGLY WORRIED BY THE APPEARANCE OF MY CAMERA, AND ASSUMED, SO SHE DECLARED, THAT WITH IT I COULD SEE HER THROUGH AND THROUGH AND KNOW HER VERY THOUGHTS.

Aban Avit's faith in a future life was invincible, and thoroughly characteristic of the Oriental mind, which accepts that faith with an assurance which should put to the blush an Occidental Agnostic. To be sure, to attain the Oriental Paradise does not depend upon the adherence in this life to that morality which distinguishes good and bad actions. It is noteworthy, that in several of these Oriental languages there is no word to express 'sin.' A cruel and vindictive man is to be shunned merely because his actions are disagreeable or inconvenient to those about him. But when he dies, and can then cause no more trouble, his memory is as cherished as a Saint's, and those who knew him will give him the customary amount of profuse wailing, and believe that his spirit passes as surely to the same 'heaven' as the kindest and gentlest of them all.

How greatly the faith of the Borneans in eternal life is indebted to their surroundings can be realized perhaps only by one who has lived in that boundless jungle, where, on every hand, Nature is in her wildest, most exuberant, most lavish mood; where life dies and is renewed in an hour. Is it any wonder that the Jungle people, with this eternal loss and eternal gain ever present, think no more of cutting down a human fellow-creature than of chopping down a tree or of plucking a gaudy flower? The jungle is an ever-present ocular proof that life follows life. Here beneath our cold skies we are every year reminded of decay and death in the withering grass, the falling leaves, and the bare branches of winter; the long waiting for Spring bids us look forward to a future away from this scene of death. In the jungle there is no death, the leaves fall while they are still green, and in a night, lo! new ones take their place; an ancient tree falls, but the mighty trunk does not lie arid and stiff to be slowly covered with pale leathery lichens; hardly has it touched the ground before it is covered with a translucent shroud of tender green, which seems but a renewal and continuation of its own life; and before the burning sun shining through the gap can scorch the delicate orchids, the gap is closed by a new eager growth and a young tree springs from the earth upturned by the broken roots. Can any dweller amid such scenes believe otherwise than that death is but an exchange of life?

Of what can be called a religion the Borneans have little; they are, to a certain extent, idolaters, and their projects are banned or blest by omens drawn from certain birds and animals, but mainly by auguries interpreted from the livers of sacrificed swine and from fowls; wherein they are no more barbarous than the ancient Romans. But the one custom, to which they all cling with a tenacity born of what is to them its proved efficacy, is the taking of human heads. Can they not recount indisputable proof after proof, drawn from their own veritable experience, that these precious influences over the domestic hearth bring the very purest of blessings, and health, and wealth to the whole household?

THE DRUDGE OF A KAYAN HOUSEHOLD.

ONE OF THE OLD, WORN-OUT DRUDGES OF A KAYAN HOUSEHOLD, WHOSE DAYS OF ACTIVE LABOR IN THE

FIELDS BEING OVER, HER DUTIES CONSIST IN CARRYING UP THE WATER FOR COOKING FROM THE RIVER. IT WAS SUCH AN OLD WOMAN AS THIS WHO WAS SACRIFICED IN THE EDUCATION OF ABAN AVIT AND HIS BROTHER.

Be it borne in mind that an enemy's head is not like the scalp of our American Indians, a mere trophy; it is an object of heartfelt veneration, an earnest of blessing to the whole community. Such is the round of life among them that a pretext for a head-hunt is readily found; the solemn ceremony of putting off the mourning for a dead Chief suggests it; or when a harvest is completed; or when a Chief takes a new wife, etc. In all these ceremonies the acquisition of new heads is of prime importance, and those, too, who did not participate in the hunt, and even very young boys, may share in the glory of this acquisition, if they will merely put on war-clothes, and before the heads are taken up into the house strike a blow at them with a parang. [The ceremonies attending head-hunts I give elsewhere.] Water sprinkled from the palm leaves, wherein the heads have been wrapped, purifies women after periods of mourning, and they may once more wear their ornaments, and bathe in the river, and the men may thereafter shave their temples. When finally hung up in the house, the heads have lost all semblance to life, and are mere blackened skulls, not exactly ornamental, it must be admitted, but by no means as repulsive as might be at first supposed.

Among the Kayans it is most strictly forbidden for any one, except the very aged, to touch these heads. Sickness, possibly death, follows a disregard of this rule; but the aged, who are at any rate on the brink of the grave, may fearlessly handle them. At a harvest festival, it is an Iban custom to take the old skulls down, and women then carry them, together with the new ones, in their dances; rice is thrust between the jaws, and arrack poured over them, that they also, to the extent of their limited capacity, may share in the feast.

This account of Aban Avit's conversation is more or less composite; the words which I have put into his mouth are not solely his, but there is none of them that I have not heard emphatically expressed by other natives; I have merely made one man the mouth-piece of several. The story of the sacrifice of the old woman for the moral and physical training of the boys, I have endeavored to give as I heard it.]

In the accompanying view of the veranda of Aban Avit's house, the skulls may be seen hanging in a cluster over the fireplace around which the people are grouped. For this photograph a trap-door in the roof had to be raised to admit light. Draped over the skulls, here and there, are pieces of bark cloth and shreds of palm leaves; the framework whereon the heads are hung is made of hoops of rattan, one inside the other, so that these invaluable relics may be arranged in a thick symmetrical cluster. Among some tribes it is customary to place the skull of a rhinoceros in the centre of the group of human skulls. This animal is so ferocious and so hard to kill that it is deemed worthy of the honor. Along the roof, half across the open trap-door, is the board mentioned above, carved at its lower edge into hooks, on which visitors hang their parangs while they sit to talk or feast with the Chief. The man with his feet resting upon the edge of the fireplace is the brother of Aban Avit, and will probably succeed to the Chiefship; his word even now seems to carry great weight in all councils. At the time of taking the photograph the house was filled with guests,—a party of peace from the Baram River, on their way to the head-waters of the Tinjar to give and take pledges of friendly relationship, and to pay off and collect indemnities for the raids and slaughterings of their fathers and grandfathers.

VERANDA OF ABAN DENG'S HOUSE ON THE APOH.

THE TROPHY-SKULLS ARE HUNG FROM A DECORATED BEAM, EXTENDING ALMOST THE WHOLE LENGTH OF THE VERANDA. IN FRONT OF THE CHIEF'S DOOR SEVERAL

SKULLS ARE TIED TOGETHER ON A FRAMEWORK OF RATTAN; THESE ARE POSSIBLY HIS PRIVATE COLLECTION.

A War Expedition

About a year and a half before my first visit to Borneo, a Chinese trader, in the upper Tinjar River, had been killed solely for the sake of his head. Killing is by no means uncommon in Borneo; but this was a murder so cold-blooded, and the victim, moreover, a Chinaman, so unprepared for the game of head-hunting, that an unusual effort was made to find and punish the murderer. Although the head, just after it was cut off, had been hung up in the veranda of a house, and although the river-bank in front had been enlivened with a 'Death-post,' whereto portions of the victim had been attached, by way of public notice that a head had just been taken, the perpetrator of the deed showed, however, a guilty reluctance in claiming any glory, or even in making himself known; furthermore, not a member of that household, nor of any household on the Tinjar River, would give the slightest clue to the identity of the murderer. All the Chiefs, hitherto trusted, told endless lies about the crime, and with such success that they believed that they had at last baffled and befooled the 'Prenta,' the *Government*.

One day, about two years after the murder, a Malay trader, who had been up among the Tinjar people for many months, and was perhaps feeling a little sore over his poor bargains, let fall to Dr. Hose, the English Resident of the Baram district, some hints that again set in motion the wheels of justice and soon fastened the guilt of that murder on Tinggi, a dweller in the house of Tama Talip. The culprit was at once summoned to appear for trial at the Baram Fort, but his people hid him and resolutely defied the Government; consequently, a reward was offered for his capture alive, or for his head, if dead. Nevertheless, the Tinjar people continued to conceal and protect Tinggi, even after an influential Chief had been deposed by the Government for his duplicity in the matter, and, possibly, for the transparent quality of the lies he manufactured. There remained, therefore, nothing to be done but to appoint an entire stranger, a native from another river, to lead an expedition against the Lerons, the tribe that was protecting Tinggi. The man thus appointed was Tama Bulan, a Kenyah, and the most influential Chief in the Baram district, who accepted the appointment and gathered a force to ascend the Tinjar. Among his followers was Juman, a Kayan Chief and the lucky and sole possessor of a gun. Tama Bulan had been strictly commanded to take Tinggi, and no one else but Tinggi; on no account was he to suffer his Kayan or Kenyah followers to kill innocent people. Juman, with a small party ascended the Tinjar, to a point opposite the house of the Lerons. Tinggi, the murderer, emerged unattended from the house, entered a light canoe, and was crossing the river, apparently to surrender himself, when, at the last moment, he seemed to change his mind, and resolved to attempt an escape. In an instant, taking advantage of the swift current, he was dashing past Juman's camp. The details of his death I had, as follows, from Juman himself: 'Tinggi came down the river, Tuan, lying flat in his canoe until he was just opposite to me and my men; then he stood up, straight, brandishing his spear and his parang, and shouting defiance to us all. But,' continued Juman, his eyes glowing with excitement, 'I was all ready, Tuan; I raised this "snappang"[8] of mine, that the Government gave me; it was loaded full of nails; and I shot that insect, Tinggi, right here, — through the breast. Over he fell backward in his boat; he kept on waving his arms; I paddled fast after him in a canoe; I got along side of him; I caught hold of his head; I pulled it over to the edge of the boat; with two chops of my parang, like that and like that, off it came.'

This head was the first Juman had ever taken, and measureless was his pride in displaying the tattooing, to which he was thereby entitled, on the back of one of his hands; the other hand was to be similarly decorated as soon as the harvesting was over. Tinggi's head he was allowed to hang from the roof of his veranda, opposite his door, in his house at Bowang Takun. Although this slaying of Tinggi was retributive justice, yet according to Borneo sentiment, it was a *causa belli*, and when I arrived at the Baram River, on a second visit to

---

[8] 'Snappang,' the Malay name for a gun, imitates the sound of the discharge. In the years following our Civil War the name, 'Ku Klux Klan,' was formed, it is said, from the sound of the cocking of a firearm.

Borneo, about three months after these events, there were already reports of retaliating expeditions led by Tinggi's brother, Kilup, in which the Tinjar people generally joined, against the peaceful dwellers on the Baram; women had been frightened from the rice-clearings by the traces of recent camp-fires, and of fresh footprints in the adjacent jungle, and doubtless would have been attacked, and killed, and decapitated, had not their husbands mounted guard each day, clad in war-coat and war-cap, and fully armed with spear, parang, and shield. Reports of new disturbances and threatened outrage came by every canoe from up the river that halted at the Baram Bazaar, until finally Dr. Hose determined to crush out this portentous feud betimes before it reached greater and, possibly, unmanageable proportions.

BORNEAN WAR COSTUME.

THE FEATHERS OF THE HORN-BILL ON THE WAR-CLOAK,
AND THE TUFTS OF HUMAN HAIR ON THE SHIELD, WHICH

THE WARRIOR HOLDS, ARE THE BADGES OF A SUCCESSFUL HEAD-HUNTER.

The whole Kayan population of the river was, moreover, somewhat in a commotion, owing to the accidental death of Oyang Luhat, one of its influential Chiefs. The control of three or four hundred people had thus fallen to his eldest son, Abun, and the large household were beginning to fret under the tedious restraints of the prolonged mourning; these restraints could be removed only by adding to the household collection a beneficent fresh head or two; consequently, under a new and vigorous young leader there was imminent danger of an extensive and formidable raid upon all the Tinjar people. Furthermore, it happened to be just at the beginning of the rainy season, when there was nothing to be done but to wait for the rice, already planted, to sprout and grow. Even in highly civilized communities, Satan finds some mischief still for idle hands to do, so, too, in Borneo what can be more natural than that days of idleness should prompt a mischievous use of spear and parang?

His Excellency, Rajah Brooke, (this wise and beneficent ruler,) has, of course, made every possible effort to eradicate the custom of head-hunting in Sarawak, but in a country without roads, and where news travels no faster than the river's sluggish current, swift retribution for any outrage is impossible; and, with the small force of Englishmen who act as his Residents, it is almost inconceivably difficult, in districts isolated by well-nigh impenetrable jungle, to follow up and arrest any offender, much more a head-hunter, whom the natives themselves, holding head-hunting to be a most praiseworthy virtue, screen to the best of their ability.

Where the decapitated victim has relatives or near and dear friends, there the Rajah's officers may possibly obtain some aid; but even under these favorable conditions, the information is reluctantly given, unless the hope is held out of a participation in the punishment or the retaliation.

In such circumstances, it is remarkable and redounds greatly to the efficiency of the Sarawak government, that exceedingly few murderers escape detection and punishment, even should it take years to trace them. The punishment is not always a death sentence; it may be a heavy fine. The veneration with which the practice of head-hunting is regarded by the tribes of the central high-lands, and the fact that they have been taught by their fathers and grandfathers that it is a religious duty, cannot but influence the Rajah and his Residents to incline to leniency in their judicial sentences on these people whenever there has been provocation, albeit slight, for the commission of the deed. Where a whole household of more than a hundred men has made an unprovoked raid upon an unsuspecting neighbor, the Rajah, on several occasions, has wisely allowed the injured tribe to make, as a kind of 'wild justice,' a retaliating raid upon the aggressors; but the expedition has been always under the direction of one of his Residents, who makes sure that only the guilty are attacked,—if unrestrained, the natives would be driven by excitement to kill all who cross their path, whether friend or foe.

To resume the story of the troublous times on the Baram. It was decided by the Government to quiet the disturbances at the very outset by administering a severe lesson to those turbulent natives on the Tinjar who still resented the legal slaying of the murderer, Tinggi; accordingly, a war expedition was planned, which should be the means of intimidating the seditious tribe, without, it was ardently hoped, the shedding of any blood, and, withal, of such an imposing character that the mere demonstration might, of itself, lead even to a lasting peace.

COUNCIL OF WAR, DURING A MARCH TO THE HOUSE OF AN ENEMY.

Dr. Hose decided, first of all, to investigate the truth of the rumours concerning the marauding Lerons. With this end in view, he decided to set out at once for the house of the young Chief, Abun, just mentioned, about one hundred and twenty miles up the Baram, where, if the rumours proved correct, his forces could be mustered.

We arrived after dark at Long Lama ('Long' meaning the *mouth of a river*, and 'Lama' being the name of a stream at whose junction with the Baram Abun's house is situated). The river's bank, sloping gradually in low, irregular terraces of sandy mud up to the house, about a hundred and fifty yards from the shore, was dotted in all directions with little fires, whereon the natives were cooking venison. A deer had been killed in the clearings, and, although the flesh is one of the greatest of delicacies, it must never be cooked in the house; the timidity of the deer will be infused into the household. By inhaling its spirit, liberated by fire, young men assimilate its timidity and become cowards in battle,—therefore the flesh is cooked in the open air, and the timid spirit at once makes its way again to the jungle. Several of the natives, when they recognized us, deserted their flesh-pots and came down to meet us, carrying fire-brands, which they waved vigorously to keep them blazing and give us light. Of course, all knew that a visit from the Resident meant something of importance, but, according to Kayan etiquette, the purpose must not be broached until we were settled in the veranda. Escorted by these torch-bearers we picked our way past the fires up the soggy, muddy bank, walked warily on the pathway of slippery logs, and so to the notched log whereby the veranda is gained.

The immense long-house, looking on its high, multitudinous piles like a gigantic centipede, stretched far away to the right and to the left into the darkness under rustling cocoanut palms; mongrel dogs barked and yapped round our heels, and from beneath the house snorting pigs rushed hither and thither in all directions. The house seemed deserted; the restrictions of mourning had banished all mirth, music, and song; the only signs of life along its whole length were three or four dim fires flickering on the clay hearths; hardly a sound was to be heard in it. With as much dignity as can be assumed when crawling on all fours up an almost perpendicular, and slippery, and notched pole, we gained the veranda, where the young Chief greeted us cordially, and ceremoniously conducted us to the clay hearth, the place of honor, in front of his own door. Fresh wood to replenish the fire was brought, and several small tin kerosene lamps, made by Chinese at the Bazaar, and without glass chimneys, were placed here and there, on the floor, and on the beams. It was not advisable, even had it been etiquette, to divulge at once the purpose of our visit, or even to allude to the Tinjar people; so dropping cross-legged about the fire, we accepted the proffered bead-work box of coarse Kayan tobacco and banana-leaf wrappers, and joined the encircling and rapidly increasing group, in a social cigarette. The talk drifted up-river and down-river, discussing crops of rice and the promise of the abundance of rattan, or of gutta, or of camphor yet to be gathered in the jungle. Occasional puffs of hot air were wafted in under the eaves, bringing with them the combined scent of the fires on the bank, of mud, and of damp chips from the logs which beneath the house were being fashioned into canoes. The brief twilight of the tropics was gone, the night was already as black as ink, although it was barely a half hour after sunset, and the insects had not yet begun the incessant din of their nocturnal medley.

Gradually, Dr. Hose led up the conversation to the killing of Tinggi and to the retaliation of the Lerons. At once eyes flashed, and every man was eager to set forth his account of the outrages; some asserted that women and children working in the rice-fields had been murdered; others maintained that certain rattan-cutters had caught sight of a large force of Tinjar people, in the jungle close by Long Lama; again, others said that the Tinjar marauders numbered hundreds, while others contended that there were, at most, but a dozen or so. Finally, it turned out that no one present had actually seen a single enemy, and the substance of the stories was so flimsy that the purpose of the expedition threatened to come to naught, when suddenly our ears caught the rhythmical and rapid thump of paddles, followed by the grating sound of the beaching of canoes. Flickering torches struggled up the bank toward the house, and, as though by telepathy, it flashed upon every one that Juman himself was at hand.

A CHIEF AND TWO SLAVES IN WAR COSTUME.

THE SLAVES ARE MAKING READY THE POISONED DARTS FOR THEIR BLOW-PIPES. IN THEIR HAMPERS ARE THE SLEEPING-MATS FOR THE CHIEF AND THEIR COOKING POTS.

Presently, sure enough, in came the hero of the hour, with fifteen or twenty followers. All took their places amid the squatting group, as unconcernedly as if their minds were as free of care, as their bodies of clothes. Juman seated himself beside us on the low platform. Again, we had to comply with the inviolable rules of Bornean propriety, and converse on any subject under heaven, save on the sole object of the visit; but this time it did not take so long to beat about the bush. After a few decorous minutes, Juman, jumping to his feet, poured forth to the assembly a harrowing account of the horrid dangers to which his household was exposed every hour of the day and night from this crowd of skulking, murderous Lerons! He spoke in Kayan, a language of soft, lingual, and prolonged vowel sounds, abruptly interspersed with short gutturals pronounced far back in the throat; and while relating his wrongs he stamped with his bare feet, turning first to this side, then to that, wildly waving his arms, snapping his fingers, and emphasising the close of each sentence by shouting 'Bahh! bahh!'—a convenient exclamation to gain time for ideas; I fear it corresponded to the cough which afflicts our own after-dinner speakers. The telling point of the speech was that the camp of the enemy had been actually discovered close to Juman's own fields, and, from the way that the jungle had been trodden down, the war-party must be in large numbers; much of the rice had been uprooted just as it was beginning to sprout, and many of their banana trees had been wantonly slashed to pieces. There were men here with Juman,—he called them forth and bade them tell their stories,—who had actually seen the encampment of the enemy, and the hundreds of footprints on the bank of the stream where they had rested. Juman was clearly an orator, and swayed at will the emotions of the assembly; volleys of grunts marked approval of his eager words; cigarettes burned quick and fast under excited puffing.

When Juman dropped on his haunches, there followed an ominous silence,—the hush before a storm. Dr. Hose at once perceived that the native blood was deeply stirred, and that these reports about the Lerons, who had no right to be in this part of the country at all, were probably correct, and would infallibly lead to an indiscriminate war. The thirst of the people for vengeance must not be absolutely thwarted, but judiciously controlled. Accordingly, he at once addressed them very earnestly, approving of their just indignation, and fearlessly telling them that the reason why their expeditions so often failed was because they lost so much time in consulting Omen Birds, that the enemy had time to prepare themselves or to decamp. Now was the hour when the lives of their wives and children depended upon instant action, and he impressively concluded by saying:—

'This time do not ask advice from birds, get ready to-night at once, and we'll all start at dawn to-morrow and chase these thieves and cowards back to their river! or else many fresh heads will hang in the houses on the Baram! But remember, that though the Government is with you in this fight, it makes war on the guilty, and on no one but the guilty. Go, therefore! Send messengers without delay, up-river and down, to summon all Kayan fighters to arms! And to be ready to join us to-morrow before the birds wake up!'

For several seconds every man sat motionless with dilated eyes and open mouth, hardly realising the joyful news. Then with one wild shout all bounded to their feet, and the whole house from end to end was staring wide awake and fairly quivering with life! Canoes were hastily launched in the darkness and dispatched up and down the black river, to bear the swift news to friendly houses miles away. The slamming of doors was incessant, dusty and long unused spears, shields, war-coats, caps, were eagerly brought from sleeping-rooms into the veranda, for inspection, or for repairs, or for fresh decorations. Clay lamps with damar-gum sizzling, sputtering, and smoking, were lit everywhere. Crouched about one lamp was a group of young men warming fresh 'Ipoh' (*arrow poison*), and smearing it on the tips of the darts for their blow-pipes. Around another, was gathered a group busily cutting new darts and shaping the pith butts to fit tightly in the bore of the blow-pipe. Others sharpened their spears and parangs, rearranging the dangling charms, which they smeared with the blood of chickens, while murmuring exhortations to them to protect the bearer from all harm and help the parang to deal death at a single blow. All the women, too, and the girls, joined in the hurry-scurry, and stitched, on the backs of war-coats, horn-bill feathers, or big butterflies embroidered in black and yellow beads. Many a love-knot was tied, that night, and fastened on parang, war-coat, and shield, and I am quite sure that some young hearts beat high with hopes of presenting, as the fairest of bridal gifts, what no female Kayan heart could possibly resist,—a lovely, fresh, human head. But, perhaps, I was too sentimental, and imputed romantic aspirations to those dusky breasts which entertained no such lodgers. For as I sat there passively watching this strange scene, so dramatic and unreal to me, and so earnest and real to the actors, I saw a girl with serious mien furtively thrust into a young warrior's hand a strip of bead-work of her own making, wherewith to ornament the scabbard of his parang. I am sorry to say that, so far from responding to any tender sentiment, the young fellow looked decidedly sheepish, and not a little puzzled by the gift, and, alas! I could not detect that he even thanked her for it. Half an hour later I saw him wandering about, dangling the precious love-token aimlessly in his hand. I concluded that she had better throw him over; such ardour as his, never leads to where glory waits.

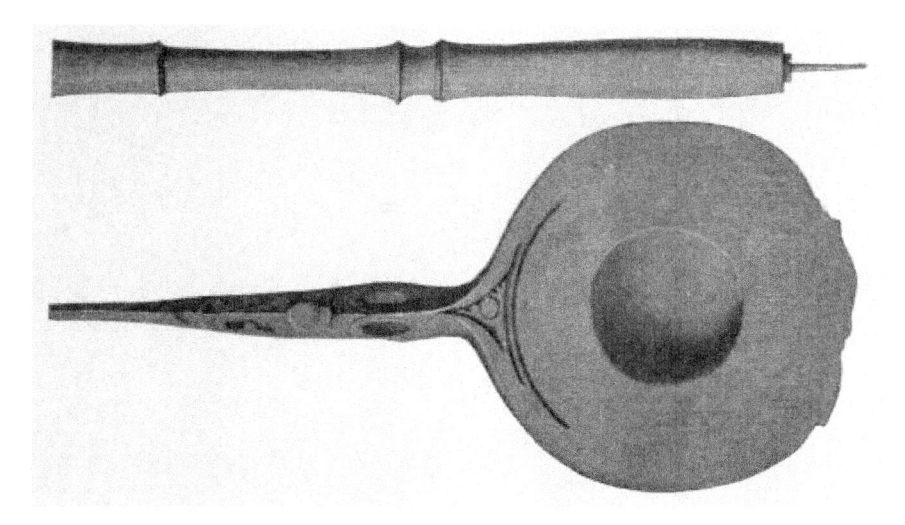

1. WOODEN FORM ON WHICH THE PITH BUTTS OF THE DARTS USED IN A BLOW-PIPE ARE SHAPED. THE PIECE OF PITH IS FASTENED ON THE POINT AT THE END, AND CUT TO THE PROPER CONE SHAPE. THE BASE OF THE CONE IS GAUGED BY THE WOODEN FORM, WHICH IS THE EXACT SIZE OF THE BORE OF THE BLOW-PIPE.

2. PALATE WHEREON ARROW POISON IS MIXED.

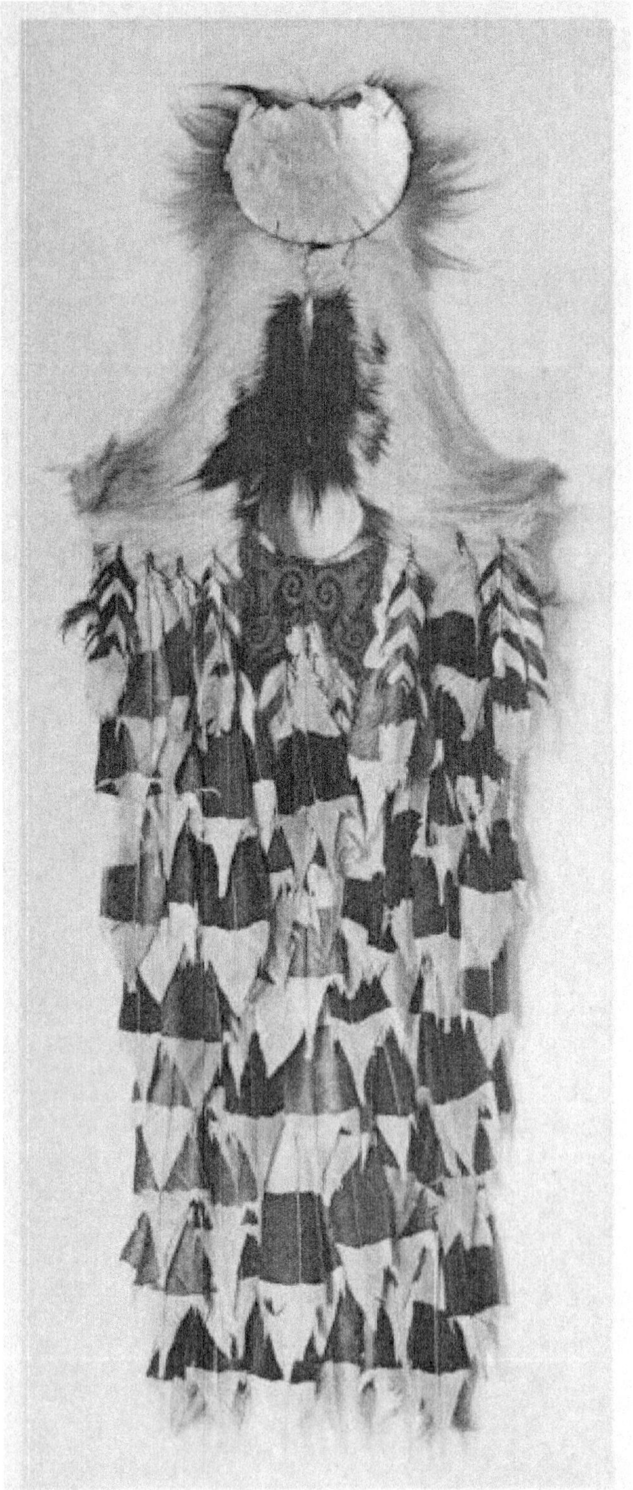

KAYAN WAR-COAT OF GOAT'S SKIN.

THE WARRIOR'S HEAD IS INSERTED THROUGH THE OPENING, AND THE PART DECORATED WITH THE FEATHERS OF A HORN-BILL PROTECTS HIS BACK, WHILE THE SHORT FLAP, WEIGHTED WITH THE PEARL SHELL, HANGS OVER HIS CHEST. ONLY THOSE WHO HAVE TAKEN HEADS ARE ENTITLED TO WEAR THE HORN-BILL FEATHERS, WHICH ARE ALWAYS TRIMMED TO POINTS WHEN USED TO DECORATE WAR-COATS. THE PEARL SHELL IS PLACED UPON THE COAT BECAUSE FROM THIS SHELL THE SPIRIT OF A WARRIOR, SLAIN IN BATTLE, MUST MAKE THE BOAT WHICH IS TO CARRY IT ACROSS THE RIVER TO THE HAPPY LAND OF THE DEAD. THE ORNAMENT OF BEAD-WORK, SHAPED LIKE A BUTTERFLY, JUST BELOW THE OPENING FOR THE HEAD, IS THE FEMININE CONTRIBUTION TOWARD THE DECORATION OF THE WAR-COAT.

Hearing vigorous stamping and loud shouting in the room of the young Chief, Abun, I entered unbidden. In the middle of the room, which was unusually large, stood an old warrior decked out in war-coat and cap, and brandishing a spear in one hand and a shield in the other; around him in a circle sat eight or ten young men watching breathlessly his every movement.

It was difficult to repress a smile at his antics; but the intense earnestness and wrapt attention of his pupils were absolute; he was instructing the novices how to lunge, guard, and parry with spear and shield. With a shrill shout and a lofty caper he dashed at an imaginary foe, warded off the attack with his shield, and, crouching low behind it, gave imaginary crippling jabs with his spear, emitting loud grunts the while, and hopping from right to left at each thrust; these thrusts were evidently fatal to the phantom foe, for, dropping his spear, the hoary instructor drew his parang, and with one chop, followed by sawing, severed an imaginary head from its body. His final explosive grunt, expressed as plain as words: 'There it is! off at last! simple as kiss your hand!' Again, he backed and sidled to show the motions when an enemy attacks in the rear; or, again, he showed how to creep stealthily, and at the same time to keep the body thoroughly covered by the shield, which, considering that this protecting article is four feet long by eighteen inches wide, cannot be called a difficult problem. Of course, the enemy was always stupid and completely deceived by the baldest feints, and inevitably fell an easy prey. But the open-eyed and open-mouthed youngsters drank in the instruction in gulps. Their instructor could not be called a handsome old man, his nose was a flattened aquiline, his lips thin and pushed far forward like a frog's; his hands were, of course, tattooed, for his knowledge of warfare had been gained in many a battle, and his contribution to the household collection of heads was large; his hair was cropped short, (probably out of respect for the late Chief,) and stood up in gray bristles all over his head; his muscular development, however, was fine for a man of his years, and his litheness and agility were remarkable.

The alcove where I sat, watching this military drill, was the sleeping platform of the old widowed mother of the Chief; her mats had been already spread for the night, before this war excitement had begun. She sat beside me, speaking earnestly and bravely to her three sons, Abun, Madong, and Batu, squatting in front of her, each busily engaged, while listening to her, in selecting from their store the best darts for their blow-pipes, and replacing with new butts any old ones which were dry or cracked. 'Be brave, sons of mine,' she said, in earnest tones, 'and remember your father, Oyang Luhat, the bravest of the brave, the friend of the Rajah, and one who obeyed every command of the Government. Bring back, I implore you, an enemy's head, that your fearless father's grave may be honoured with a fragment of it. Obey the orders of the Tuan Resident; if he forbids you to kill, then come back empty handed rather than disobey the Prenta. If you are killed, of course I shall wail and lament for you; but I am old, and shall meet you soon again with your father in Long Julán, where all brave warriors go who die in battle or by accident. And you, Batu, [the youngest, about eighteen years old,] be not headstrong, but follow your brothers and take their advice in everything.'

A WAR-CANOE, OR A RACING-CANOE, MADE FROM A SINGLE LOG.

IT IS ONE HUNDRED AND TWENTY FEET LONG AND HOLDS QUITE EASILY A HUNDRED MEN.

Her words were so simple and direct, and, withal, uttered in that soft, flowing language which I had learned to like so well, that, I confess, it never entered my mind at the time that her personal appearance was far from prepossessing. I saw in her only a modern instance of the Spartan mother, and quite forgot her few and blackened teeth, and her slit ear-lobes, enormously elongated by her mourning ear-rings of heavy wood. She sat on the floor half leaning back against the wall, with only a strip of blue cotton cloth (not immaculate) around her waist, and covering as far as the knee her thin, wrinkled, and tattooed legs, while she was addressing her three boys, of whom she was very proud. Her eyes, dimmed from age and from the daily glare of the sun, rested first on one, then on another, but most frequently on the youngest, Batu, whose marriage was to take place as soon as the tattooing on the legs of his bride was finished. Evidently her mother's heart feared lest this high prize of his enamoured hopes, coupled with his youth, might spur him on to hazard more danger than his brothers. The ardour of the hour was contagious, and I saw (honesty bids me acknowledge) nothing unnatural or unmotherly in these prayers to her sons to bring home a freshly severed head, to hang in consecrated repose above the domestic hearth or on an honoured father's grave.

In the veranda, all the bustle and excitement were continued; fresh recruits kept constantly arriving from neighbouring houses, and from rice-clearings, where men often pass the night in small huts. Outside, in front of the house, in the granaries for rice, there was also much commotion, the commissariat department must not be overlooked; a good store of rice had to be packed in baskets and bags of a size convenient for handling. In this work, the youngsters could help, and the sturdy little chaps, infected with the excitement of their elders, forgot sleep, and shouted and laughed as they darted here and there, and stumbled in the dark, carrying the baskets down to the canoes at the river's edge.

Long before the excited stir and confusion had subsided, we were stretched out on our mats upon the floor to snatch a few hours of sleep before dawn; whether or not the natives slept at all is doubtful; when we awoke at the first streaks of gray in the east, the bustle of embarking was at its height.

Just as the first red beams of level light came gleaming down the long stretch of the river, five of the most energetic canoes swung out from the shore, and a mighty shout went up from their sixty or seventy paddlers; the foam and spray dashed and sparkled and glittered from the paddles; the thwarts creaked in their rattan bindings as the canoes fairly bent and quivered under the powerful strokes. Away they darted up-stream racing for the lead, the snow-white feathers in the warriors' caps and on the war-coats, glittered like burnished silver as they fluttered and caught the glancing sunlight.

Every few minutes, canoes from down-stream, filled with warriors in panoply, came into view, just touched at the landing, asked a few breathless, excited questions, swerved off, and dashed after the leaders. The women, in a long line, leaned over the railing of the veranda, and, let us hope, 'rained influence;' certain it is that between the puffs of their cigarettes they broadly smiled encouragement to their lovers and husbands, who (it pains me to add) paid absolutely no attention to them. When ten or twelve canoes had started off, we followed in our big canoe, manned by Ibans from the Baram Fort, who, though of a different tribe, love fighting as passionately as do the Kayans. Not to be outdone, we started off with as brave a splash and as vigorous a shout as the best of them, and very soon had caught up with the main body of canoes that were just behind those that were the first to break the placid water and catch the full beams of the rising sun.

Indeed, it was a thrilling scene! It was war, savage war, and a war of savages. However it might end, be it bloody or bloodless, now at the outset fierce eagerness lit up all faces, and a frenzy for blood had mounted to every brain.

As we rounded a turn of the river we came to a sudden pause. The advance guard of five canoes had hauled up to the shore. On a narrow sandy bank an excited crowd of warriors were kindling a fire and putting up poles and arches of sticks cut along their whole length into curled shavings,—a bird of good omen had been seen on the right side! An exhilarating proof that, although the usual rites had been neglected, the blessed birds were, after all, propitious. The fire, an unfailing messenger from man to the omniscient Omen-givers, now announced to the birds that their favour was greatly appreciated. All the maturer men, pre-eminent among them our old friend, the whilom instructor in the warlike use of shield and spear, evidently also a pronounced and respectable conservative, were overjoyed, and danced, and shouted, round the fire before returning to their boats. Although no such spur was needed, yet unquestionably this favourable omen imparted a fierce exultant joy to all, and we started off with redoubled zeal.

FIGURE-HEAD OF A LONG WAR-CANOE.

THE MAN IS AN IBAN OF THE REJANG DISTRICT, NOW SETTLED ON THE BARAM. HIS COAT IS OF NATIVE MANUFACTURE AND DESIGN.

The canoes kept fairly close together all day, but as the sun mounted higher and higher, and was at last directly overhead, the paddling became somewhat less vigorous; cumbersome war-coats and caps were placed in a heap in the centre of each boat. Three or four times we all halted and cooled ourselves off by a plunge in the stream, which, now that we had passed the lowlands, ran beautifully clear. Whenever we approached friendly houses, the paddling became furious, the shoutings and cries from all throats were renewed; to which, as a response, several canoes full of eager warriors would unfailingly push out from shore to join us. Then again was the air filled with a wild din of savage whoops and halloos, and thrills of excitement ran from boat to boat.

Late in the afternoon, under the westering sun, we reached Juman's house at Bowang Takun; the house is a large one standing at some little distance back from the river and almost hidden under a luxuriant grove of cocoanut palms. Why the spot should be called *Onion Lake*, seeing that there are neither onions nor lakes there, is as inexplicable as some of the Bornean conventional tattoo designs. There is a slimy pond, to be sure, near the house, which as it is water might suggest a lake, and its exceedingly bad odor might supply a reminder of the vegetable.

As the day's journey closed at Juman's house, Juman very naturally claimed the privilege of acting as host to this large party. Furthermore, was he not the indirect, — but most happy cause, of this delightful war? Was not its joyous pretext to avenge his wrongs? Surely it was his pleasant duty then to feed the warriors royally. (And let me say in parenthesis that to supply, at a few hours' notice, food and lodging for four or five hundred men might well task any hospitality save that of a Bornean.) Accordingly, his boats had pushed on ahead at the double quick, and reached his house several hours before us. When the forty or fifty canoes (with an average of at least ten men to a canoe) drew up to Juman's beach, the slaughtering of pigs and fowls was still going on, and great troughs full of boiled rice were in preparation. In order not to be in the way, the whole army filled in the spare time by bathing in the river, and by washing their chawats, (*waist-cloths*,) which were spread out on the pebbly beach, and, until they were dried, the owners remained in the water. Before dark, all were summoned to the supper, which was spread in the veranda for the common folk, and in Juman's own room for the select few. In two rows on the floor down the centre of the whole length of Juman's room, where we dined, were squares of banana leaf, each one piled high with boiled rice, and beside each cover stood a little bowl of wood or of coarse china, filled with cubes of boiled pork and chicken. Between the rows, about every three feet, were large wooden bowls heaped with pulverised salted fish; these bowls were in common, all hands might dive into them for a savory pinch. As soon as all were squatted, some began to fall to at once; whereupon Juman shouted the obligatory welcome, 'Kuman plahei plahei,' which, as I have said, means *eat slowly*. He had no shade of fear that his guests would not eat heartily,—the duration of the meal must be long,—'the linked sweetness long drawn out.' Mrs. Juman and little Miss Juman (I failed to catch their names when I was presented), and several little Jumans were ubiquitous in their zeal that all should be helped, that every one should have plenty; when this was assured, they sat on one side and helped themselves. It was a remarkably quiet feast, all attention was absorbed in disposing of the food with neatness, and, in spite of the injunction of Kuman plahei plahei, with dispatch. Considering that all the eating was performed without knife, fork, spoon, or even chopsticks, the cleanliness with which they all ate, brought a blush to our cheeks when we contemplated the quantity of rice scattered about our places when we had finished.

Darkness closed in soon after supper; the men all gathered in groups in the veranda. Again and again the stories about the hiding-place of the enemy were rehearsed, and those who had been among the fortunate discoverers of this hiding-place never lacked an interested party of listeners, who accepted implicitly every embellishment which each repetition brought forth. The plans for the expedition to the clearings on the following day were discussed, and, in a sort of Council of War, it was finally decided that the whole band should preserve as closed ranks as possible, and sedulously use every expedient in the jungle to indicate to the foe their formidable numbers. In case the enemy had scattered only to reassemble, its scouts would become aware of the perfectly equipped and enormous force with which it had to deal. (I mention these details to show that this expedition was not a mere armed mob, but that the leaders had some inkling of the rudiments of genuine tactics.) Every one was keen for the fight; a protracted peace on the Baram had made the people restless; the heads hanging from the rafters in the houses were becoming exceedingly dusty, and their beneficent virtue was, possibly, evaporating.

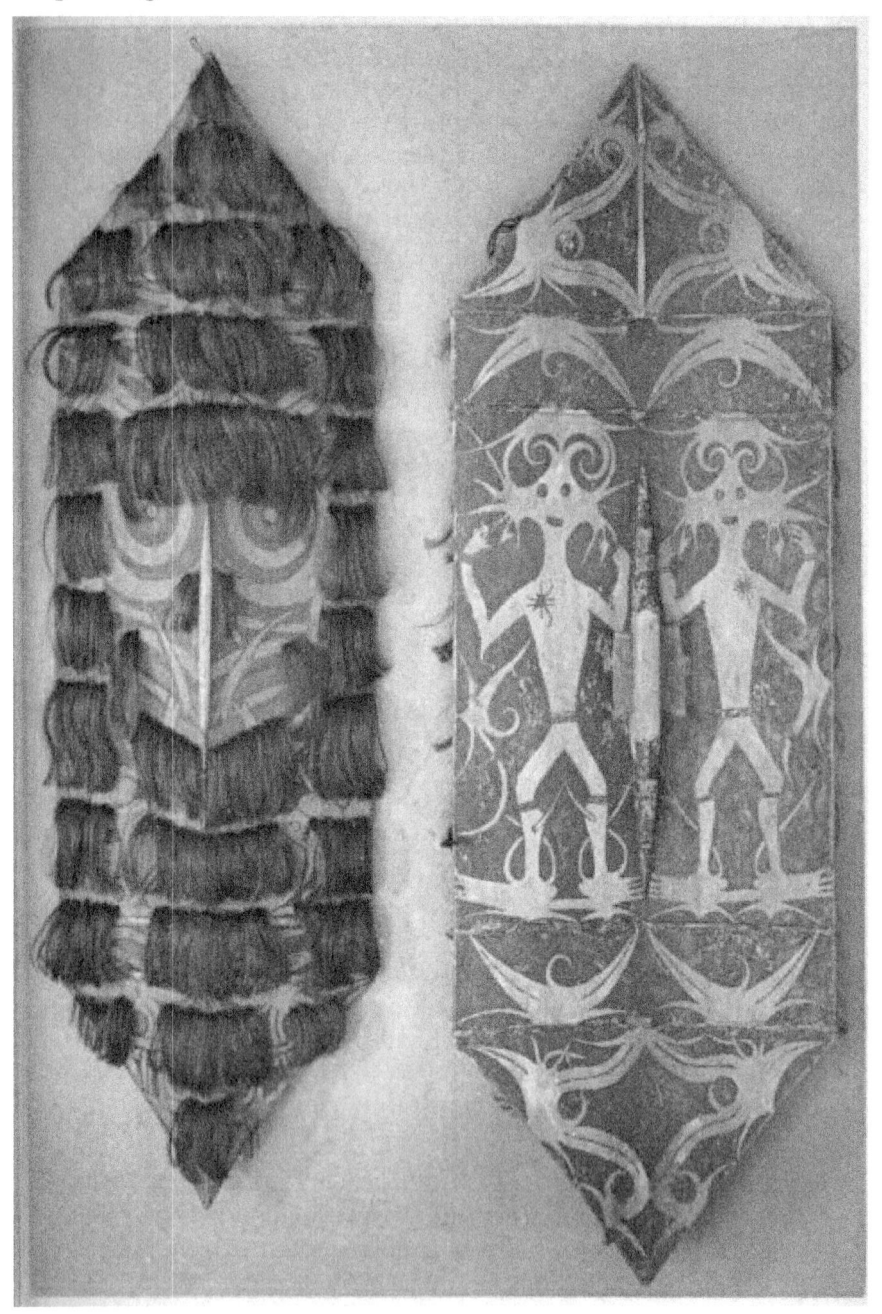

KELAVIT BOK — A HAIRY SHIELD.

ON THE OUTSIDE IS PAINTED A SQUATTING FIGURE, WITH THE ARMS HOOKED UNDER THE BEND OF THE KNEES, AND WITH A LARGE, GRINNING FACE, AND WIDE, STARING EYES AND LONG TUSKS. COVERING THE PAINTING ARE ROWS AND TUFTS OF HUMAN HAIR, CUT FROM THE HEADS OF SLAIN ENEMIES. ON THE INSIDE OF THE SHIELDS ARE USUALLY FIGURES OF MEN OR WOMEN; IT IS SAID THAT THE FIGURES OF WOMEN ARE PAINTED THERE SO THAT THE WARRIOR MAY BE CONSTANTLY REMINDED OF HIS WIFE AND FAMILY AT HOME, FOR WHOSE BENEFIT AND HONOUR HE IS STRIVING TO BRING BACK A FRESH HEAD. IN THE SHIELD HERE PHOTOGRAPHED, THE PATTERNS ABOVE AND BELOW THE FIGURES ARE EVIDENTLY DESIGNED FROM THE PECULIAR CURVES OF THE BEAK AND HORNY CREST OF THE HORN-BILL, THE WAR-BIRD OF ALL THE TRIBES. THESE DESIGNS ARE ALMOST INVARIABLE IN THE DECORATION OF KAYAN SHIELDS.

By the time, however, that all the excited rumors of the number of the foe, and of its movements, had been thoroughly sifted, I think I could detect indications that several of the older and cooler headed Chiefs began to waver in their belief that there would be after all any desperate conflict; possibly even, that this fierce show, with all the paraphernalia of war, would in itself prove all-sufficient, and that the enemy would be so intimidated that it would make no stand.

As the evening wore on and the damar lamps burned low with fitful sputters, I deserted the Council of War, and joined a group where care had been cast to the winds, and, by tacit consent, the evening before the battle was to be as gay and festive as possible. A youth was playing on the kaluri, and a sharp-featured man of middle age was the bard; he had a deep bass voice and seemed to be widely recognized as the possessor of an endless repertoire of songs,—every song that was called for, be it war-like, be it pastoral, be it of love, or be it of the nursery, he was familiar with, and at once launched into the solo, while the rest joined in the refrain.

I could not follow word for word these Kayan songs, which are often, no doubt, quite ancient. The unwritten languages of all the Polynesian races are subject to remarkably rapid modifications; wherefore the songs and legends which preserve their original form are very difficult for modern and foreign ears to understand. Juman sat cross-legged next to me, and interpreted to me in Malay, from time to time, fragments of the songs; one, I remember, had a very *catchy* rhythm with a constant refrain '*Tama Poyong kapei paha, Ara wi wi ará.*' According to Juman, it was a woful ballad rehearsing the lament of a young girl to her mother because she had been commanded to marry 'Tama Poyong, with the twisted leg;' her plaintive objections to Tama Poyong as a husband, on various grounds, sent Juman and all the rest of the group into such fits of laughter that they could hardly join in the chorus, and, of course, I laughed in sympathy. Another song was of the workers in the fields, and then followed a minute account of the harvest-festival, when women dress like men in nothing but a chawat, and parade about the house in a long procession carrying shield, parang, and spear. The solo singer sat in the centre of the group, and with a smile glanced here and there about him in a half-embarrassed way, keeping time to his song by twirling the free end of his chawat round and round in front of him, and at times, for emphasis, whacking it down on his knee. Whenever women were represented as speaking, he broke into a high falsetto.

So the evening wore on till one by one the singers crept away, and soon, wrapped in their long, white cotton coverings, were stretched along the veranda like a row of corpses in shrouds.

The next morning the excitement in getting off in the boats that there had been at Long Lama was repeated. Eight or ten more canoes from up-river joined us just as we set out, making the total number of the fleet at least sixty, carrying about six hundred,—truly a very formidable army of keen, savage warriors. After ascending the river a short distance, the canoes fell into single file and turned into a narrow tributary stream, leading up to the rice-clearings.

On both sides, trees arched over the stream in a dense canopy; thick with orchids, ferns, and vines, which sent their blossoms, roots, and tendrils down, in heavy masses, almost sweeping our heads; gorgeous butterflies flickered and fluttered in their uncertain flight just above the surface of the water or gathered, like flaming jewels, on patches of mud on the banks; hordes of monkeys, aroused by the unusual bustle and turmoil on the river, peered, and chattered, and jeered at us from a safe distance above; while the harsh and deep-toned calls of the horn-bills boomed and echoed from the depths of the jungle.

POLING CANOES OVER SWIFT BUT SHALLOW RAPIDS.

For several hours we zigzagged up the stream, following the deeper courses where the current ran less swift, under shady, far-reaching boughs, whose tips dabbled in the rippling water; gradually the stream narrowed and ran between rocks and pebbled islands. Paddles were ineffectual against the swift current, and the men halted to cut poles. One by one, the long line of canoes again moved off, the men grunting in chorus at each shove of the poles, whose successive movements travelled along the line like the rippling legs of a centipede; the man in the bow raises his pole and sweeps it ahead for a fresh hold, then the next man behind, on the opposite side of the boat, does likewise with the same motion, and so down the whole line, each waiting till the man in front has his pole firmly fixed. Then all the twenty together, with a profound and mighty grunt, give a shove that sends the boat ahead for fifteen or twenty feet.

By this time, we had approached so near to the lurking-place of the enemy that it was deemed advisable to have scouts sent ahead, especially to see that there were no trees on the banks which had been partially chopped through and were kept in position only by the vines binding them to adjoining trees; a fatal trap for enemies often used by the Borneans. When the trees are half cut through, it needs but a single blow with a parang to sever the vines that hold it and then down it goes crashing on the boats of an enemy, and while the occupants flounder in the water and are entangled among broken branches, nothing is easier than to reap an abundant and soothing harvest of human heads.

Thus we slowly toiled up the shallow water in the crawling canoes, while scouts kept abreast in the jungle, cutting a path for themselves in the dense tangle of thorny palms and rattans. Foremost among them were Abun, the Chief, and his youthful and ardent brother, Batu. They were as alert as hawks, peering everywhere for indications of the earnestly desired foe. Every now and then my eyes were dazzled by flashes from a diamond-shaped decoration on Abun's war-cap. When we disembarked at noon I found that this glittering jewel was a tin trade-mark stamped in familiar letters: 'Devoe's Brilliant Kerosene Oil.'

For some inexplicable reason, the Borneans never breakfast before starting on any expedition; but, once started, they always seem to choose the most inopportune time for their first meal; just when they have fallen fairly into the swing of paddling or poling, they must needs land and build fires for cooking rice. Even war permits no exception to this exasperating custom; so at noon the whole fleet pulled up on a 'karangan,' or pebbly island, where, in fulfillment of the strategy planned the night before, fully a hundred fires were kindled under as many earthen pots, and over a widely extended area. While the rice was boiling, some energetic workers constructed a shelter with boughs and large palm leaves to protect the Chiefs and the 'Kalunan putih,' (*white men,*) from the vertical rays of the sun, which beat down pitilessly in this wide expanse of the stream, where a tributary, almost equal in size, joined its broad waters. The smoke drifted hazily and lazily into the thick, ever-dripping jungle, and the water swirled over the smooth hidden rocks and broke into 'unnumbered smiles' in the flecks of sunshine. War-caps and coats were laid aside, and for an hour there was rest for warriors, filled with peace and rice. It is to be feared that under this soothing influence the pristine enthusiasm which marked the start was slightly ebbing; 'weary seemed the oar, and weary the wandering fields of barren foam;' there is no knowing how much longer that hour would have lasted. Juman was keeping himself a little in the background, now that his alarming reports were so soon to be tested. Of a sudden the note of instant war was struck by Ma Obat, (*Father of Medicine,*) of most fierce aspect, but a braggart and at heart a coward; one of his eye-sockets was empty and in the other rolled a bloodshot orb, whose red lids, from which the lashes had been plucked, were everted. He started up, and, with a shout to his men to be quick, or they would never reach the enemy, bustled down to his boat, slipping his head through his war-coat and girding on his parang, as he went.

This sudden call broke the spell, and in a moment all were scurrying to the boats, but not before every peg whereon the pots had rested was with scrupulous care pulled up, and the embers scattered; — nothing brings worse luck to a war-party than the omission of this last duty in breaking camp. One by one the canoes started off again up-stream; sometimes making their way with difficulty between boulders, then again gliding swiftly over placid pools, the poles rattling and splashing on the pebbly bottom. Before long, we reached the head of navigation, and here at last were the rice-clearings, — the very ground whereon the foe had lately trod. For half a mile or more on the left bank of the river, the jungle had been cleared and the surface burnt, leaving only tall charred stumps of trees. Here and there were scattered thatched huts on high poles, where the guardians of the fields sleep at night; and all the undulating ground about the scraggy charred tree stems, was clothed thick with the lush, translucent green of sprouting rice.

THE WAR-PARTY HALTED ON A 'KARANGAN' TO COOK BREAKFAST.

The path now led up the bed of the stream, here dwindled to a mere brook; the foliage was dense all about us, and all were obliged to advance as stealthily as possible. Every face was set, with keen eyes darting in every direction, and every muscle tense. Not an instant but was fraught to all with possible death; at any moment might come the sudden sharp sting of a poisoned arrow from an invisible, noiseless blow-pipe. No one picked his steps,—eyes could not be spared for that. The trembling of a leaf might mean a fatal wound. It was a thrilling, impressive hour. I suppose my heart would have beat quicker, had I not had a firm conviction that the victims of the unerring blow-pipe would be natives, not white men. Once I looked over my shoulder, and smiled at Abun just behind me, with the repoussé legend 'Devoe's oil' glittering on his cap. He did not return the smile, but gravely shook his head, in deprecation of all lightmindedness in such a fateful time. Suddenly there was a commotion in the advance guard, loud cries and vehement talking. Then a quick movement forward. I thought we had actually encountered the enemy, but just as suddenly every man came to a halt and spears were grounded. Our foremost scouts had come upon the camping-ground of the wily Lerons; a capacious shelter of interlacing shrubs and overspread with large leaves had been discovered; the earth was blackened and deep with the ashes from their fires; round about, we found the jungle beaten down, and while we were closely examining these recent traces, one of our scouts came back in great excitement to lead us to the edge of the clearing, where a treacherous ambush had been made, whence a watch could be kept on the labourers in the rice-fields and a sudden onslaught made upon any unwary women or unarmed men.

The last doubt was now dispelled. Intruders with evil intent had been skulking in the neighborhood, in considerable numbers, and very recently,—but whither had they fled? Possibly, they were in hiding, awaiting a favorable chance to attack, or else, after we had given up the pursuit, to return to their deserted ambush.

The little army, gathered on the banks and in the dry bed of the stream, waited patiently until the scouts had returned from fruitlessly searching the jungle far and wide. Then a council of war was convened upon the karangan. It was of no use to advance further unless to attack some household on the Tinjar;—this was not advisable; no one knew with certainty from whose house these hostile intruders had come, and indiscriminate vengeance was out of the question where the Prenta was in the lead.

It was futile to attempt pursuit. The enemy was equipped for land travel, which we were not, and, as they had at least a day's start, we could not hope to catch up with them. Bitter was the disappointment to all. Many vehemently declared that they were willing to go on, without rest or food, by night and day, only let them taste the glorious excitement of a fight for heads. Ma Obat turned his one seeing but unsightly eye on Dr. Hose, and boldly said, (unblushingly of course, and in a vainglorious tone,) 'If the Tuan will let me go with only a few of my men, I promise I'll bring back heads; if I don't find these Lerons I know where to find some Ivans [thus pronounced by Kayans] collecting gutta and rattans.' After this display of courage in killing unarmed victims, and of obedience to the Government, he assumed an expression of great ferocity, and rolled his cyclopean eye round the circle to note the effect of his words. To any one who knew how untutored, how undisciplined, how childlike are the minds of these savages, it could hardly have been discouraging, certainly not surprising, to see how many were the nods of approval which followed this treasonable speech; the zealous old 'fencing-master' was, as might be expected, decidedly on Ma Obat's side, and a grizzled old warrior, who, during the discussion, had seized the opportunity of cooling himself off in a pool directly in view of the assembly, cried out, waving his arms and lying flat on his back in the water, 'That's the talk! that's right! I'll go with Ma Obat! and we'll kill any one we meet, Ivan, Leron, Punan! any one is better than no one.'

PARTY OF ARMED WARRIORS ON A NARROW TRAIL IN THE JUNGLE.

Ma Obat clearly knew his audience. I think he had really voiced the universal sentiment. Fortunately, the Resident was present, and the supreme head; never for a moment would he allow the possibility of such an unbridled expedition to have a lodgement in their minds. He turned to Abun, who had more men under his command than any other Chief, and to him put the question whether he would be willing to lead an expedition into the country of the Lerons, and solemnly promise that none but Leron men should be killed. The young fellow had a hard struggle; ardently as he longed to approve his lately inherited Chiefship by leading a head-hunt, and piously as he desired to honour his father's grave with a fresh head, he knew the heavy fines the Government would impose on his House if innocent people were killed, and he distrusted the precipitate temper of his followers. All eyes were fixed on him as, for several seconds, he sat silent, gazing intently at a little pile of pebbles he was pushing up with his widespread toes. Then without lifting his eyes he almost whispered to the Resident, 'Tuan, I cannot promise so much for my men. Every one of them has known me as a mere boy. Although they follow me for my father's sake, I cannot promise they will do as I command when we get in sight of any dweller on the Tinjar, armed or unarmed. No, I cannot lead the expedition and keep this promise.'

At this reply, a grunt of unmistakable disapproval was emitted by the whole circle, and, to prevent at once any more insubordinate offers like Ma Obat's, Dr. Hose immediately ended all discussion by a diplomatic speech, delivered after their fashion with great emphasis, and brought them all round (mere children as they are) to believe that the expedition had been a brilliant, absolute success. Was it not manifest that the enemy had scattered, and fled in wild disorder before them? Had not the real object of the war been gained? Were they not glorious conquerors, every one of them, since all danger to women and children had been removed? What hostile Leron would now dare to lurk about the rice-clearings, after he had noted the traces of this resolute army of invincible warriors? The only thing to do now was to start an enormous peace expedition into the Tinjar country, and put an end, once for all, to the present feuds by the payment and collection of 'Usut' [indemnity] and by the performance of 'Jawa' [a sham battle].

The speech was greeted with a shout as triumphant as if they saw the backs of their enemy disappearing before them; they sprang to their feet, and spears, shields, and parangs clattered, and plumes waved, and so clearly were they victors, that, in imagination, each warrior had a foeman's head dangling at his belt.

One and all turned to retrace their steps. Where but an hour before, in strained silence, we had crept stealthily, now, that all danger of a lurking foe was dispelled, we scrambled along, laughing, shouting, clattering iron-shod spears on the stones, and hurrying to be first at the boats. Abun, Madong, and Batu did not share in this exultant mood; they alone seemed down-hearted; they and their household must continue to endure the burdensome restrictions of mourning.

It was during this straggling march that the 'fencing-master,' who was, it appears, a Past-Master in knowledge of all rites and usages of war, and his word law, announced that in a case like the present, where a war-party had failed to bring home a head because the enemy had scattered, it was quite in accordance with time-honoured, head-hunting custom to borrow a head; the benign influence, from a relic thus rejuvenated by posing as a head freshly taken, would then be diffused in its adopted home. This announcement amazingly heartened the young brothers.

We now shot in a few hours through rapids and over rocks, where, on our way up, we had toiled almost all day long. As the sun slowly declined, the faster we raced, helter-skelter; spray was flying, paddles thumping, the canoes, creaking and grinding over the rocks, dashed together in a mad race to be the first to reach Juman's house and proclaim the glorious news that we had put the enemy to flight. The canoe wherein I sat, was one of the earliest to reach Bowang Takun, and I could, therefore, count the canoes as they came darting through the dense leafy arch where the smaller stream entered the Baram. There were in all sixty by the count. No sooner were they drawn up on the sloping bank, than their occupants, numbering at least six hundred, were one and all, dashing and splashing in the water. [Indeed, it might be almost asserted that the Kayans and Kenyahs live as much in the water as out of it. Although they may have been wading alongside of their canoes all day, yet there is never a halt of even a few minutes that they do not divest themselves of their one garment and at least extend themselves in the water, if it is not deep enough for swimming. It would be as monstrous for a Kayan boy not to know how to swim as for a white boy not to know how to run.]

A STEALTHY APPROACH TO THE HOUSE OF AN ENEMY.

After the restful bath and the cooking of the evening meal, on the bank,—this time we were not Juman's guests,—the expedition began to disband. Those who lived only a short distance up or down the river heaped their cumbersome accoutrements in their canoes and glided off into the darkness.

Abun's party had a pious duty to perform; accordingly, we spent the night at Bowang Takun, where Abun was going to borrow the head. The loan was transacted with minutest care; the head was reverently lifted from its resting-place by a very old man, whose remnant of days on earth was nearly spent, and who, therefore, shrank less, than a younger man would shrink, from a touch which is sure to be followed by speedy death. From the moment that the skull was touched a deep solemnity fell on all. No laugh, no jest, no light word broke the reverence of what all felt to be a holy act. The skull was carefully swathed in palm leaves and tied under the bow of Abun's boat, so that it just grazed the water.

Early on the following morning we all set out for Long Lama, Abun's boat in the lead, and without stopping all that day we drifted silently down with the slow current under a scorching sun. Abun's canoe and one or two others pushed on a little faster than the rest, and when at about five o'clock in the afternoon we were distant from Long Lama only one turn of the river, we found that they had there disembarked, and had already prepared a wonderfully decorated and elaborate camp; there the whole party must remain for the night, and not be even seen by any member of Abun's household till dawn of the next day. All around the tent-like shelter of palm leaves were horizontal poles resting on forked sticks, whereon were hung the war-coats and caps, and the almost solid wall, thereby made, was completed by the shields, which were leaned against it to fill in any gaps. Spear-points glittered everywhere, and in front of this hut, or shelter, there was reared an archway of sticks, whereof the bark had been cut up in curled frills along the whole length.[9] Down near the edge of the water was a pile of green bamboo joints decorated with bands of plaited palm leaf; in these the rice must be cooked, and not in earthen pots,—possibly an instance of the tendency in all ceremonial rites to return to the most primitive methods.[10]

[In the accompanying photograph, Madong, the second son, is the well-built young fellow in the foreground; next to him is a young warrior whose name, I think, is Jok; then comes Abun, the Chief, with one hand resting on his shield; immediately on his left is Batu, the youngest son; and in front of him the elderly man, with close-cropped hair and upturned face, is the 'fencing-master.' At his feet is the pile of bamboo joints, and near them several hampers containing rolls of palm-leaf matting, whereon the natives sleep. In the background are the rows of war-coats and shields. I was at a disadvantage in taking this photograph; the light from the last rays of the setting sun was poor, and the support for my camera was an unstable sand-bank.]

The taboo against visiting the house did not extend to Dr. Hose and myself, nor to Dr. Hose's Iban crew; none of us belonged to the household; so we left the Kayans at their sacred encampment, and were soon settled for the night amid all the comforts the house of Abun could afford.

---

[9] Poles cut into shavings in this manner have a significance which even the Borneans have lost sight of; they never could or would give any reason therefor except that it was 'the custom.'

[10] Dr. Morris Jastrow, Jr., *Journal of Am. Oriental Soc.*, 1900, xxi., p. 30 et seq.

THE RETURN FROM A HEAD-HUNT.

THE CAMP OF ABUN'S FOLLOWERS ON THE EVENING BEFORE THE RETURN TO THEIR HOUSE WITH THE BORROWED HEAD, WHICH WAS TO REMOVE THE RESTRICTIONS IMPOSED BY THE MOURNING FOR A DEAD CHIEF.

At the very first faint glimmer of dawn I was awakened by an unusual stir throughout the house. The women and children and the few men who were so unfortunate as to have been obliged to remain behind, were all collecting along the edge of the veranda below the eaves, whence they could get a view of the river. Just at the very instant that the sun sent its first shaft of level light down the long expanse of river we heard coming from up-stream, a solemn, low, deep-toned chant, or rather humming, in harmony. There were no articulate words, only a continuous sound, in different keys, from treble to bass, of the double vowel *oo*, as in *boom*. A minute later the long line of canoes, lashed three abreast, slowly rounded the turn, and drifted toward the house. The men were all standing erect on the thwarts arrayed in all their many coloured war-clothes, with bands of plaited palm leaves around their knees and elbows and also on every spear and paddle. Only a few were at the paddles, merely enough to steer the procession, while all the others stood as motionless as statues, holding their spears upright and the point of their shields resting at their feet. On and on they slowly glided, propelled, it almost seemed, by this inexpressibly solemn dirge, which was wafting this sacred skull to a home it must for ever bless. The brilliant colours of the war-coats flashed brighter every minute as the sun rose higher, and lit up the framework of the wondrous pageant;—the cloudless blue sky over-head, the myriad spangled ripples of the glistening river beneath the dark masses of heavy foliage, suggesting, yet hiding, the ever-mysterious jungle, the hushed, awe-stricken group of women and children, awaiting the warriors' return, and over all, the silence of earth and sky, broken only by the modulated cadences of that impressive harmony. On, on, they glided until the three foremost canoes touched the bank; then Abun alighted and unloosed the skull, still in its coverings of palm leaves, from the bow of his boat. In order to watch the ceremony more narrowly, I left the veranda as the boats neared the beach, and I shall not soon forget Abun's solemn, absorbed demeanour. I could not catch his eye, and, unlike his usual self, he took not the smallest notice of my presence, nor did any of the others. Every face wore the wrapt expression of a profoundly religious rite. Without intermitting the chant, Abun, bearing the skull, led the procession in single file to the up-river end of the house. [The skull was now representing a freshly taken head, and there was no longer any danger to those who touched it.] When they were all gathered, still chanting, in a close group, the old 'fencing-master' stepped out to the front with a blow-pipe, and, looking in the direction of the Tinjar River (still chanting), addressed a vehement warning to the enemy, and then (still chanting) raised the blow-pipe to his lips, and blew a dart high in the air to carry the message to them. The chanting instantly ceased, and all gave a wild, exultant shout! The skull was placed upon the ground and its wrappings broken, and on four stakes near by were placed the bleeding fragments of a chicken which the 'fencing-master' had torn apart as if it were a piece of paper. Each warrior, in turn, then advanced and gravely brandished his parang over the skull, and, walking past the four stakes, smeared the blood of the chicken on his knees, and addressed the spirit of the fowl in a prayer to 'protect him from all dangers, to impart strength and courage, and drive out all pains and stiffness from his bones.' After they had passed the last stake they gave a loud, shrill shout, leaped high in the air, and ran quickly up the notched log into the house.

By this ceremony each one cast off the taboo of mourning. When all those who had actually been on the expedition had performed it, then followed those who had been obliged to remain at home; and after them, the small boys, even those who were scarcely able to walk.

Everyone, without exception, must be adorned with bands of palm-leaf strips bound round their knees and elbows, and must be dressed in war-clothes. The small boys, however, wore only war-caps, not decorated with horn-bill feathers, but with the skull of a horn-bill, or the long feathers of the Argus pheasant. Those who were too tiny to hold a parang were carried by their fathers, and their little hands were guided while a feeble stroke was made at the head. Between their little lips several grains of rice, boiled in a bamboo joint, were then put, to symbolize that they too had been in a warriors' camp and partaken of warriors' fare. Then they were carried past the stakes, and smeared with the blood, while the father uttered the prayer for them, and, in place of the leap and manly shout, gave a bound in the air, and an explosive exclamation, before carrying them hurriedly up to the veranda.

As soon as every male inmate of the house, from feeble age to toddling infancy, had performed this rite, in a flash the charm of the taboo was snapt! In a twinkling, every corner in the house seemed turned into a barber's chair. Ever since the death of Oyang Luhat, the late Chief, no hair had been trimmed, and long locks, so unsightly to Kayan eyes, had grown on the temples of the exquisite youths and fastidious loungers, who, before the taboo, figured as the 'glass of fashion,' as they certainly are always the 'mould of form.' Turn and turn about they scraped each other, and when the operation was finished, (which, judging from the character of the knives, must have been a fine lesson in the endurance of agony,) each one carefully gathered up the hair, and, rolling it in a ball, spit vigorously on it, and threw it as far as he could out of the veranda. I imagine this was done with the idea of preventing any one from collecting the hair, and thereby working a charm against the owner; or it may be that spitting upon the hair exorcises any evil Spirit lurking in it. I asked many a one why it was done, but the only reply was, 'Adat seja'—*merely custom*.

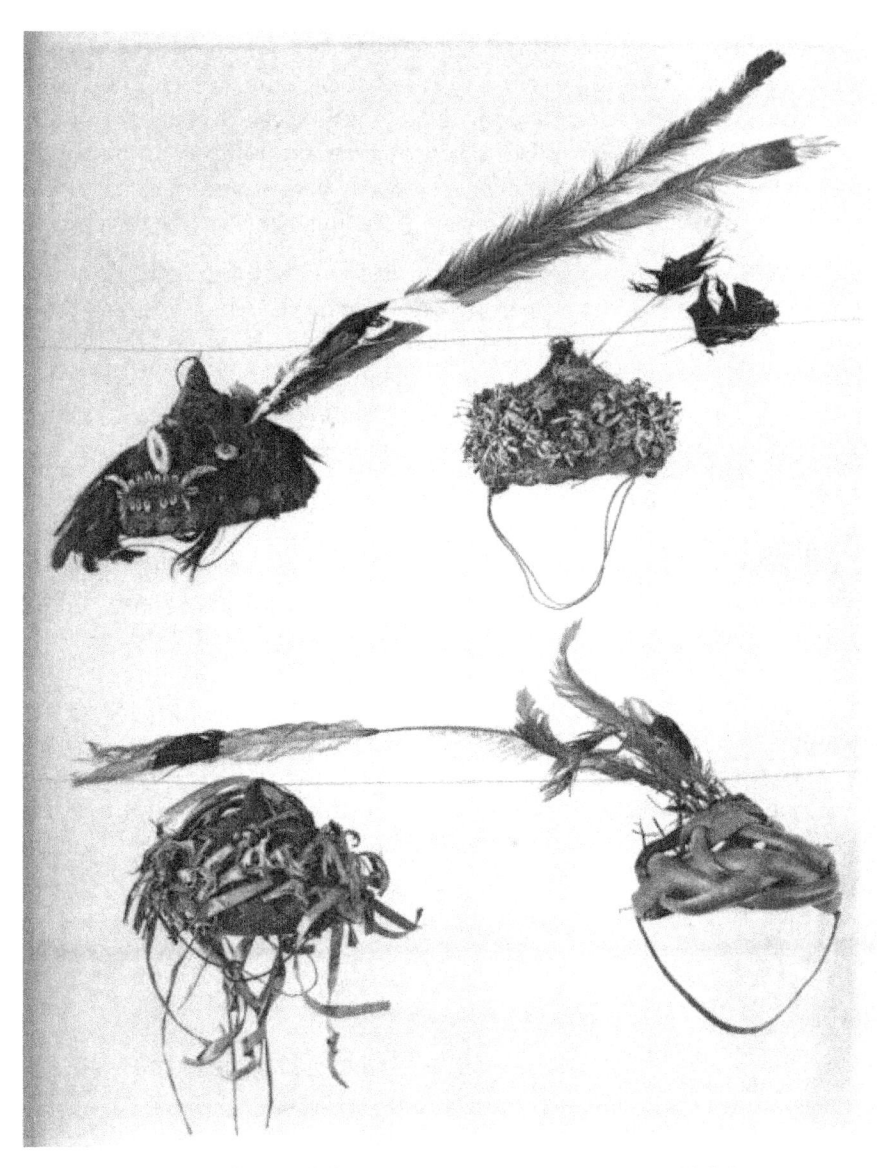

WAR-CAPS OF RATTAN AND SPLIT BAMBOO.

[In connection with this instance of a possible survival of primitive religion, let me mention that in this remote region I found an example of another well known ancient custom:—wooden images are fashioned in the likeness of an enemy, and placed in the jungle; as the wooden representative decays the original sickens and dies.[11] In 'The

---

[11] See *The Golden Bough*, Frazer, vol. i., p. 15.

Free Museum of Science and Art,' in Philadelphia, two of these images are preserved. They represent Dr. Hose and Tama Bulan. They were made by the Lerons after the killing of Tinggi, to be revenged on these two arch-foes. They were discovered by a friendly native and brought to Dr. Hose, whose image happily shows as yet no sign of decay; from the last reports the original also was in excellent health. See next page.]

Of course, it is quite unbefitting for women to go through the rite of slashing at the head; they never go on war expeditions. Therefore, they are freed from their mourning by being sprinkled with water dipped from the river in the palm leaves wherewith the head has been wrapped. Thereafter they resume their ornaments of bead-work, their ponderous brass ear-rings, and don fillets of gaily coloured cloth.

When every member of the household has been freed from the taboo by these rites, a fragment of the skull, wrapped in palm leaves, is attached to a long rope of bamboo twigs, and solemnly carried to the grave of the Chief, which, in the present case, was about half a mile down-stream. In the path which the sons and near relatives have to take to reach the grave, a living chicken, with its legs tied, is placed, and on it each one, in passing, must tread, (the poor fowl does not survive more than two or three footfalls.) The fragment of skull, lifted on the tip of a long bamboo pole, is hung to the edge of the ornamentation on top of the grave. When this is finished, all that can be possibly done to honour a dead Bornean Chief has been performed.

Wooden effigies of Dr. Hose and Tama Bulan, which were left to decay in the jungle, and thereby accomplish the death of the originals. One-half natural size.

I think the one on the left is Dr. Hose.

At night, the men who were away in the rice-fields, when the war-party returned, attain their freedom by smearing with the blood of fowls a little piece of wood cut into a brush of fine strips at one end; this brush they fasten on the side of one of their large basket-work fish-traps, placed on the floor of the veranda, and against this ensanguined brush they rub their knees, before uttering their prayer and giving the shout and the leap which the warriors gave outside the house. The fish-trap, on this occasion, they call their *Father*; 'it catches everything it sees, and is afraid of nothing.'

GRAVE OF OYONG LUHAT, THE FORMER CHIEF AT LONG LAMA.

A PIECE OF THE SKULL BORROWED TO TAKE THE PLACE OF A FRESHLY TAKEN HEAD HAS BEEN PLACED ON THE FLAT ROOF ABOVE THE COFFIN, AND THE LONG STREAMER OF SHREDDED PALM LEAVES ATTACHED TO THIS HALLOWED FRAGMENT OF SKULL STILL HANGS FROM THE TOP OF THE GRAVE. THE BODY OF THE CHIEF RESTS IN A COFFIN HEWN OUT OF A LOG AND PLACED HORIZONTALLY ACROSS THE

TOP OF THE HIGH COLUMN. OVER THE COFFIN IS FASTENED A LARGE, SQUARE SLAB OF WOOD, CUT FROM A FLAT BUTTRESS ROOT OF A TAPANG TREE. THE STICKS PROJECTING FROM THE SQUARE TOP OF THE GRAVE ARE STRUNG WITH CIGARETTES, WHICH CARRY MESSAGES FROM THOSE WHO MADE THEM TO FRIENDS AND RELATIVES IN THE NEXT WORLD.

All hours of the next day are devoted to a promiscuous slaughter of pigs and chickens, and to the preparation of a great feast; every one contributes a pig or a fowl, according to his means; and on every pig's liver the fateful omens must be deciphered. At intervals, along the whole length of the interminable veranda, are little enclosures wherein sit the shrewd old Dayongs, whose exhortations, before the slaughter, are potent with the pigs to have nice, lucky livers. As each pig, with its legs tied, is brought and laid before the Dayong to be exhorted and then killed, the owner pays the Dayong a small fee of a few beads, a strip of cloth, or the blade of a parang; after this preliminary fee-giving (a custom, not unknown elsewhere), the owner enters the little enclosure, and, seating himself beside a large gong, proceeds to bang it with a stick, and make as much din as possible; all the while the Dayong lectures and exhorts the wretched pig. The owner while beating the gong pays absolutely no attention to the Dayong's words, which may be possibly etiquette, but is certainly not surprising,—not a syllable could be audible above the deafening squealing, clattering, banging resounding on all sides. Very likely the Dayong desires to have his platitudes overheard by no one except by the pig, whose attention to duty is every now and then enforced by a vigorous thump in the side from the fist, or a dig in the ribs from the thumb of his ghostly exhorter. When the Dayong thinks the auspicious moment has arrived, and that the swine has caught the drift of the exhortation, and has obligingly modified the streakings of his liver, he plunges a knife in the animal's throat, catches the spouting blood in a bowl, and, before life is extinct, rips open the paunch, and extracts the dripping liver, whereon, in characters legible only to the Dayong, the pig had inscribed an assured knowledge of the future. Now and then, an avaricious Dayong will persist in reading dreadful portents on the liver; of course, a second pig must be brought, and a second fee paid; and so on until the Dayong is satisfied, then at once the signs become good. On the present occasion eighty-five pigs and sixty fowls were sacrificed. The young boys who have been on the expedition are made to feel that they are to be numbered among the warriors, by being compelled, on that first evening after their return from the head-hunt, to cook their own supper of pork and rice, and to sleep in the veranda among the grown-up men.

The pork is cut into small cubes and boiled in bamboo joints; a very pleasant flavor is thereby imparted to the meat, if you can shut your eyes very tight to the fingers that prepare it.

After the feast was cooked and served in wooden trays and bowls, we all squatted here and there about the veranda, and helped ourselves to the toothsome delicacies of parboiled pork and chicken, excellent boiled rice, pulverized salted fish, and bananas. Then dusty and musty cords were cut on many a jar of 'Borak,' or sweetened rice beer, and the festive cup, either half a cocoanut or blue pressed-glass tumbler, was passed from lip to lip. Speeches were made, in which the invincible bravery of every warrior was proclaimed, and frightful threats were hinted as to the fate of the Lerons, had they not fled like the cowards that they are. Festival songs and war-dances, with kaluri accompaniment, followed. When the jars of Borak were drained to the dregs, one by one the exhausted warriors crept to bed, saturated with the serene joy of duty done, glory gained, and honour paid to their departed Chief.

Even after all these ceremonies and the feast, the house is not utterly free from taboo: for ten days no work may be done in the clearings, nor may the men go for rattans or any jungle product. There is always a foundation of wisdom for these taboos. Thus, to keep the men collected in or near the house for a number of days, after a head-hunting raid, is a wise provision: the house cannot be surprised unawares by a retaliating force.

Thus ended this memorable War Expedition of the Kayans and Kenyahs of the Baram against the Lerons of the Tinjar, to vindicate Juman for the legal killing of Tinggi and drive the Lerons back to their own district, — a typical expedition, save alone that the Omen Birds were not consulted, and that it did not end in a wild and wanton raid on innocent people.

WAR-COAT AND CAP MADE OF THE SKIN OF A MANIS.

'Jawa' or Peace-Making

During the rainy months, when all work in the fields is suspended, and Nature herself attends to the rice, every path in the jungle leads idle feet to mischief, and, if war be forbidden by the Prenta, pent-up energy may find a wild outlet in boisterous protestations of peace, provided only that these protestations have at least a suggestion of war.

After our war expedition up the Baram just narrated, barely a fortnight elapsed before we were organizing a great Peace-making with those very people of the Tinjar who had been our foes. Tama Bulan, Tama Usong, Aban Deng, and Juman, the chiefest Chiefs of the Kayans and Kenyahs, with all their numerous warriors, were eager to join in the Peace-making, and pledge themselves to the Tinjar people for the friendliness of all the dwellers on the Baram and its tributaries.

Accordingly, the Baram Chiefs were summoned to the Fort, and the day before this great army of peace-makers set out, Dr. Hose invited these Chiefs and their adherents to a lavish feast at his house. The viands were prepared according to the taste of the guests, and, to make all feel perfectly at home, served on the floor of the veranda; the arrack, however, was of extra Chinese brew, and, of course, superior and very much stronger than the diluted, home-brewed liquor to which they were accustomed. Consequently, the hilarity and fluency of song and speech, upon a liberal and well-laid foundation of boiled pork, chicken, rice, and salted fish, was exuberant, but never boisterous. Perhaps the presence of so many powerful Chiefs, above all, that of the all-powerful Resident, had a restraining influence. We all sat down (should I not say, squatted?) at about four in the afternoon, and the last of the guests departed to their quarters in the Bazaar at about eleven o'clock at night. About fifteen pounds of tobacco were consumed, three good-sized pigs were stowed away, and the Chinese shop-keepers alone know how many jars of arrack were unsealed. Tama Bulan and Tama Usong were the last to leave the scene of revelry, and we watched (I must admit with great relief) their dusky figures disappear down the path, as, linked arm in arm, they meandered off in the broad moonlight toward the Bazaar.

Juman, for the second time the important member of an expedition, failed to appear, and since it was partly on his account that the trouble between the people of the two rivers had arisen, the Peace-making would be incomplete without him. In Borneo, after past wrongs, peace and good-fellowship cannot be gained by simple asseverations; there must be always a palpable exchange of beads, highly prized jars, brass gongs, etc., as an indemnity. The perpetrator of the wrong, or one of his descendants, must be present with his adherents to join in the sham fight, known as the 'Jawa.' The canoes of the peace-party were laden accordingly with articles for exchange, and with the paraphernalia of the men who were to engage in the sham fight.

At an early hour on the morning after the feast, we started up-river in the Government's steam launch, for which the river is navigable for at least sixty miles above the Fort; behind us trailed the long line of canoes with the peace-makers,—a pretty woe-begone, head-achey looking lot, after the Chinese arrack of the night before. As the day wore on and we steamed slowly up against the strong current, dodging the ponderous logs that swept past, one by one the Chiefs climbed up from their canoes and sat limp and taciturn around us on the small deck of the steamer. Still no sign of Juman and his party. We had expected to meet him before we turned off into the Tinjar River. So necessary a personage could not be left behind; therefore, a letter was left for him at the mouth of the Tinjar. On a large sheet of paper, we painted a picture of a steam boat heading up-stream with inky volumes of smoke issuing from the funnel and a long line of canoes in tow; underneath was a gigantic hand pointing up-stream. This letter was fastened in a cleft pole stuck up on the bank; then we steamed at full speed up the large tributary.

A CHARM AGAINST FEVER.

THE BARRIER AND CHARMS DEVISED BY THE DAYONG TO WARD OFF EVIL SPIRITS FROM THE HOUSE OF THE LELAK CLAN, AND TO DRIVE AWAY THE DEMONS WHO WERE ALREADY AFFLICTING THE HEAD-MAN OF THE HOUSE WITH FEVER AND TRYING TO LURE THE SOUL OUT OF HIS BODY.

A lovely feature peculiar to the Tinjar River is the hills cultivated with rice. On the lower reaches of the Baram, the flat, swampy ground extends for a mile or more from the river on both sides. Here, clearings extend over low undulating hills, and at this season of the year the rice was already six inches tall, and its tender emerald green was unspeakably refreshing after the dark foliage of the jungle. Twice we passed groups of men and women busily weeding the fields; but, poor wretches, as if their toil were not enough, they must all needs be clad in heavy war-cloaks; they had heard, so they said, that there was an enormous head-hunting army on the way from the Baram, and they were in hourly terror of being attacked and killed. We allayed their fears, and were delighted to learn that the fame of our War Expedition had travelled so bravely and had lost nothing in transmission.

Early in the afternoon we reached the household of the Lelaks, and halted for the night, to allow Juman to catch up with us. The old man of the house, whose adherents were not numerous enough to entitle him to the rank of a 'Penghulu,' and whose wealth was insufficient for the title of 'Orang Kaya' (*Rich Man*), merely presided over his household by reason of his age, and was known simply as the 'Orang Tuah' (*Old Man*). On our arrival, we were told that he was almost at death's door from an attack of fever, and that every resource known to Dayong art had been tried in vain; evidently, the evil Spirits had resolved to entice his soul away, in spite of the elaborate barrier which the Dayongs had professionally erected in front of his house.

This barrier consisted of a circle of stakes cut, at intervals down their sides, into curled shavings; in the centre of the circle stood a high, squared pole painted with stripes of red and black; at about four feet from the ground, and again near its top, were cross-bars piercing it from front to back and from side to side. At its base stood an earthen jar filled with water, and round about outside the circle was a bristling thicket or sort of *chevaux de frise* of posts and stakes cut into manifold fringes of shavings, and several cleft sticks about three feet high, holding in the cleft an egg. To the Dayongs, these curled shavings and cleft sticks have a profound meaning which they either did not know or did not wish to divulge. All these prophylactics were, however, in vain; the evil Spirits obstinately and perversely refused to depart from the old man. Not being an angel, I pressed fearlessly within this charmed ground, and even took photographs there in spite of Tama Bulan's solemn warning. He would not go near the barrier, and in awed tones warned me that just as sure as I touched any of those stakes I would have horrid dreams and most assuredly be clutched by a ghost and hideously scarred for life; should the ghost chance to clutch me by the throat, I would choke to death and never wake.[12]

After I had taken the photograph, we paid a visit to the old man as he lay feverishly tossing and turning on his hard board bed. I administered to him a placebo in the form of an assurance that I had skilfully caught and imprisoned the evil Spirits in my 'box-with-an-eye' (*my camera*), and they would trouble him no more; then, abandoning the 'faith cure,' I administered a generous dose of quinine.

The Lelaks are an unusually industrious household; they cultivate an abundance of rice and keep it stored for rainy days, in granaries which, although they are far away from their dwellings and hidden in the jungle, they decorate with graceful designs in black paint upon a white ground. In their houses, also, almost every beam-end is carved into barbaric figures of men or of monkeys in twisted positions with

---

[12] See page 68 and photograph.

arms and legs interlacing; also many of the upright posts supporting the roof have carved in them deep niches to serve as seats.

In the evening, under the benign effects of a hearty meal of rice and fish and of numerous cigarettes, Tama Bulan became jovial, and his broad, genial smile beamed to right and left on all as he sat with his back against one of the carved house-posts, and proposed that we the guests should be entertained with some of the dances for which the Lelak women are famous. Of course, the women were coquettishly shy at first and scurried off to their rooms. Tama Bulan was not, however, to be thus put off or put down, but appealed to the Orang Tuah to send searching parties for the best dancers. Then he turned to Dr. Hose, and, in a metaphor of which he was fond, said, chuckling, 'Tuan, this fishing doesn't seem to be very successful; all the good, plump fish have gone up-stream, and left us nothing but these bony ones;' here he nodded toward some old and thin beldames, calling them by the names of the poorer kinds of fish which generally are thrown away; but when, a few moments later, three young girls, dressed in their best skirts and with bright-coloured fillets round their heads, shuffled coyly out from their rooms ready for the dance, he lit a fresh cigarette and settled back comfortably in his seat, saying, 'Aha! Here are plump fish worth looking at.'

DECORATED STORE HOUSE FOR RICE.

THE PLANT GROWING DENSELY AROUND IT, IS WILD TAPIOCA.

The dance was like that of almost all of the Malay and allied races, more waving of the arms and swaying of the body than movements of the feet. It was exceedingly like the dances of the Javanese, wherein movements of hands and wrists are the chief features. It appeared to be a solemn performance; instead of the fixed, mechanical smile of our ballet dancers, there was a stare of constrained solemnity verging on a scowl.

The effect on the dancers themselves was marked; demure as were their motions, their excitement was great. One of them suddenly ceased and, leaning against the wall, declared that she was exhausted with the strain. Although the movements of the dance had been slow and gentle, she was undeniably almost in an ecstatic trance, with eyes half closed and breathing labored.

Very different were the Kayan dances which followed; the men vied with each other in wild leaps and shouts, springing high in the air and coming down on their knees, all the while battling with imaginary foes; slashing with their parang and waving their shield in rhythmical time to the drone of the kaluri.

Our hand-clapping by way of applause caused great laughter and astonishment, and the ever-present small boys imitated it in high glee. Their only fashion of showing approval or wonder is by a loud cluck with the tongue. Once on a time, when we happened to stop at a house which, during the selection of a rice-field, was under a 'lali' or *restriction*, (no stranger may then enter and no inmate leave it,) Dr. Hiller and myself were urgently requested to pace up and down in front of the house, after we had stripped ourselves to the waist, so that the inmates might have the privilege of seeing our Japanese tattooing. They had all gathered in a row behind the railing of the veranda, and as we passed along below, the succession of explosive clucks of unbounded admiration sounded like musketry in the distance. Eagerness to see our tattooing broke down for us many a barrier. Although the Borneans themselves are masters in the art, nevertheless they use but one colour, and could not believe that the variegated Japanese designs were not painted, instead of pricked in. Many a time this incredulity proved a sore trial, by subjecting us to vigorous attempts at rubbing off the colour with a dirty thumb, well moistened on the tongue. Here also at the Lelak house, at Tama Bulan's urgent request, I stripped to the waist, and the sight of Hori Chiyo's best handiwork on my back so inspired one elderly woman, that, after the chorus of clucks had subsided, she burst into song, which, being in the Lelak dialect, I was unable to understand, but was assured it was extremely complimentary.

The guest chambers in a Lelak house are boxes about five feet square, suspended from the roof, and to which access can be gained only by a ladder. Possibly, this is for the comfort of the guest; possibly, it is in order that he may not have too much liberty. We preferred, however, the floor of the veranda, but before morning I realized the error; three times was I awakened by an incubus of a dog curling himself up for sleep on my chest.

Late in the night, the whole house was aroused by the arrival of Juman and his adherents; he had read our letter and made the best time he could against the strong current. The expedition was now complete, and the following morning we abandoned the steamer and started off in canoes.

The Orang Tuah of the Lelaks maintained that my box-with-one-eye was better than all the Dayongs, and that of a surety I had effectively captured the evil Spirits; he was so much better that he insisted on going along with us. I must acknowledge I was none too well pleased with his determination; he was exceedingly feeble, and should he die the blame would be surely imputed to me.

Continuously along our route the numbers of the peace-makers were augmented by boat-loads from the houses that we passed, all anxious to join in the feasting which took place wherever we halted, and all wanted to be present at the final grand ratification in the house of Tama Aping Buling at the head-waters, where Kilup and Juman, bitter enemies, were to meet, and be reconciled.

Late in the afternoon during a terrific thunder-storm, we arrived at Tama Liri's house, and although he is a Penghulu of importance, his house is a disgrace and he himself a troublesome thorn to the Sarawak Government. In the first place, there was no notched log whereby to cross the wide stretch of muddy bank; to get to the house we should have been compelled to wade through mud knee deep, had not the Kayans and Kenyahs in our party devoted themselves energetically to showing the Berawans what could be done in the way of rapid work. In pelting sheets of rain and deafening peals of thunder they dragged forth a great fallen tree-trunk and cut notches in it. The Chief and his people, meanwhile, who ought to have been helping, sat at their ease up in the house and looked down unconcernedly. In the second place, Tama Liri's house is built upon such ramshackle poles that they could not support the weight of boards, and, consequently, the flooring is of bamboo strips, and in places so weak that all were afraid that the whole flimsy structure would tumble about their ears. The Baram folk were by no means in a good temper when at last they gained the shelter of Tama Liri's veranda. In the evening all the Chiefs took a malicious pleasure in telling their host what a miserable shanty he had instead of a house, and expressing the hope that by the time they revisited him he would have built a new one. In the midst of these vivacious observations, which did not seem, in the least, to disturb our stolid host, Tama Usong begged me to lend him my box of matches; on receiving it he passed it over to Tama Liri with the suave remark, 'Here, Blood-brother, are some posts for your house; they are better than those you have, and you can buy more in the Bazaar, very cheap.' All the Baram people, and even some of Tama Liri's own followers, snorted and laughed at this stroke of wit, but the host adroitly diverted their thoughts by instantly expatiating on the pig, six spans long! which Aban Liah (not he himself, but his neighbor Aban Liah) was going to kill for the feast when we arrived at his house. Tama Liri added that it would have been better, of course, if it were eight spans long; this would have been the kind *he* would kill were *he* giving a feast. Tama Bulan was not in as good spirits as on the preceding evening. He was depressed by the illness of his nephew, Wan, who had been ailing ever since reaching the Baram Fort, and now, from exposure in the heavy rain during an attack of fever, was in the first stage of pneumonia and verging on delirium. Tama Bulan begged me to give him some medicine; but remembering the disagreeable time that I had in his own house, in consequence of the death of an inmate, I demurred, preferring to shift the responsibility on the Dayongs and the livers of pigs and entrails of chickens.

Tama Bulan assured me, however, that he had absolute confidence in my medicine, and always had, even at the time of Lueng's death, when her brother, who thought we had poisoned her, wanted to kill Dr. Hiller and myself. 'Besides,' he added, 'it will be so inconvenient to have Wan die in the house of Tama Liri; of all men, he will be the very one to demand immense compensation for the ill-luck brought on his miserable old house.' Thereupon, I did all in my power for the boy; but in the morning, when the time came to leave, he was only a very little better, and it would have been highly dangerous to move him down to the boats. With great regret we were obliged to leave behind the dear old Kenyah Chief to take care of his good-for-nothing nephew. We had depended upon Tama Bulan to make the peace-ceremonies go off smoothly, and in strict adherence to Borneo customs. Wan's father, a half-brother of Tama Bulan, was continually making trouble between the Kenyahs and the Sarawak Government, until Dr. Hose one day obtained possession of an invaluable charm of his, consisting of a small misshapen hen's egg, whereon he based all his good luck. Only by the ever-present threat that his egg would be broken by Dr. Hose at the least sign of treason on his part, can he be controlled and kept peaceable, even, I believe, to this hour. Owing to the sins of the father, I was not quite so compassionate as I might have been, for this handsome but arrogant youth, who was now the cause of our losing the assistance of Tama Bulan. I left my watch with the dutiful old uncle, and exact diagrams of the positions of its hands when the medicines were to be given. Our next stage was to be but a short one: if Wan were better on the following day, Tama Bulan could catch up with us; if he were worse, my advice was that he should be moved to the boats carefully and an attempt made to get him home. Tama Bulan said he would much rather have him die in the canoe than in Tama Liri's house. Judging by the general lack of recuperative power in the Borneo people when they are seriously ill, and by the small probability that my instructions would be strictly obeyed, I thought Wan was doomed, and so expressed myself to Tama Bulan, with the hope, at the same time, that the medicine would be efficacious.

RIVER BANK IN FRONT OF A LONG-HOUSE.

Joined by Tama Liri and a number of his adherents, we set out for the house of Aban Avit; Tama Bulan dolefully and regretfully bade us good-bye, wishing us 'Salamat jalan' — *a lucky journey.*

Aban Avit, also a Berawan, proved to be as much a credit to the tribe as Tama Liri is a disgrace; his house is strongly built, well floored, well roofed with iron-wood shingles, decorated here and there with carvings, and, around doors and along partition walls, ornamented with borders of loops and circles and dots painted in black and white by the Chief's own hand. (Elsewhere I have described the house with some minuteness.)

No longer under Tama Bulan's influence, the other Kayan Chiefs began to behave in a foolish and stubborn manner.

Tama Usong flatly refused to come up to the house because he disliked Aban Avit, and sulked in his boat on the other side of the river, preferring to endure torrents of rain at night rather than forget old scores until the very hour of the grand ratification of peace and amity at Tama Aping Buling's. His absence, however, was not felt; the house was full of strangers; an old, sad-faced Chief, named Laki Jok

Orong, had arrived only the day before, from the Rejang, and was on his way to the Baram, whither he was escorting a middle-aged woman who three years previously had been abducted from her home, and ever since held captive in a Rejang River house. Curiously enough, Dr. Kükenthal, on a visit to the lower Baram, had happened to photograph this very woman before her abduction,[13] and had sent a copy of the portrait to her family. Having discovered the house wherein the woman was detained, some of her friends set out to obtain her release. By means of this photograph, which they took with them, they were enabled to establish her identity beyond dispute, and brought her away. The features in the photograph were still recognisable, even under a thick coating of finger-marks. The woman herself now had possession of it, and, proudly unwrapping it from its many coverings of dirty cotton cloth and dried palm leaves, passed it round the circle.

Laki Jok Orong had a sad tale to tell of the oppression of his people by one Owang Taha, a half-breed Malay, and a sub-Resident for the Government, in the upper Rejang River. When he once got fairly started, he kept up the screed in a whining, lugubrious monotone that droned on and on till his audience, by desertions and by new arrivals, was changed several times, and at last engaged in general conversation; but none the less, the droning plaint of the Rejang Chief still went on and on. The seven or eight long, straggling hairs which he suffered to grow on his lip, above the right corner of his mouth waggled and waved, and in his ears the ornaments, carved out of a horn-bill's crest to represent tiger-cat's teeth, alternately pointed up and down as he dolefully shook his head over the never-ending rehearsal of his wrongs. I retired to my dark-tent, developed a dozen or more negatives, packed away all my trays and chemicals, and then when I rejoined the circle around the fire in the veranda, still from the outer edge of darkness quavered Jok Orong's voice as persistent as ever, — and as unheeded.

---

[13] Dr. Willy Kükenthal, *Forschungsreise in den Molukken und in Borneo*, 1896, Tafel 42.

SOME CANOES OF THE PEACE-PARTY IN A QUIET REACH
BETWEEN RAPIDS.

Early in the next forenoon, Tama Bulan and six of his best paddlers came swiftly up-stream to tell us that Wan was much better, but that they had decided to take him home with all speed. Of course, that Tama Bulan should turn round and immediately go back to Tama Liri's was not for a moment to be thought of, and, although it was early in the day, jars of arrack were brought out, and the sullen Tama Usong and Juman, persuaded thereto by Tama Bulan, joined us in the veranda, and the unwearied Laki Jok Orong seized a fresh opportunity to indulge in the luxury of woe, and to begin, and continue the recital of innumerable wrongs. The etiquette in drinking toasts is the reverse of ours; with us, he who is toasted remains seated, generally with a sickly, self-conscious smile, while all the others rise and drink to him. In Borneo, however, the toast is the only one who rises and is the only one to drink, and he must leave no heel-taps; it is the company who remain seated, and break into a deafening humming and *oo-oo*-ing, which are kept up until the last drop is drained. Possibly, the custom arises from the fact that there are rarely cups enough to go round, and one sticky, begrimed, glass tumbler, or else a carved bamboo cup, (rarely used now-a-days,) must perforce pass from lip to lip. That there had been such things as bamboo drinking-cups, we discovered by mere accident from a song, commonly sung at these feasts, which runs:—'I offer to you the glittering cup, I offer to you the bamboo cup.' The words have a jingling rhythm:—

> Akui mejee tebok klingee
> Ara wi wi ará
> Aku meju tebok bulu
> Ara wi wi ará.

'Tebok Bulu,'—Bamboo Drinking-cup.

Never having seen in use, as cups, aught else but pressed-glass tumblers or cocoanut shells, we asked what was meant by 'tebok bulu' and, by way of answer, a rummage began among the old mats and baskets piled on the rafters; whereupon, several bamboo cups were found, coated with dust and soot. They were carved into a sort of lip like a pitcher on the upper edge, and on the sides were decorated with engraved scrolls, bands, and circles. Tama Bulan was delighted to see them, and said he remembered well when there was no other kind of cup than the tebok bulu. He insisted that one should be washed out immediately and put to use, inasmuch as arrack always tasted far better from the bamboo. To Jok Orong, being a guest from afar, was accorded the honor of the first drink, and the *oo-oo*-ing was so thunderous that in his nervousness most of the arrack trickled down where his shirt front might have been. Then came Tama Bulan's turn, and without the wink of an eyelid he drained the cup, and then gave a cleanly wipe round his mouth with the long, dangling end of his waist-cloth. So the flowing bowl passed round; one after another the Chiefs were toasted and *oo-oo*-ed, and Jok Orong's perpetual-motion tongue was again set free, but instead of recapitulating his endless wrongs, he now divulged, for the first time, the true object of his visit. Having first privately conferred with Tama Bulan and obtained the latter's hearty approval of his purpose, he formally announced to the whole company that he was on his way to the Baram Fort to convey to Dr. Hose, whom he now unexpectedly met on the road, the earnest wishes of the people of the Batang Kayan River, in Dutch Borneo, to emigrate to the Baram district, and place themselves under the protecting Government of Rajah Brooke. It was the very thing that Dr. Hose had been hoping to hear for some time past. It was especially fortunate that Tama Bulan happened to be on hand, and could give his weighty assurances that the immigrants would meet with cordial welcome. As a tangible proof of the friendship of the Kayans and Kenyahs of the Baram, a large bundle of presents was made up for Jok Orong to carry back with him. Tama Bulan purchased at once from Aban Avit two large brass gongs as his contribution, (a really lavish present;) Aban Avit sent a highly prized clay jar; Tama Usong and Juman contributed parangs and spear-heads, and Dr. Hose sent a bolt of white cotton cloth, three bolts of Turkey red, a bottle of Scotch whiskey, and, with his usual happy tact, a bundle of candles; these, he explained to Jok Orong, were to light the footsteps of the new comers and guide them to a land of ease and plenty,—a gift and a message exactly in accord with their own sentimental symbolism; and six months later, when a large number of these Batang Kayan people did move over to the Baram, the Chiefs all came to Dr. Hose and laid these candles before him in the court-room of the Fort.

RIVER SCENE IN THE HEART OF BORNEO.

When the arrack was getting low and the lament of Jok Orong was beginning afresh, Tama Bulan arose to take his leave. All the people of the house, even the women and children, marched out in single file and took their places on the plank walk leading to the river-bank, and even on the notched log at the very edge of the water. As the brave old Kenyan Chief's canoe swung out, all those who stood on the shore waved their large disc-like hats, shouting farewells and wishes for his safe journey home. He leaned far out from under the palm-leaf screen of his canoe, and with a broad smile, revealing a gleam of his shining black teeth, waved his hat and shouted success to the Great Peace-party; the swift current caught his boat, and it dashed out of sight round the turn of the river. There is unquestionably an unusual personal force in this middle-aged Kenyah Chief's character; not a tribe that does not respect his name and speak of him with admiration mingled almost with reverence. In my book of photographs, which I carried about with me to overcome the objections of timid souls to having their portraits taken, Tama Bulan's portrait soon became framed with a black margin of thumb-marks, and his features much dimmed by constant fingering,—the natives are never content simply to look at a portrait, but always insist on passing their hands over it; in landscapes, no matter how familiar the scene, they take no interest whatever. Tama Bulan's influence cannot be attributed to fierce looks; his expression is, on the contrary, gentle and benign; nor is his presence commanding, but yet, when he once gives an order or pronounces judgement, there seems to be no thought of disobedience or of appeal. Certainly, he has one characteristic: keenness; we once asked him if he knew what was meant when, in talking English among ourselves, we said 'T. B.' (his initials); he at once replied, 'I think, Tuan, you are, probably, talking about me.' We were led to ask because we noticed several times that he looked up swiftly when these initials were uttered.

By the time that all the arrack had been quaffed, the promiscuous household of Aban Avit was somewhat demoralized; nevertheless, we picked out a party of eight or ten sober men to escort us to the top of an adjoining hill, whence we could get the bearings of several mountains which would give us cross-bearings when we reached the really hilly country. It was an exceedingly difficult ascent, although the hill was only five hundred feet high; so dense was the jungle with thorny palms, rattans, and the roots of 'buttress trees,' that we had to cut every step of our way to the top. When we reached the summit we were just as much closed in by trees as when we were at the foot. As a sight of the horizon was essential, there was no help for it but to sacrifice some of the grand old trees; so our men were set to work with their axes, and in a few minutes one after another of the venerable giants went toppling down the precipitous hillside, carrying smaller trees in their fall and making a crashing roar that reverberated from mountain to mountain like veritable peals of thunder. Then were disclosed views of the surrounding mountains through the open windows in the foliage, and we were enabled to take the bearings of Mt. Dulit, and Mt. Mulu, and the peaks of a low range of lime-stone hills that were to the south-westward near the coast.

The next day, during our toilsome paddling up-river, we overtook an old Chief named Jamma and his party, also on the way to Tama Aping Buling's to participate in the Peace ceremonies.

Jamma had the reputation of having at all times a marvellously good opinion of himself, and on this occasion was travelling in grand state with gong-players in the bow of his boat discoursing that tinkling, staccato music, of which, it seems, he was an ardent admirer.

LAKI JOK ORONG, A REJANG RIVER CHIEF.

THE ORNAMENTS IN HIS EARS ARE CARVED OUT OF THE BEAK OF A HORN-BILL, IN IMITATION OF TIGER-CAT'S TEETH.

The instrument known as the 'Kromong' is an importation from Brunei, the ancient capital of Borneo, and consists of a series of eleven small brass gongs laid on ropes of rice straw and struck with a wooden beater. The result is perfect in time but absolutely devoid of melody; it is merely running up and down the imperfect scale of gongs in sequence, or beginning at the deepest toned, or largest gong, with the left hand, the third in the series is struck with the right hand, then the second with the left and the fourth with the right, and so up the line of all the eleven gongs, the left hand following the right at an interval of one gong. At a distance, possibly at a very great distance, the sound wafted across the water is really not unpleasant, recalling the gurgling and tinkling of a woodland brook; but close at hand its jangling monotony is beyond words exasperating.

Jamma, to whom was due this running accompaniment, is the nephew of the redoubtable Aban Jau, who, in the wild days before Sir Charles Brooke became Rajah of the Baram district, was the ruler over all the people of the Tinjar. For years he defied the Sarawak Government, and with his numerous and formidable household of eight hundred people was the terror of the whole region. His house was over a quarter of a mile in length, and was well stocked with brass swivel-guns brought from Brunei. But he was finally overpowered by the Rajah's trained Iban soldiers and forced to submit to the laws and the taxes of Sarawak. Mild and moderate as these were, they were too galling to Aban Jau, and he soon after migrated to the regions of 'Bulun Matai,' — the Land of the Dead, — his household was scattered, and nothing now remains of his long-house except rows of decaying posts stretching far away into a thick, impenetrable overgrowth of palms, gigantic ferns, and tangled vines. To judge of the dead uncle by the living nephew, it cannot be said that the breed is improved; the nephew, Jamma, is a decidedly repulsive old fellow in spite of his musical strain. At the time I made his acquaintance he was sadly in need of a razor, or rather, of a pair of tweezers; a five days' scraggly growth of grizzled bristles covered his chin and cheeks; to aid his failing eyes he wore a pair of huge, circular, brass-rimmed spectacles, evidently a bargain, purchased at random from a Chinese trader; their focus did not in the least comply with the formula of his eye-sight, and made him squinny up his eyes in a number of wrinkles that would puzzle Cocker. The eyes behind the glasses resembled those of an Orang Utan; the whites were a dirty, blood-shot brown, and the iris appeared to have overrun and left a stain around it. His eyebrows and eyelashes had been pulled out, and beneath the lower lids hung wrinkled and flabby bags of skin. His upper lip was long, and came down to a point in the middle, and his lower lip was thick and everted, exposing the pale, moist, inner surface. His nose was broad and flat, and the nostrils opened directly forward and apparently into the cavities of his skull. On his head a thin, unhealthy-looking crop of whitish hair stood up, like a scrubbing-brush, where it was not covered by the very dirty and faded blue and white jockey cap of canton flannel, which he wore with unmeasured pride and with a 'peace in the consciousness of being well dressed,' which all his 'religion could not bestow.' The stretched lobe of his right ear had given way, and one long end dangled down on his chest and whipped from side to side whenever he moved his head quickly. Long experience has taught me utterly to distrust personal appearance at first sight, but in Jamma's case a prolonged acquaintance confirmed a belief that his intense ugliness had struck in.

The Peace-party was by this time assuming large proportions; constant additions were made to it from the houses along the river, and late in the afternoon, after a vigorous and inevitable outburst from Jamma's gongs, we pulled up at the high sandy bank in front of the house of Tama Aping Pang. Here, beyond the region of mosquitoes, and while darkness was closing in, cooking fires were built along the shore.

After the evening meal was finished and universal benevolence was diffused by soothing cigarettes, all the Kayans went up into the house to assist Juman in the rite of 'Usut'—that is, of obliterating a feud. The interchange of Usut is obligatory between the descendants of enemies whenever they first enter each other's houses; they may have met many times on most friendly terms in the jungle or in the houses of neighbours, but they must not take shelter under one another's roof until they have appeased the wrongs done by and against their ancestors. The simple rite of giving Usut for ancestral wrongs is expanded into the performance of Jawa when, in addition, the descendants have been themselves wrongdoers.

Up the notched log we all mounted to the veranda and seated ourselves in a circle on the floor. Juman and Tama Aping Pang, a short and squat little man, with a decidedly Mongolian face, sat cross-legged and facing each other. Juman began the ceremony by flinging down a roughly made iron spear-head into the centre of the circle; thereupon Jamma, still wearing his goggles and his blue and white jockey cap, arose to officiate. Upon the flat surface of the spear-head a young chicken was at once decapitated, then torn to pieces, and its warm blood smeared thickly over the point. The hideous Jamma thereupon proclaimed, in the guttural grunts of the Sibop language, that all enmity between the Houses of Tama Aping Pang and Juman was at an end, and hereafter neither of them could be reproached with having allowed the slaughter of their ancestors to go unavenged. Whereupon sundry beads and trinkets were exchanged more as a formality than on account of their value, and some blood from the spear-point having been rubbed either on the chest or arms of everyone present, including ourselves, Juman and all his clan at once hailed Tama Aping Pang and all his clan, as friends. No carousing followed, and the weary Kayans soon retired to the river-bank and to their canoes to sleep.

This house of Tama Aping Pang is famed for its manufacture of 'Sumpits,' or blow-pipes. All along on the partition wall of the veranda, I noticed that they were stacked in all stages of manufacture, from the rough-hewn and thick staves up to the drilled and polished tubes. The best Sumpits are made of a hard, close-grained, reddish wood of a tree called 'Niagang.' This is used not only on account of its hardness but also because it is exceedingly straight and has very few knots. A staff of wood about eight feet long is shaved down until it is about three and a half inches in diameter; it is then inserted in a hole in the floor of the house, and so secured that one end remains five or six inches above the floor; over it a man stands with a long, slender rod of iron flattened to a rough edge at one end; this edge an assistant keeps constantly true to the centre of the long staff, while the man raises and drops the drill perpendicularly. Gradually a bore of about a quarter of an inch in diameter is thus produced. It is an exceedingly slow process; it takes at least eight or nine hours to drill through the whole length of the staff. The bore is now smoothed, first, by means of fine sand or clay smeared on a slim rattan, which is pulled through it many times rapidly backward and forward. It is then ready for polishing with another piece of rattan ending in a loop or a cleft, wherein leaves, like the bamboo, rich in silica, are bound; it is thus polished until it shines almost as brilliantly as a gun-barrel. The staff is now trimmed down to the diameter of about an inch and a half at the mouth, and to an inch at the muzzle, and then scraped and smoothed with knives and shark-skin files. If the tube happen to be slightly sprung, the curve is overcome by a broad iron spear-head bound on at the muzzle; when the pipe is held horizontally the weight of the iron counteracts the curve.

Some of the more highly finished blow-pipes are furnished with a sight, called by the Kayans 'Bitan,' ingeniously made of a cowrie shell imbedded in gutta-percha near the muzzle, with the slit-like opening turned upward and parallel with the shaft; again, others have an iron sight, near the muzzle, bound on with rattan. I have never seen any carved ornamentation on a blow-pipe except a plate of bone inlaid with strips of lead, at the mouth-end. 'Sumpitan' is the Malay name for the weapon; the Kayans call it 'Leput,' and the Punans simply 'Put;' Ibans, who clip and elide Malay words, drop the ending *an*, and call it 'Sumpit.' All these names are, possibly, derived from an imitation of the sound when the dart is blown through the tube and the tongue closes the opening with a quick pat.

Before our departure next morning there was lively trading in the specialty of the house. The house itself was really a notable monument of industry and artistic taste; many of the projecting beam-ends were carved and the partition walls decorated with borders and frescoes in black and red. For a bolt of red cloth I bought the elaborately carved door of a dwelling-room, whereof the photograph is on the opposite page.

Our next destination was the house of the crafty and treacherous Aban Liah, once a respected Penghulu, but on account of his duplicity in connection with the murder of the Chinaman by Tinggi, (set forth in the preceding pages,) the Government had degraded him. His house was selected, nevertheless, as a rendezvous for the whole Peace-party before ascending the river to the house of Tama Aping Billing, just then the candidate for the Penghulu-ship of the upper Tinjar, and also for Aban Liah's seat in the Council Negri.

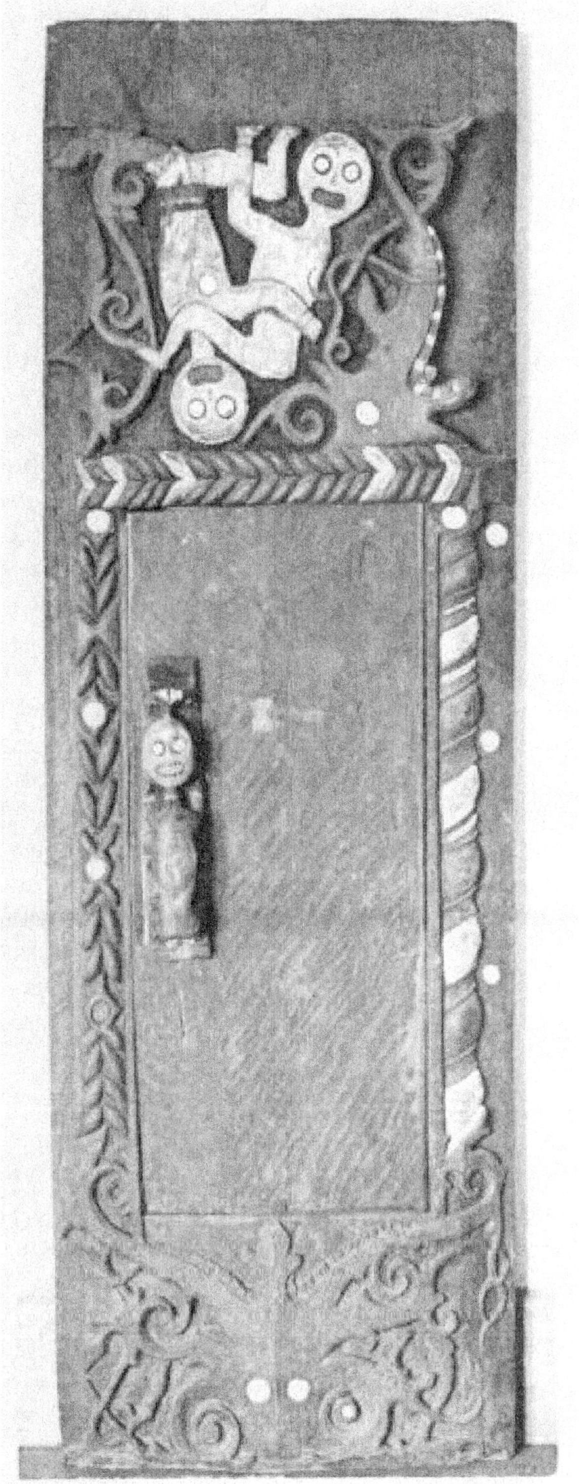

A DOOR-FRAME FROM THE HOUSE OF TAMA APING PANG, A SIBOP.

THE TWO LITTLE FIGURES ABOVE THE DOOR WERE SAID TO REPRESENT WAWA MONKEYS. THE CARVING TO THE RIGHT OF THEM IS, I BELIEVE, THE CONVENTIONALIZED HEAD OF A PIG. BELOW THE DOOR THE SAME DESIGN IS REPEATED, BUT REVERSED AND DOUBLE.

After the halt for luncheon, at mid-day, old Jamma courteously invited me into his boat, and in order to overcome my prejudice against him I accepted his invitation. He verily tried his best to make me comfortable; arranged mats and rolls of cloth for me to recline on; started up the gong-beater to his deafening and lugubrious work; told me with assiduous attention the names of the small tributary streams which we passed, and zealously pointed out one where some of his men had gone on a collecting trip for the 'thing that smells,'—a circumlocution for camphor,—he was afraid to pronounce the name lest it bring bad luck to his collectors. That the river was pre-empted was manifest; across its mouth had been stretched a rope of rattan, and from it dangled wooden models of parangs, billiongs, (axes) and spears. These models indicated that the river was claimed by the camphor collectors; to disregard this warning exposed the offender to the malignity of all evil Spirits. The only way whereby such a taboo may be counteracted is to build a fire, and erect over it an arch of twigs and sticks cut at the ends and down the sides into curled shavings; when the fire burns up briskly, he who would break the taboo must carefully explain to the fire that he is a near friend to the claimants of the river, and entreat the flame and the smoke to convey his message of good-will both to them and to the Spirits of the jungle. After this ceremony he may, in perfect safety, pass under the rattan, and ascend the river.

In the course of this entertaining and instructive conversation, Jamma suddenly, and apparently for the first time, caught sight of my briar-wood pipe, and, apropos of nothing, exclaimed, 'What a pity it is that the Tuan did not bring with him several pipes like the one he is now smoking.' The mystery of his devotion to me was at once solved! Here was the secret of his hospitality; alack, I did not respond; blind to the palpable hint, I simply replied that it was indeed a pity, a great pity; I often liked to change my pipes, but that this one was so exceptionally sweet that I had brought no other. He had counted on my handing it over to him with alacrity, and at once his manner changed from 'gay to grave, from lively to severe;' the rest of the journey was passed in an obstinate silence, unbroken save by the banging of his brazen gongs.

Aban Liah began to show his evil disposition from the very moment we pulled up at his house; he insisted that Juman should never enter his house until Usut had been paid. This seemed designed to thwart the whole Peace-making; not only would much time be consumed in discussing the payment of Usut which was not due to Aban Liah, but furthermore the ceremony of Jawa and total settlement of Usut had been planned to take place in a day or two at Tama Aping Buling's. Dr. Hose put a stop at once to all this nonsense by emphatically telling Aban Liah that Juman was now travelling with the Government, — that is, with Dr. Hose himself, — and as the Government intended to enter any house that was convenient, Juman should follow. I am thus particular in giving these details because of their tragic consequence to Aban Liah. In response, Aban Liah gave a grunt, and, muttering, shut himself up at once in his private room, where he sulked for half an hour, while the Kayans and Kenyahs were making themselves quite at home in his veranda. When they were all seated in groups, Dr. Hose went to the room and dragged forth the pouting, grumbling, obstinate old creature, and although the two men, Aban Liah and Juman, were perfectly well acquainted with each other, Dr. Hose made an elaborate ceremony of introducing them, as though they had never met before; this formal introduction really seemed to obliterate all previous hard feeling, and Aban Liah unbent as though graciously meeting a new acquaintance. Shortly afterward, our host cleared a space in his room for us, spread fresh mats, and put his fireplace at the disposal of our Chinese cook. When we all sat chatting in the veranda, Aban Liah seized the occasion to expatiate on the magnificent proportions of the pig that he was going to kill for us on the morrow, affirming that it was seven spans long (this was one span better than Tama Liri had held out to us), and very, *very* fat! His arrack also was of an especially fine brand, and plenty of it, too, in jars dusty with age.

Suddenly, messengers hurried in to announce that the Lerons from the house of the Leppu Anans close by, and friends and relatives of Tinggi, were on their way down-river to go through the ceremony of Jawa with Juman and his clan.

ABAN LIAH.

A BERAWAN CHIEF, WHO, DURING THE PEACE-MAKING, DIED OF A GUILTY CONSCIENCE.

The greatest excitement at once ensued; all jumped to their feet and began talking and gesticulating wildly. Dr. Hose, fearing that a real fight, instead of a sham one, might be the result, hurried up-river in a light canoe, to meet the approaching participators in the Jawa, and to restrain their zeal. These people, be it remembered, had vowed to kill Dr. Hose on sight, and had even made death-dealing images both of him and of Tama Bulan, as I have already mentioned. Dr. Hose's absolute disregard of their bloodthirsty threats and machinations disarmed them completely; he boarded their canoe in the most friendly manner and accompanied them down-stream.

When they were opposite to Aban Liah's house, the bravest in their party fired three or four blank shots from an old muzzle-loading gun. This salute Juman was bound to answer from the house. His gun was a breech-loader, but unfortunately so old, battered, and loose in its joints that a man at the stock stood in as much danger as a man at the muzzle. Juman's apology for his reluctance to fire it off was—(literally translated) 'Tuan, will you shoot off this snappang for me; I am afraid its engine has the fever.' My assistant, Lewis Etzel, discharged it twice for him, and then made the hair of the Lerons stand on-end by discharging from his Winchester rifle six shots, in rapid succession. After this exchange of salutes, the Lerons disembarked and entered the house at the up-river end. After all were assembled in a dense crowd, panting with excitement, their eyes dilated and flashing, they paused for a second and then gave a wild yell, like a jeer of derision, and began stamping their feet on the rattling boards. It was truly deafening. Instantly Juman and his people were on their feet. There was a quick, frenzied dash, with yells and stamps, until they stood face to face. This was the instant that the sham, weaponless fight should have taken place, leaving black eyes and torn ears. For a moment, it seemed as though over-excitement would lead to a deeper tragedy. The reaction came unexpectedly from Juman, the chief actor in this dramatic show (which in sooth it really was). Juman, brave enough before a single man, Tinggi, was here overcome by an attack of—what shall I call it?—stage fright? The next moment we saw him wilt and ignominiously retreat from the affray. The wild hubbub subsided weakly. Criticisms of Juman's conduct were at once loudly, freely, and universally expressed. But, unabashed, he stoutly maintained that he had fulfilled all that was required of him, and that now was the time for Usut. The Lerons had killed many of his ancestors in days of yore, and he demanded of them, as a salve for his wounded feelings, five 'Tawaks'—(large bronze gongs made in Java) and five small gongs, (worth in all about three hundred Mexican dollars.) This considerable sum, the Lerons protested, was far too high a price to pay for wounds inflicted on Juman's ancestors and his own feelings; finally, after much haggling and many excited gesticulations on both sides, a compromise was struck on one Tawak, one small gong, and a 'Lukut sekála,' one of those invaluable beads, prized above all others by Kayans, Kenyahs, and Ibans.

(I tried my best to solve the mysterious value of these beads, but in vain. They are by no means brilliant or showy; indeed, quite the contrary, they are rather dull and ugly; of about half an inch in diameter, and on the four quarters there is a little many-pointed star of dull yellow on a dark background. They look a good deal like old Venetian glass, but whence they originally came, or wherein consists their charm, the natives themselves could not or would not tell. Once on a time, some astute Chinese traders, counting on an assured fortune, sent a Lukut sekála to Germany, where it was copied with really marvellous fidelity. With these faultless imitations they were certain that they could deceive the natives, but the latter detected the counterfeit beads at once, and, although willing to purchase the forgeries, would pay but a pittance for them.)

By the terms of the Usut, whenever the Lerons should pay a return visit to Juman, he pledged himself to restore the Lukut sekála.

As soon as Juman's Usut was finally settled with the Lerons, Aban Liah's vaunted seven-span pig was brought forward for inspection and admiration. Tama Liri at once fell to measuring it off; when his last span reached the animal's snout, he arose, and, gazing round on the circle and wagging his head with a beaming and triumphant smile, announced that after all the pig was barely *five* spans long. The chorus of clucks of surprise with which this announcement was greeted did not, however, in the least disconcert the boastful and deceitful old host.

A CONTINGENT OF THE PEACE-PARTY.

Jamma, still resplendent in his dirty blue and white jockey cap and prodigious goggles, hustled about in a most officious manner, directing the guests and members of the household where to sit, and what to do, always in a half-apologetic tone, as if the host, Aban Liah, should be pardoned for not exactly knowing what was proper. Tama Talip, the Chief of the Lerons, now that everything in the way of Usut had been paid and snugly stowed, took his seat among the Kayans and Kenyahs, and denounced Juman's demands and rehearsed the deaths among his forebears due to Juman's bloodthirsty family. Juman listened stolidly, evidently not a little pleased to hear how very brave his ancestors had been. The talk went round the circle, and Jok Orong began again to drone forth the endless tale of his woes. The dreary knowledge of what this implied proved too much for the patience of the white contingent of the Peace-party, and we all crept unobserved out of the circle, and, having found, on the banks of the river, an upturned canoe, reclined thereon, and lazily watched in the gloaming the gigantic fruit-bats, ('flying foxes' they are called,) which were now thickly visible in all quarters of the sky and all bending their flight in one direction, toward their nocturnal feeding-ground. They imparted an antediluvian appearance to the sombre scene, and we seemed to have travelled back into a remote geologic period, among the pterodactyls. Not even the golden rays of level sunlight gleaming forth from beneath lowering clouds on the horizon could dispel this solemnity. At our feet sluggishly glided the darkening river, emerging, and again lost, from under the dense jungle on its banks, whence here and there tall, slender, tufted palms rose into the silent air from the unbroken green massed about their feet. On the opposite bank, in the distance, abruptly towered Mount Dulit, whose purple peaks were glowing with the last rays of sunlight. And 'all the air a solemn stillness' held, save when at intervals the muffled murmur of Jok Orong's woes reached us from the house behind, but did not mar the scene; it partook of the nature of eternity and infinity; we felt that *labitur et labetur in omne volubilis aevum.*

On the next day a great feast was held; as one of the most important, nay, most vital, of preliminaries, the slaughter of the pigs took place, and the inspection of their livers for favorable or unfavorable omens. The pigs were brought up with their four feet tied together, and laid in a row outside the circle of Chiefs and elders in the veranda. Tama Talip, the Chief of the Lerons as well as an adopted father of Tinggi, whom Juman had slain, begged Dr. Hose to talk to a pig before it was killed, and enjoin it to divulge by its liver whether or not the Government was right in ordering the death of Tinggi. Dr. Hose consented to harangue the swine, but with much shrewdness, warned the assemblage, in advance, that no matter what the victim's liver might indicate, he had pursued the course that seemed right to him, and would do so again in spite of all the livers of a thousand pigs. He stood forth in the centre of the circle, where the pig was lying, and paused solemnly for all conversation to cease; in spite, however, of the gravity of his bearing, and the sacredness of the occasion, some of the light-headed rabble, outside the circle, kept up a gabbling, whereupon he shouted at them in a voice so loud and stern, that their teeth chattered, and old Jamma's hair stood up stiffer than before. In the pin-drop silence that followed, he suddenly gave the unsuspecting swine a vigorous kick to enforce attention, whereto, by an aggrieved squeal, the animal responded that it was all ears. His harangue was then addressed, partly to the pig and partly to the Lerons, almost in the following words:—'Lerons, it is not one of our customs to ask from a pig what is in the hearts of men, but you people of up-river have faith in this custom and believe that a pig knows your feelings, [cries of 'Betúl! Betúl!'—True! True!] I will on this occasion adopt your custom and talk to this pig. You tell me that this pig understands Malay, so I will talk in that language, that all may understand, Kayans, Kenyahs, Sibops, Berawans, and Lerons. Know then, that it was neither Juman nor Tama Bulan who slew Tinggi and his brother Sidup, but I, the Government, did it, and none other. If you have any fault to find, find it with me. Remember that, you, Tama Talip, there! And now, O sacred pig, tell us who is in the wrong and who is in the right. [Here, the pig receives another and vigorous call upon its attention, and responds befittingly.] If men of the Tinjar kill people, I will order men from the Baram to find the murderers and slay them. If men of the Baram kill people, I will order Tinjar men to find the murderers and slay them. Let this declaration of mine sink into your livers, all you people from both rivers, and never forget it.' With these concluding words, he stamped his foot so suddenly and so loudly, that the old men, already awed by the silence and the solemnity of the hour, jumped almost from the floor, and Jamma shook his goggles off. Immediately the cry arose,—'Kill the pig instantly, that he may hear nothing else to influence him!' The poor beast was then quickly seized and taken to one side, and its neck sawed through with a dull parang, and before its death-struggles were fully over, its warm liver was deposited in a wooden bowl, and passed round the assembly for close inspection. They all tried to look extremely wise and expressed their opinions in a grave undertone to their neighbors; an old man, with one eye and a faded green velvet smoking-cap, winked and blinked at it, and then pensively resumed the mastication of a betel nut. Jamma pawed and fingered the liver all over, but maintained an ominous silence. Tama Talip screwed his mouth up on one side with a foreboding expression, clasped his hands over his knees, and began rocking backward and forward. The atmosphere became charged with perplexity and deep anxiety. Evidently, the fateful liver was only possibly favorable, and certainly dubious. The gall-bladder extended down nearly to the edge of the liver, and the small lobe which lies beside it was thin and long; so far, these features meant long life and prosperity. The chief points, which involved perplexity not unmixed with deep dismay, were that the lobe which represented the Government, was small, hard, and firm, while its inner border was ominously like a cord set into the surrounding substance; and, worst of all, above the attachment of the gall-bladder was an unprecedented, deeply indented scar, as if some of the liver had actually melted away! Consternation began to deepen. It was a hazardous minute for the Government. But Dr. Hose rose to the occasion, and at once proclaimed to all the clear and manifest interpretation of the extraordinary message from the pig. He asserted that the liver most unmistakably revealed to them, by the hardness of its lobe, the strength and unswerving justice of the Government, and that it was most difficult to break, while at the same time, it was as clear as noon-day that the thick, cord-like border showed how firmly the Government was united to the best interests of the people. Then turning to the scar above the gall-bladder, he made their very souls quiver and their flesh creep, by declaring that it unquestionably foretold the speedy and inevitable death of some very important Chief! (A little wholesome terror is a happy solvent in governing these people.) Several of the Chiefs present would have turned pale, if they could, at this frightful, terrifying revelation, but possibly they consoled themselves with the thought, hitherto unacknowledged by their self-conceit, that perhaps they were not so very, very important after all.

No one dared raise a dissenting voice to Dr. Hose's lucid and manifest interpretation. A good instance, by the way, of one of the sources of his influence over them; he always contrives to turn to the Government's account their superstitions and fears.

Aban Liah, our host, was the most apprehensive of all present. He well knew that he had once been all-important in his tribe, and that he had been unfaithful and treacherous to the Government; wherefore, the better to conceal his deadly fear, and revive his courage, he had his large jars of arrack brought out, and ostentatiously cut the dusty stiff rattans which bound down the covers. The first drink was tendered to the interminable Jok Orong, the guest from the Rejang, to whom all desired to show friendship and promise protection to his people should they move into the Baram district. He gulped down the drink quickly, but not so quickly that the crowd had not time enough to stamp and shout in the customary manner so mightily that the house most alarmingly trembled, creaked, and swayed, until caution prompted us to secure safe positions over good, strong beams; no accident happened, however, although a tremendous uproar accompanied the quaffing by each Chief. Before the second round of drinks, Dr. Hose insisted that they should deliver their speeches and protestations of peace while their brains were still unclouded, and as a preliminary the officious Jamma killed a fowl over a bowl of water, and then with a brush of wood cut into a tuft of shavings at one end spattered the blood and water over the audience. Then, still holding the blood-smeared brush in his hand, he launched into a vehement harangue, proclaiming this to be the very greatest of all Peace-makings that had ever been known on the banks of the Tinjar, and that the pig's liver had shown them clearly and truly the strength and benefit of the Government. When he had nearly shaken off his absurd goggles and his jockey cap had assumed a jaunty air on the back of his head, he handed the bloodied brush over to Juman, who at once jumped to his feet, and in the Kayan language began to tell in a truly sensible way how he and Tama Bulan had been commanded by the Government to bring Tinggi to justice. He then deliberately narrated all the details of the killing, (which must have been pleasant to the ears of Tama Talip, the adopted father of Tinggi,) but gradually he worked himself up to a high pitch of excitement, beating the air with his arms, see-sawing backward and forward, and emphasising the close of each sentence by shouting 'Bahh! Bahh!' He asserted that he was but the servant of the Government when he killed Tinggi, and so staunch was his loyalty that, should the Government command him to kill his dear friend Tama Usong, he would hold it to be his duty to obey. His excitement soon over-mastered him, and when he began to indulge in bravado, and offer to engage any one member of Tinggi's family in single combat, we deemed it high time to pull him down into his seat, and then plied him with congratulations, just as though he had fully rounded off his speech and finished all he wanted to say.

LIAN AVIT, A LEPPU ANNAN, WITH TIPANG, HIS WIFE, WHO IS STANDING, AND HER TWO SISTERS.

THE WOODEN FIGURES BEHIND THEM HAVE BEEN PLACED NEAR THE PATHWAY LEADING TO THE HOUSE, TO FRIGHTEN AWAY EVIL SPIRITS. THESE FIGURES ARE NOT WORSHIPPED AS IDOLS, NOR ARE OFFERINGS OR SACRIFICES MADE TO THEM,

BUT THEY ARE REGARDED TO A CERTAIN EXTENT WITH REVERENCE. INASMUCH AS TO TOUCH THEM OR TREAT THEM DISRESPECTFULLY ENDANGERS THE OFFENDER TO TERRIBLE DREAMS AT NIGHT AND TO BEING SEIZED BY GHOSTLY HANDS, WHICH WILL LEAVE LASTING SCARS.

While he was on his feet, drinks had been passing around quietly and some of the older men, whose heads were none too strong, began to feel alcoholic effects. Old Aban Anyi, a devoted follower of Tama Usong, and a hero of many battles, who once told me with pride that he had killed many men, any quantity of women, and no end of children, hearing Juman boast that he would kill Tama Usong if he were so ordered by the Government, tried to get on his feet to challenge such braggart talk, but Tama Usong himself grabbed him forcibly by the back of his waist-cloth and thumped him down to his seat again, where he sat mumbling and protesting until soothed and silenced with another drink. The bloody '*pla*,' or wooden brush, was next passed to Aban Liah, but his speech was weak and very apologetic throughout; he asserted that the Government had treated him badly by degrading him just because he did not tell the whereabouts of the murderers, Tinggi and Sidup; indeed, he never knew who the murderers were. Now the fact was that we knew, and all his hearers knew, that he had lied egregiously and persistently about the murderers, and had even concealed them in his own house. All this had been fully proved after the murderers had been killed. It was the sufficing cause of his loss of the Penghulu-ship.

Tama Usong's turn came next to declare his good will to the people of the Tinjar, and before he began, a large cup of arrack was thrust upon him. The contents of the jars had become, by this time, nearly exhausted; consequently this cupfull had been dipped up from the dregs, and Tama Usong gulped into his mouth several large pasty lumps of fermented rice. In the embarrassment caused by holding the pla (which seems to be essential to public speaking) he blew the kernels of rice accidentally, but directly in his host's face. The arrack was painfully present in his rambling and incoherent speech, to which no one paid any attention. At its conclusion all the Chiefs drank in turn from the same cup, and the formal part of the programme of the meeting ended.

Having gathered about him a fresh and untried audience, Jok Orong started in again with his endless, life-long tale of woe, which, we knew, only too well, would last until the arrack was utterly exhausted as well as his hearers; we, therefore, left them incontinently, preferring the peace and quiet of the Leppu Anan house, a short distance up-river, to the fingered feast of stewed fat pork with which Aban Liah was about to regale his guests.

The Leppu Anans are a clan from the Rejang, which not long before had been driven over to the Baram district by a threatened onslaught of the Ibans, who by some underhand means had obtained permission from the Government to attack them with a regularly organized force. Dr. Hose, hearing that this expedition had started, and knowing that the permission had been granted to the Ibans on false pretexts, and inasmuch as in this matter of life and death there was no time to communicate with the Government, instantly sent swift messengers to the homes of the Leppu Anans, telling them to fly for their lives, and promising them protection if they settled on the Tinjar. It was a terrible journey for the poor innocent creatures, loaded down, as they were, with all their household effects and retarded in their haste by the care for the women and children. Many of them, I was told, were so exhausted that they actually crawled and dragged themselves on all fours down the hills which separate the Rejang and Tinjar valleys.

The Ibans, consequently, found the Leppu Anan houses deserted and stripped of everything movable. Whereupon, not to be baulked of all spoils whatever, they attacked some of the friendly houses, the abodes of the very people who, on their journey up-river, had cheerily and kindly wished them success in their head-hunting. To the Bornean a head is a head, whether of friend or foe; so on this occasion the Ibans returned to their homes laden with spoils of their friends and enriched with heads which had not been on the shoulders of those against whom they had set out.

The Leppu Anans, in their new house, although they still harboured the small clan of Lerons who had vowed vengeance on Dr. Hose, nevertheless regarded Dr. Hose as their preserver, and no trouble taken in his behalf could be too great. They are quiet and gentle in their manners and very clean in their persons and about the house. We noticed with much relief that they did not throng about us, asking such inane questions the minute that we had landed, as, 'When did you arrive?' or, when helping us to disembark, 'Did you come in a boat?' questions which are really not at all unusual even from the very men who have been paddling your boat all day long. Possibly, true etiquette demands such questions among the natives themselves, who, for some occult reason, always desire their actual arrival and departure to pass unnoticed.

These Leppu Anans were intensely interested in my photographs, and literally climbed on each other's shoulders to see them. In their anxiety to touch the page itself, they nearly crushed the lucky holder of the book. The picture which excited their unstinted admiration is of two Ibans bargaining for the sale of a highly prized Chinese jar; they read the meaning of it at once, explaining it over and over to each other; but opinion was divided as to the balance of trade; some thought the owner was a fool to refuse the pile of silver dollars which the purchaser was offering, while others contended that the man who offered so mean a sum for so fine a jar must have been crazy. (When I showed the photograph to the wife of the man who had posed for me as the owner, she was extremely indignant, protesting that I had no right to represent Angas as such a fool! No sensible man would ever refuse that pile of money for such a common old jar. She felt actually defrauded of all that wealth, and I am sure she looked on me as a thief.)

At noon the next day the Peace-party, which we had left to finish up the 'seven' span pig at Aban Liah's, came up-river, and we all set out together on the last stage of the journey to Tama Aping Buling's.

It was an exciting day's travel; the rapids were extremely swift, and the Kayans, Kenyahs, Sibops, Berawans, Leppu Anans, and Lerons became inextricably intermingled in forcing their canoes past dangerous rocks and through narrows where the water rushed with almost irresistible power. Every man of the large assemblage was at the highest tension of excitement in anticipation of the stirring ceremonies close at hand, which after all, in the twinkling of an eye, by the merest accident, or by some trivial flaw in etiquette amid so large a body of hostile clans, might be converted to bloody battle.

When Tama Bulan was forced to leave us and turn back with his sick nephew, he provided, with usual forethought, a small pig, which was to be swiftly forwarded to Tama Aping Buling's in advance of the Peace-party. In punctillious observance of native customs on such exalted occasions as the present, the pig must be sacrificed on the beach before the Kayans and Kenyahs disembarked. We were positively assured by Aban Liah on leaving his house, that the piglet had been sent on ahead the night before to Tama Aping Buling's house at Long Dapoi; wherefore, when the Peace-party arrived, everything would be ceremoniously carried out. Our boat, a little in advance of the others, was gliding smoothly on a long stretch of quiet water just above turbulent rapids, when we were met by some men in a canoe from Tama Aping Buling's; a short excited announcement from them revealed to us that all was not going rightly up-river; accordingly, we changed to their lighter boat, and sped up-stream, leaving our luggage and the Peace-party to follow as they could. The men who poled the canoe could talk but very little of any language but Sibop, so we hardly knew what was amiss until we arrived at the house. On the beach, we were met by Tama Aping Buling himself, almost in tears; before we could get fairly out of the boat, he squatted down, and, in a voice of despair, said, 'Oh, Tuan Prenta, what shall be done! No pig has been sent to sacrifice when the Kayans arrive. There will be war instead of peace.' It was even so. That old traitor, Aban Liah, had purposely kept back Tama Bulan's pig in order that the Peace-making should be a failure, and that his rival, Tama Aping Buling, should get into trouble. Dr. Hose instantly turned and started down-stream to meet the Kayans, and keep them down-river until Aban Liah should either restore the pig or procure another and send it on ahead of them. Aban Liah was serenely imperturbable when accused to his face of the theft of the pig, and of his plot to create trouble; but eventually Dr. Hose's unsparing denunciation, combined with the sullen threats of the tired Kayans, eager for the comfortable shelter of a house for the night, forced him actually to leave the party, and paddle off down-river to buy or borrow the indispensable little pig.

IBANS BARGAINING OVER THE SALE OF VALUABLE CHINESE JARS.

THE OFFER OF FIFTY MEXICAN DOLLARS IS TREATED WITH HAUGHTY REFUSAL. THE TWO MEN POSED THEMSELVES, AFTER MY SUGGESTION, FOR THE SUBJECT OF THE PICTURE.

They told us afterward that at house after house he was rebuffed, and, although there were plenty of pigs everywhere, not one could he borrow, beg, or steal, so universally disliked was he for his mean, tricky ways. Night came before he finally succeeded in procuring the sacrifice, so that the wearied Kayans were forced to sleep in their canoes, or in huts of boughs which they built on a pebbly island in midstream, and endure a drenching deluge of rain, illumined by such blinding lightning and deafening thunder as only the Tropics know.

The house built by Tama Aping Buling stands on the north bank of the river, just opposite to the mouth of the Dapoi, a large tributary. It is about two hundred feet from the river, on a high bank which slopes gradually to a wide pebbly beach. The house was only recently finished at that time, and had cost interminable labor; many of the piles whereon it was built were at least twenty inches in diameter, and supported the floor fully fifteen feet from the ground. The veranda was broad and well floored with wide, hewn planks, and roofed with shingles of billian wood, not nailed to the rafters, but tied on with strips of rattan. One end of the house was not yet quite finished, and shingles only partially covered it. This incomplete state was not, however, without its uses; it supplied Tama Aping Buling, while showing his house to us, with a chance to make a remark, which, hackneyed and threadbare as it is among them, is always uttered apparently in the belief that it will be received with all the applause of a novel and brilliant idea. With a wave of his hand toward the roofless rafters, Tama Aping explained, 'This end of the house is occupied by Laki Langit and his children,' which, interpreted, means, 'Grandfather Sky and his children—the stars!' We had heard the witticism so often that it was hard to force a smile,—but we did. Let him among us, who, in describing 'full dress,' has never called it 'war-paint' or 'best bib and tucker,' cast the first reproach at the unsophisticated Borneans.

Early on the following morning the wee pig was sacrificed on the beach and there left in its gore. Such a sacrifice, when made in ratification of a compact, renders the flesh inedible to all participants in the ceremony; hence the diminutive size of the pig. On the present occasion Aban Liah's enforced pig was so extremely small, that I saw a lean and hungry dog seize it by the head after the sacrifice was over, and, slinging the body over his back, make off toward some tall grass, where he probably devoured the whole carcass at one meal,—possibly, at one gulp.

The sacrifice of the pig was certainly a beginning, but it did not seem to expedite the other ceremonies to be performed in the veranda of the house. The Kayans, never enthusiastic over this Peace-making, (which is not a fraternisation, but only an agreement not to kill each other on unprovoked raids,) were sulking in their huts on the karangans, under the pretext of drying themselves. All the while Tama Aping Buling and his clan, and the other Tinjar Chiefs and their clans, sat wearily waiting in the veranda for the Kayans to appear. There were several false reports that they were coming, and each time the host, Tama Aping, invariably alleged that most important matters needed attention in his private room, and as invariably had to be dragged, trembling, from his little dark sleeping-box, where he was crouching, to attend to the reception of his guests. One cause of Tama Aping's conduct was dread lest it should leak out that he had been largely instrumental in giving the Government the information which eventually led to the detection of Tinggi and his brother, Sidup, both of whom had been, in point of fact, at one time inmates of his house; should this treachery become known, his own people, even, would turn against him, and his life would not be worth a black bead.

TAMA APING BULING'S HOUSE ON THE TINJAR.
THE SCENE OF THE NOTABLE PEACE-MAKING.

The forenoon passed; the day wore on to afternoon,—still no Kayans; we began to fear that they had turned back and had given up all idea of peace-making.

Jamma of the flabby, unhealthy lips, talked interminably, and his goggles seemed to grow bigger and his jockey cap dirtier every minute. Tama Talip silently munched betel nut, and squirted the blood-red juice incessantly through a crack in the floor. Aban Liah was depressed in spirit, and sat sullenly twisting an extinguished cigarette between his fingers. We became thoroughly wearied of the whole assemblage, and, unattended, paddled across the river to a grassy point where we could watch for the coming of the Kayans, and, at least for awhile, get rid of the natives. Even this watching became intolerable, and finally we decided to go up the clear Dapoi River a short distance and take a swim. Of course, this was the very time through the perversity of luck, that the Kayans decided to go up to the house, and we, unfortunately, were not on hand. Kilup, one of Tinggi's brothers, took it upon himself to be the leader of a small Jawa party, and did not even wait for Juman to disembark from his canoe, but ran full speed down to the beach, and with his parang drawn,—a violation of propriety absolutely forbidden in every well-conducted Jawa—actually chopped at Juman's boat and slashed the palm-leaf covering. They told us afterward that Juman behaved bravely, and sat unmoved in his boat,—his serenity was possibly due to the knowledge that the 'snappang,' albeit with the 'fever-stricken engine,' was at his side, and that, if necessity arose, its discharge would prove fatal to some one, either to himself or to Kilup. By the time we returned from our bath the excitement had subsided, but none the less, Tama Aping Buling remained secluded in the depths of his private apartments. Dr. Hose at once summoned Kilup before him, and incontinently imposed on him a fine of one tawak,—equivalent to thirty dollars, a really heavy fine. Kilup sat unmoved during his sentence, and then arose slowly and swaggered off to his room, where he was told to remain until sent for, under penalty of another fine, or, possibly, imprisonment in the Baram Fort.

The Kayans were very naturally greatly incensed at such treatment; certainly they had a right to expect a little more hospitality after their dolorous night in the soaking rain.

By way of precaution against too much zeal in the approaching sham fight, we made the Tinjar people place about half-way down the veranda a high, square platform, used ordinarily as a sleeping-shelf for guests; this would tend to keep the two forces apart and check too quick an onslaught. When this was done, Tama Liri was deputed to go down to the river and conduct the Kayans to the veranda. It is an inexcusable breach of decorum for any strangers outside the house, to pass in front of a Chief's door, before ascending to the veranda; guests, therefore, from down-river should enter at the down-river end of the house, and *vice versâ*. Tama Liri knew this as well as he knew his name; but, solely to stir up more trouble, he conducted the Kayans who came from down-river to the up-river end of the house, which involved a direct insult to Tama Aping Buling. Of course, the Kayans remonstrated, but too late; and then, to retrieve the insult, had to tramp almost the whole length of the house in the mud and slime beneath the veranda; this added fresh fuel to the fire already burning in their breasts.

The Lerons, Sibops, Berawans, and Leppu Anans gathered at the up river end of the veranda, to await the entrance of the Kayans, and we placed ourselves midway, so as to be on hand to moderate, if possible, too realistic a sham fight.

The Kayans and Kenyahs came quietly up the notched log, and halted in a close crowd until the last man had fairly entered the veranda. Standing thus within the house of one who had always been an enemy, and confronting their deadly foes, it is no wonder that they were trembling with excitement; their eyes were glancing suspiciously in all directions to detect any signs of treachery or the sight of concealed weapons. Suddenly, with one impulse, they began yelling, stamping, waving their arms, and leaping in the air. Immediately the Tinjar people joined in; in a second the whole veranda from end to end became a perfect pandemonium of shrieking, frenzied, gymnastic savages. Not a step did they advance toward each other, although everywhere there were furious, threatening gestures.

This appalling scene was kept up for fully a minute, and then the frightful turbulence gradually quieted down. Dr. Hose at once seized Juman by the arm and led him, followed by his people, right in among their bitter enemies; then glancing round quickly to see that no one had a weapon in hand, instantly proposed that they should all once more jump and stamp together, and he himself led off with a resounding stamp and a terrific shout. Juman followed, then another and another, until, in a trice, once more the house was trembling beneath them, and the rafters echoing; but this time friends and foes were almost shoulder to shoulder. The inanity, I think, of the proceeding slowly dawned on them; the shouting did not last as long as before; it became more and more feeble; at last it ceased suddenly, and they all sat down. Little by little the ice of mutual distrust began to thaw; here and there men who had been mortal foes were sitting cheek by jowl, engaged in friendly conversation.

At this stage, it was the host's clear duty to bring out his arrack; his guests might at once have pledged each other, and friendship might have been cemented; but Tama Aping Buling was in his sleeping-room, probably buried beneath a pile of mats.

Speeches were made by Jamma, Aban Liah, and Juman, but they lacked earnestness and cordiality, and, at their conclusion, the pigs whose livers were to foretell the issue of this Peace-making and the futurity of the participants, were dragged into the centre of the assembly. As each one was brought in, it was harangued by the Dayongs, and adjured to tell the truth and to intercede with the Spirits to drive out all animosity from the people of the two rivers. The largest pig was reserved as the 'Government's pig,' and had been selected on account of its size and beauty, but it did not turn out to be exactly what the Government would have chosen as its fittest representative. It was an albino, with lack-lustre, whitish eyes and a pale, mottled snout; it lay so still that I half expected it was about to cheat the sacrifice by dying a natural death. Of course, it fell to Dr. Hose's lot to exhort this pig *ante mortem* to proclaim truthfully *post mortem*, by infallible omens in its liver, whether or not the Government's course was right; but he gave the natives clearly to understand that, whatever the omens might be, they would not in the least influence him in the management of Government affairs; and that he followed the custom merely to please them. Thereupon, he prodded the pale-eyed and anæmic pig with his foot, to arouse its earnest attention, but no responsive grunt nor indignant squeal came from that cadaverous representative of the Government; it lay imperturbably still and blinked. As soon as his words ceased, the pig was dragged to one side, its throat cut, and its liver at once dexterously extracted. When this organ, which proved to be unusually large, was passed round among the Chiefs and among those who were skilled in the interpretation of auguries, it was pronounced with one accord to be in its every aspect most favourable; but, in an unlucky moment, just as it was about to be taken away, some one, inquisitively, lifted one of the lobes to examine the under surface, and instantly a convulsive horror and shuddering recoil ran through the whole assemblage, — a large, foul abscess was disclosed!

Once before, on this expedition, had the natives been shocked by a fateful foreboding of death, and now, for a second time, in yet clearer terms, had this death-warrant been delivered. On the first occasion, at Tama Liri's house, their horrified eyes had noted a deep scar, and now with inexpressible dismay they beheld a corroding ulcer.

Dr. Hose, in solemn tones, again repeated the true interpretation of the blood-curdling portent: — *a faithless, scheming Chief*, who was secretly hostile to the Rajah and to his people, would *very shortly die a miserable, inevitable death*! Again the liver was passed round the awe-stricken circle; in vain they summoned their best ingenuity in suggesting a less dreadful interpretation, but it was only too clear that Dr. Hose's words bore every impress of truth.

Old Aban Liah, of whose hostility to the Government there had been such recent proofs, sat a little outside the circle, and when the liver with its death warrant was passed over to him, he waved it aside, and in tones that reminded me vividly of Shylock, and almost in Shylock's very words, said, tremulously, 'Let me go away; I am not well;' and then added, apologetically: 'the smell of this beastly, warm, raw flesh has made me ill. I must go.' And he got up, with dazed looks, and went with uncertain steps to his room.

An hour or two later, in the evening, some of his friends came and begged me to go see him. To my surprise, I found him in a high fever and semi-delirious. I directed them to wrap him up warmly, to produce a sweat, and advised them to remove him to his own home as soon as possible. I supposed that he would be all right in the morning, when the effects of the feasting at his house the day before had passed off. I never dreamed that his illness would have a fatal termination.

Neither Aban Liah's sudden illness, nor his absence, interfered with the Peace-making. Kilup was summoned from his room, and in the presence of the assembled tribes he was given such a vehement rating by the Government that he probably remembers it to this hour, and he was furthermore warned that even threatening language was punishable.

Still no arrack was broached, nor feast spread. At the slightest noise or excitement, off sped Tama Aping Buling to his room, and there remained in seclusion until all was again quiet. He had, in truth, more cause for alarm than the others; his wife, his children, and all the women of the household were dependent on him for protection in any outbreak of hostility; his guests had to look but after their own safety; these guests were now peaceable, but in a flash they might become mortal foes in deadly conflict.

Old Jamma was always to the fore, talking incessantly and making effusive attempts to ingratiate himself with everybody; but if all present shared my feelings, his thick, everted lips, and eyes distorted behind those prodigious goggles, would have checked every throb of sympathy. Furthermore, he had unaccountably changed his jockey cap for a war-cap of Tiger skin, with which he fairly terrified the Kayans. A skin of the great tiger is something so terrible to many of the natives that they dare not even touch it; an oath bound by a tiger's tooth or tiger's skin is one of their most solemn pledges. The Kenyahs and Sibops are the only tribes who may touch a Tiger's skin with impunity.

It was not until afternoon had deepened into night that the feast and the arrack were brought out. The roar that went up when Juman drained the first cup could have been heard certainly for a mile, and the stamping was stupendous. In fact, under the weight of the three hundred jumping men, the floor sagged fully six inches, and the huge piles, whereon the house was built, swerved and sank deeper into the earth. Thus it went on, one toast after another, and roar upon roar; then they made speeches fervid with alcohol. Jamma talked rank, open treason when his tongue was loosened, and claimed the whole Tinjar River as a direct inheritance from his Uncle, Aban Jau; the Rajah had no right to be there, and the Government obstructed instead of helped the people. Very little attention, however, was paid to him, either by the assemblage, or by Dr. Hose, a neglect which cut him deeply; he ached to be of sufficient importance to receive a rebuke from the Government, but Dr. Hose merely replied, 'We must all bear in mind the source whence these silly remarks come; I think you'll all agree that they are not of the slightest consequence.'

The drinking, the stamping, and the shouting were kept up throughout the night, and, to our great content, the Kayan guests behaved well and restrained themselves within bounds. Jamma and his clan were the only flagrant offenders, talking treason and indulging in threats.

A smell of fermented arrack, stale fumes of rank tobacco, maudlin gabble from drunken men, the snarling and yelping of dogs, the clucking and cackling of poultry, the wailing of children, and the crying of babies, pervaded the world into which we awoke in Tama Aping Buling's house the morning after the great Peace-making carouse.

Suddenly, above all sounds, arose repeated, piercing shrieks from terror-stricken women, excited shouting of men, slamming of doors, and the clatter of bare feet fleeing over the loose, rattling boards of the veranda. The master of the house flung himself, trembling, into our room and breathlessly announced that one of his men, overcome by the night's debauch, had gone 'amok'—as he said,—and, armed with parang and shield, had sworn to hack in pieces all whom he met; he was now rushing from room to room slashing right and left at the terrified and fugitive inmates. Two or three brave men had climbed to the loft above the partitions between the private rooms, and, with poles, were trying to beat down and disarm the maniac and lasso him with loops of rattan.

A man who runs amok both expects and desires to be killed, but endeavors to slaughter beforehand as many victims as possible. Dr. Hose caught up a long and heavy pestle used for husking rice, and we all hurried out in the veranda, armed with our revolvers, to assist in the capture of this most dangerous ruffian; and, since he desired to be killed, we were quite ready to gratify him. Just as we came opposite the room from which the maniac had driven the occupants, frantic with terror, the man himself rushed forth directly in front of Dr. Hose, but the latter was ready for him with a greeting which was as well-directed and cordial as it was unexpected. By one waive of the long pestle, his shield was instantly thrust aside, and there followed a disconcerting and most demoralising prod full in the pit of the stomach. All his valiant 'amok' collapsed, and, with eyes rolling in his head, he staggered back through the doorway and plumped down, with a flop, on the floor. Instantly the men overhead, with their rattan loops, had him encircled round the waist, and a vigorous pull suspended him in mid-air from a cross-beam; with their poles they knocked the weapons from his hands, and then, like a spider with a fly, they had him quickly swathed with rattans and bound hand and foot. The next thing was to take him to his own room, and leave him thus confined until he had recovered his senses. But while they were carrying him thither, the ever-officious, and withal treacherous, Jamma, staggered impetuously forward, and, vehemently insisting that the maniac should be set free, actually began to grapple with the carriers. In a twinkling, his wrist was seized by Dr. Hose, and he was whirled round; then, after executing an astonishing and dizzy pirouette, he lost his balance and went skimming along the floor, until, with a reverberating thump, his head struck the wall, and he lay motionless. Some friends ran to him and propped him up. He made no attempt to rise, but only blinked his bloodshot eyes, denuded for once of the goggles, and kept gasping, panting forth: 'Why did the Government strike me? Why did the Government strike me?' Finding his question unanswered, he lapsed into silence, and put in practice the ingenious idea of feigning death, wherein he was much helped by a sudden rush of alcoholic fumes to his head. His nephew and a few devoted friends lost not an instant's time in laying out the corpse, and, seated beside the limp body, immediately struck up a funeral wail over his sad, untimely demise. It really seemed possible that the man might be dead, so, at Dr. Hose's request, I examined him, but no trace of injury could I find on the corpse but a severe, darkly coloured bruise on its forehead; when, however, this bruise was bathed with arnica, I noticed that it wholly disappeared, and the discoloration was transferred to the absorbent cotton, and that the skin presented an unbroken surface. When I attempted to examine his eyes, the wrinkled resistance of the lids showed me his inflexible determination to remain dead.

 Disgusted with the whole household, we had our luggage incontinently carried down to the boats; then, after speeding the Kayans and Kenyahs, now in a benign and peaceful mood, on their homeward journey, the Great, Historic, Ceremonial Peace-making came to an end. It had been a veritable and a notable success throughout; old scores had been settled by exchange of Usut and by the Jawa, and return visits had been planned; barring Aban Liah's antagonism and illness, Kilup's bad behavior, and the incident with Jamma just related, everything had gone off more smoothly than we had any reason to expect, considering the undisciplined, grown-up children with whom we had to deal. We were, nevertheless, truly glad to be rid of the responsibility of a party so large, and of material so inflammable.

We decided to continue our journey, and ascend the Dapoi River, to visit some Punans,—a nomadic tribe, who had recently encamped near the head-waters of the stream.

Just as we were pushing off in our canoe, a wild figure, with arms waving, and face distorted with malignant rage, dashed down the log-walk to the beach; there it turned and faced the house. It was Jamma, the corpse. Snatching off his war-cap of Tiger skin, he waved it, backward and forward above his head with frantic gestures, toward the house. We did not care to wait for the upshot of these remarkable antics, but pursued our tranquil course up the Dapoi, inhaling peace and repose beneath the over-arching boughs festooned with ferns and orchids.

SIBOP WOMEN AT THE HOUSE OF TAMA BALAN DENG.

Late in the afternoon, we landed at the house of Tama Balan Deng, a Sibop Chief, who received us kindly, and most hospitably gave up to us his own room, wherein throughout every minute of the entire night we were the objects of awestruck curiosity to his whole household, the larger part of whom had never before seen a white man; they sat immovably huddled together at one side of the room, and were the last objects that we saw on going to sleep, and when we awoke at dawn they were noiselessly creeping away.

Early in the day, to our surprise, Tama Aping Buling arrived in his canoe, in a state of painful excitement over Jamma's conduct of the day before, whose antics were now explained. As soon as we had left, the old rascal, tired of being a corpse, fell into a violent rage with the universe, and had stormed down to the beach, and there had cursed with his awful Tiger skin cap every bit of timber in the house, together with all its inmates, big and little, old and young, and all the Kayans, root and branch, who had been in it, and ended up with the white men who had half-killed him. The house, as I said above, had just been built, at a cost of infinite labor and great expense; but after such a blood-curdling curse had been launched at it, to Tama Aping Buling's superstitious mind, the domicile was for ever banned and ruined. The object of the poor fellow's hurried visit was to ask Dr. Hose if he did not think it best that the whole structure should be immediately destroyed; it took much serious argument from Dr. Hose to dissuade the disconsolate Tama Aping from the determination to empty his house of all movables and then set fire to it.

This account of Jamma's malevolence did not exhaust Tama Aping's budget. He brought the latest news of Aban Liah, whom we had last seen stricken down by the dreadful omen in the pig's liver. The most skilful Dayongs had been summoned to keep the soul of the old Berawan Chief from wholly deserting his body, and, at last reports, they had grave doubts as to their success in finding whither it had temporarily flown, unless several additional parang blades and three or four more bolts of cloth were given to them, wherewith they could bribe the Spirits who were luring far away the soul of Aban Liah; they were sorely afraid that, in spite of all their exertions, the soul would evade them and slip off to Bulun Matai. We despatched the necessary spiritual bribes, and then continued our journey to the home of the Punans.

Four days afterward, when we left the Dapoi and again turned into the Tinjar, we stopped at the scene of the Great Peace making, and there we learned the end of Aban Liah's tragic story. The fate foretold so clearly by the liver of the Government's albino pig had been fulfilled. The conscience-stricken soul of the faithless Aban Liah had, indeed, departed to the Fields of the Dead. From the moment that he saw that ulcerous liver, and realized its plain indication to himself he sickened, became delirious, and within forty-eight hours was dead!

There happened to be in one of the boats of our party an old woman, a distant relative of Aban Liah, and when the news of his death was first shouted to us from a boat which we met on the river, this old creature withdrew a short distance from the bank, and, squatting down on the sand, proceeded to emit a solo of heart-rending wails for the dead, rehearsing his good qualities in a jerky and descending chromatic scale, beginning at high C and ending when her breath gave out; then, after a deep inspiration, the wailing strain was resumed. All the while she was glancing around to see the effect it had upon us, and also to see what was going on up and down the river while she was busy in sorrowing for the defunct; she knew, quite as well as we, what a thorough-paced old rascal he was, and how far better it was for all his household that he was dead and out of the way. When she had reeled off a due amount of profound sorrow, she re-embarked, and was as chatty and gay as possible until we reached the dead Chief's house; there it behooved her to roar again for appearance's sake. We went up to the house of mourning to pay our respects to the household and be witness to their grief. At the hour of our arrival, there happened to be a lull in the wailing, but the appearance of visitors of such august importance at once demanded a resumption, not only of gong-beating, but also of the recitation of the estimable, noble character of the departed. The obtrusive old Jamma was again to the fore, all animosity forgotten in his eagerness to display his extreme grief; out of respect for the dead he had discarded his jockey cap and goggles. Several other Chiefs from neighbouring houses and ourselves were led to places of honor in front of the bier, whereon lay Aban Liah, sealed up in a coffin hewn out of Durian wood. The bier was draped with some cotton cloth, which we recognized as that which we had sent as a bribe to the Spirits, and on posts at the four corners were hung the Chief's most valuable beads, his parang, shield, and spear, and a number of musical instruments; it was expected that he would hold a high position among the minstrels and warriors in Bulun Matai. As soon as the chief men had conducted us to our places, they squatted beside us, and, covering their faces with their hands to hide the scalding tears that did not flow, they began to moan and groan in a style which was, perhaps, quite as symbolical to them of true sorrow as black crape and nodding plumes are to us.

At this moment, the women of the dead man's immediate family issued from his private room, clad in high-pointed yellow hoods of bark-cloth, which flowing down enveloped them from head to foot; they gathered about the head of the coffin, and wailed to the accompaniment of several deep-toned gongs. This same rite had been repeated for every visitor who had come to the Chief's house since his death; they were in good practice. All members of the household were in their dirtiest and most worn-out habiliments; every ornament had been discarded; girdles of beads had been replaced by belts of twisted rattan, and weights made of pebbles wrapped in bark-cloth had been substituted for metal ear-rings; many of the men and some of the women had smeared themselves with soot from the cooking-pots, and no one had bathed in the river since the demise of the Chief, four or five days before. They were certainly repulsive in appearance. This wailing lasted but a scant five minutes, and then the women retired, and the men withdrew their hands from their eyes; of course, not a tear had been shed. With the elasticity of youth, — for they are all mere children, — they were at once interested in hearing of the expedition we were about to make to the summit of a mountain near by, and were laughing and joking over the Ghosts and Sprites that we were sure to meet in that mysterious moss-jungle continually shrouded in mists.

It is the custom among the Berawans to keep a corpse in the house for several months, varying the length of time in accordance with the rank or wealth of the deceased; sometimes the body may have to remain unburied until after the harvest. On the third or fourth day after death, the body is squeezed into a large jar, which has been carefully cut apart at its largest diameter, so that the body does not have to be forced through the narrow neck. It is in the lower half that the corpse is placed in a cramped, squatting position; the upper half is then fitted on tightly, and the crack sealed up with resinous gum. The jar is then placed in a corner of the veranda, and a pipe of hollow bamboo is inserted to drain off to the ground below the fluids resulting from decomposition. It occasionally happens that gases accumulate inside the jar, and cannot escape through the tube, owing to a stoppage, and then an explosion follows.

The Berawans believe that shortly after death the spirits of the dead return from Bulun Matai, to see that their relatives and friends are displaying the due amount of grief by performing the proper ceremonies. Should a spirit find that it has been neglected and forgotten, it curses the culprits, and they become blind, deaf, or lame. If all has been done to show befitting grief and respect,—if the mourners have been on a raid and secured a nice head wherewith to decorate the grave or the household hearth,—then the spirit retires to the nether world, never again to return.

In former days, on the death of any influential Chief, if his people were either too lazy or too cowardly to go head-hunting, a male or female slave was purchased and sacrificed in honor of the dead. From near and far, friends were invited to take part in the high ceremony. When the poor wretch of a slave was thrust into a cage of bamboo and rattan, he knew perfectly well the death by torture to which he was destined. In this cage he was confined for a week or more, until all the guests had assembled and a feast was prepared. On the appointed day, after every one had feasted and a blood-thirsty instinct had been stimulated to a high pitch by arrack, each one in turn thrust a spear into the slave. No one was allowed to give a fatal thrust until every one to the last man had felt the delight of drawing blood from living, human flesh. We were told by the Berawans that the slaves often survived six or seven hundred wounds, until death from loss of blood set them free. The corpse of the victim was then taken to the grave of the Chief, and the head cut off and placed on a pole overhanging the grave. Frequently, some of the guests worked themselves into such a blood-thirsty frenzy that they bit pieces from the body, and were vehemently applauded when they swallowed the raw morsel at a gulp.

It is, probably, in conformity with the same idea of a head-hunt in honor of the memory of the deceased, that the tribe of Malanaus, on their return from a burial, engage in a mock battle with those who remained behind to guard the house, and throw at them mud and imitation javelins made of light pith.

The body of Aban Liah, although a Berawan, was not placed in a jar, but, as I have said, in a coffin, and would be kept in the house, so they told us, for three months, until the end of the harvest. The people darkly hinted at the absolute necessity of their obtaining, at that time, a fresh human head. But Dr. Hose warned them of the sure consequences following every violation of the solemn compact and rites of peace which they had just concluded.

We left them in their grief, and set out on our trip to the summit of Mt. Dulit, one of the lofty range that forms the watershed between the Rejang and the Baram Rivers. When we turned into the little stream that flows down the side of the mountain, we noticed lying on one of the banks the huge, stately Durian tree, (worth a livelihood to a whole household on account of its much-prized fruit,) which had been already cut down just to make a monumental support for the coffin of the good-for-nothing old Aban Liah. The giant pole was to be elaborately carved and painted, and, when the Chief's body was ready to be placed in position, this huge trunk would be erected near the bank of the river, a little below his house.

Whatever might have been its origin, it is not now easy to determine what emotion it is which prompts the Borneans to decorate elaborately the depositories of their dead; at first glance, it seems as if it must be affectionate remembrance and a devotion to the habitation of the soul even after the soul has left it. But, certainly among the Borneans, demonstrative affection is, I should say, an exceedingly rare trait; their lives are almost as purely individual and selfish as are the examples Nature sets before them at every turn in the jungle. During the time that a child is still nursing at the mother's breast, there is that instinctive, protective parental affection observable in all mating animals; but after the child is weaned and is able to toddle, it is allowed to ramble pretty much where it will, and to take its educational bumps and tumbles without parental worry. Mother Nature provides the only clothes it wears, and, after her own healing, scarifying fashion, darns and patches the rents and tears that they may receive. Among the young boys and girls there is a sort of playmate affection, whenever self-sacrifice is not necessary, and where the one who plans the game or sport always expects to be and is the principal player. Between adults, be they the nearest of kin or be they even lovers, I think I am safe in saying that there is no such thing as unselfish love; a youth would never think of resigning a comfortable place in a boat to his father, or to his mother, or to his sister, or even to his sweetheart. When a man comes back from a long, and perhaps dangerous, expedition, he does not fall into the arms of his family amid tears of joy and welcome; but he walks up the notched log and stalks along the public veranda, looking neither to the right nor to the left until he deposits his burden opposite his own door, and there he sits down, lights a cigarette, and tries to act and look as if he had just come in from the rice-field after a day's work.[14] There is not a greeting of any kind whatsoever exchanged on either side; but after a while, and little by little, an admiring group of men and boys gather round, and slowly he unbends, telling scraps of news about friends or foes in the country whence he is come, until at last he is haranguing the people and acting 'Sir Oracle' in the centre of a circle of gaping mouths and unwinking eyes. It is the same were he about to start off on an expedition; no kerchiefs are waved to him nor do eyes stream with tears as his canoe pushes off from the shore; he goes down to the boat with his parcels in just the same matter-of-fact manner as if he were only going to cross the river for fire-wood. I have seen Bornean mothers, fathers, and sweethearts, part from those who ought to have been dear to them, and who were about to set out on distant expeditions of a peaceful nature, or on long war expeditions of a dangerous nature, but I remember only one solitary instance where there were any tears or the slightest show of reluctance at parting; that one instance was the parting of a sister from a brother who had come over on a visit to the house into which she had married quite recently. The woman in this case did really show a downright love for her snaggle-toothed and hideous brother; she hung upon his neck, sobbing and wailing, trying her best to hold him back, and pleading with him not to go; he patted her on the shoulder, seemed very self-conscious and exceedingly bored; finally, extricating himself rather rudely from her arms, he stalked toward the notched log and descended, looking straight in front of him. Possibly it was, on the woman's part, more homesickness than love for her brother. From the Arctics to the Tropics, be it ever so humdrum, there's no place like home.

---

[14] See also, to the same effect, *The Golden Bough*, vol. i., p. 26.

GRAVE OF THE WIFE OF ORANG KAYA TEMANGANG LAWI.

THE CORPSE WAS PLACED IN A SQUATTING POSITION IN A DEEP PIT, HOLLOWED OUT AT THE UPPER END OF THE

COLUMN AND COVERED OVER WITH A LARGE TRIANGULAR SLAB OF WOOD, CUT FROM THE ROOT OF A BUTTRESS TREE. THE ORNAMENTATION IS COMPOSED OF WHITE CHINA BOWLS AND PLATES, FASTENED ON WITH GUTTA-PERCHA

Among certain tribes, the body of a Chief swathed in cloths is placed within the upper end of a tree trunk hollowed out for the purpose, and a large slab of wood cut from a 'buttress tree' is fastened on top. The photograph, on the opposite page, is that of the grave of a Chief's wife, and I am sure that in its erection and ornamentation no jot of affection was felt by the husband, Temangang Lawi, than whom no more heartless old head-hunter, and slayer of women and children, exists in Borneo. His only idea in spending so much time and money on the grave of his wife was his own glorification. The white spots on the column are china bowls and saucers stuck on with damar gum; the flags and streamers on top are strips of white and red cloth, possibly to keep off birds of prey; possibly a remnant of the Mongolian idea that anything moving and fluttering in the wind attracts or distracts the attention of the Spirits.

Again, other tribes enclose their dead in coffins which are placed in miniature houses on the top of high poles, sometimes on single poles, again on two or even four poles. These little houses are decorated with open-work carving along the ridge-pole and down the angles of the roof, and with painting on the sides. Not infrequently small wooden figures of men are placed standing on the roof or climbing up the poles; possibly, these are effigies of the slaves which in former times were sacrificed at the burial.

Natural surroundings and the habitations of the living have, of course, a great influence on the methods of disposing of the dead. In mountainous, stony districts, the primitive form of burial is apt to be in cairns or in caves; in lowlands, where land is swampy, burial in trees, out of the way of beasts of prey, is adopted. In those districts of Borneo where the jungle is so dense that it is well-nigh impossible to dig a grave through the impenetrable, interlocking roots of trees, a burial on poles follows of necessity. Where the river-banks are constantly changing with every freshet, burial in such soft soil would not be permanent. I think, therefore, that it is more than likely that burial on high pedestals was, in the first instance, a result of natural surroundings, and the elaborate decorations are for the glorification of the living, and not for the dead. In Borneo, there are no carnivorous animals to dig up bodies, but it is by no means unknown that men exceedingly anxious to win admiration as head-hunters obtain from graves the coveted prize, be it of friend or of foe; therefore, the more inaccessible the body, the less is the likelihood that the market for heads will become over-stocked. In the Naga Hills of Eastern Assam, where the natives live in communities much like the Borneans, some of the tribes bury their dead in the village streets; others dig graves just outside the door of the house, or, when the body is perhaps that of a young unmarried girl or a child, the grave is made even inside the door. There was I acknowledge, much pathos in the explanation once given to me by a Naga, whose child was buried inside his house, that if his little girl were buried out in the jungle or under the open sky, she would be 'very much frightened at night.' The simple and unostentatious mounds made by the Nagas over their dead, bear more evidence, I think, of their affection than do the gaudily decorated tombs erected by the tribes of Borneo, and yet in their daily lives the Nagas are not one whit more demonstrative than the Borneans.

When, after two days of hard climbing through virgin jungle, we reached the topmost peak of Dulit, which is almost exactly five thousand feet high, dense clouds shut off our view of the valley below, but the last rays of the sun were slanting through endless aisles and marvellous recesses of emerald moss, and from far below, and beneath the clouds, came the dull booming of a deep-toned tawak from the house of the dead Aban Liah, announcing fresh mourners at his coffin.

The great Peace-party had at least brought peace to that scheming, turbulent old soul, whose body now rests in the valley of the Tinjar.

THE MOSS-COVERED JUNGLE ON THE SUMMIT OF MT. DULIT.

SPHAGNOUS MOSS AND OVERGROWN LYCOPODIUMS COVER THE GROUND AND ENVELOPE EVERY TWIG AND BRANCH, TRANSFORMING THE JUNGLE INTO A LABYRINTH OF ALLEYS AND GROTTOS, DRIPPING WITH MOISTURE AND LIT BY FLECKS OF SUNLIGHT, WHICH, FALLING UPON THE SPARKLING DROPS, ILLUMINE THESE SILENT DEPTHS WITH A SOFT, GREEN LIGHT.

On the opposite page is a photograph taken on the summit of Mt. Dulit. The heavy drapery which covers every tree and branch, almost every leaf, is a sphagnous moss, breast-high and many feet in thickness. I beseech the reader to summon to his memory the most vivid, emerald green he has ever beheld; and then intensify it by a cloudless, tropical sun, at high noon; and then, in addition to this, let every burnished leaflet glow and sparkle with myriads of iridescent drops fed by the warm, heavy mists which constantly sweep over the mountain.

No words can describe the endless shades of 'greenth' which are revealed in the vistas formed by overhanging masses, where here and there the rays of the sun pierce the cavernous recesses; of which, most assuredly, this is the first photograph that has ever been taken.

Personal Embellishment

Early in the morning of the third day of our journey up the Baram, to visit Tama Bulan, far in the interior of Borneo, we stopped at a long-house, and as I saw the women descend on their errand to the river for water I was utterly amazed at their costume, and rubbed my eyes to make sure I was not dreaming. I looked and rubbed, and rubbed and looked! It was no illusion! The women who were descending the long notched logs to the river's edge wore on their thighs and legs beautiful blue silk *tricots* or 'tights,' of an elaborate open-work pattern! and on their hands and forearms delicate black silk mits! I was not prepared for this elegant toilette in the Jungle, and my bewildering amazement continued until, on nearer inspection, I found that the airy tracery which I had mistaken for silken tights was tattooing.

I will not enter on any discussion of the origin or purpose of tattooing:—whether or not it began in the mark which God set on Cain after the killing of Abel, or as to its religious, or tribal, or social purposes, but will simply set forth the customs in regard to it as I observed them among the Kayans and Kenyahs, the patterns, and the mode of performing it. Inasmuch as the details will be dry and extremely uninteresting, and, in reference to the patterns, given with minuteness, because these patterns are in their general features almost immutable and are supposed to be symbolic, I would advise my readers to skip the following pages, and examine only the photographs, merely premising that, since Nature has inscribed at the entrance to the Torrid Zone, 'All clothes abandon, ye who enter here,' I fancy no one will dispute that, as a substitution for clothes, pervasive tattooing provides a device both attractive and modest.

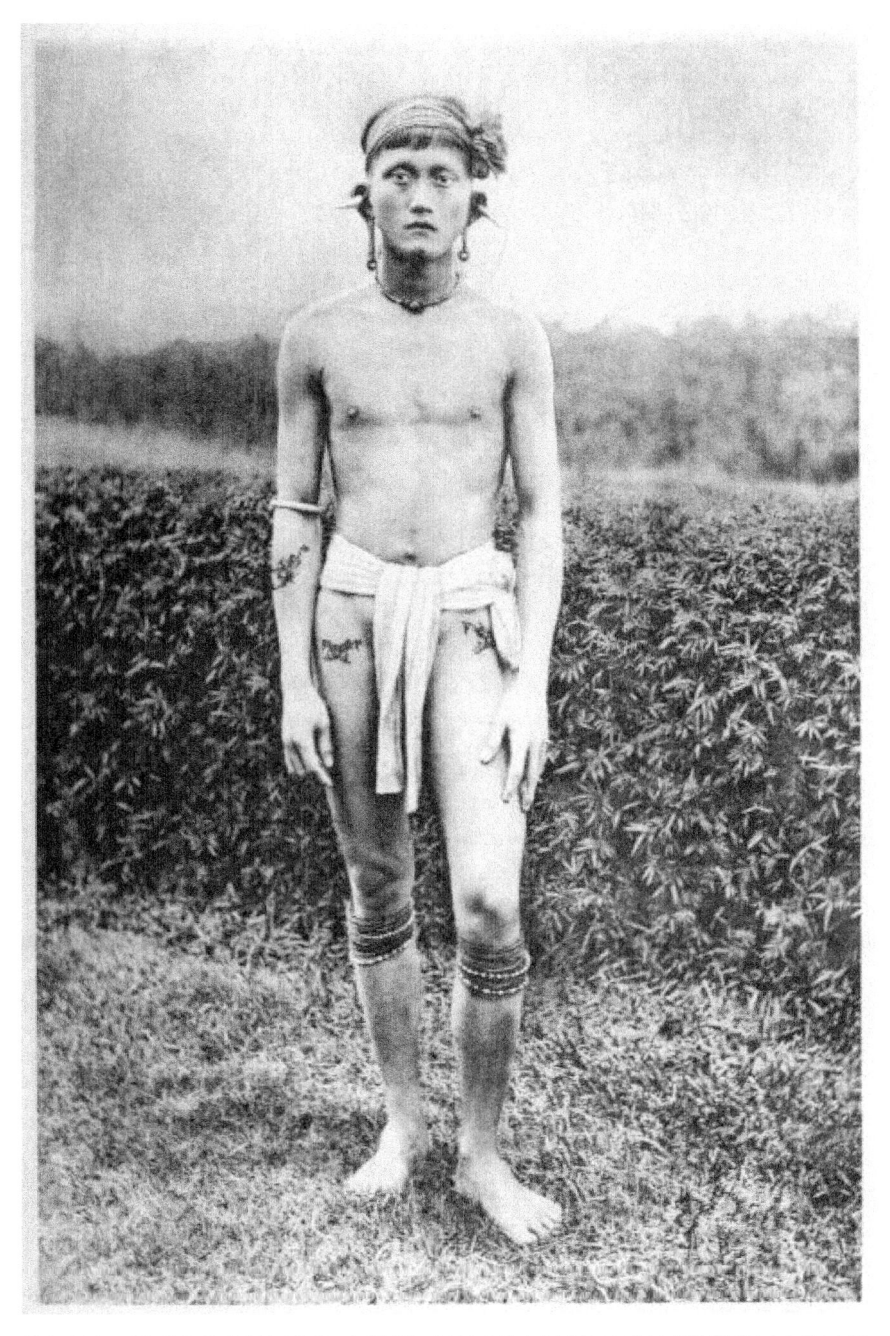

BATU – YOUNGEST SON OF THE KAYAN CHIEF OYONG LUHAT. HIS TATTOOING IS CHARACTERISTIC OF THE KAYANS OF THE BARAM DISTRICT, EXCEPT THAT HIS HANDS DO NOT

BEAR THE MARKS DENOTING A SUCCESSFUL HEAD-HUNTER; THE TIGER-CAT'S TEETH IN HIS EARS SHOW, HOWEVER, THAT HE HAS BEEN ON HEAD-HUNTING EXPEDITIONS AND HAS ATTAINED THE RANK OF A WARRIOR. AFTER THE EAR HAS BEEN STRETCHED TO THE DESIRED LENGTH, ONE SMALL COPPER RING IS USUALLY ALL THAT IS WORN, MERELY TO KEEP THE LOBE FROM CONTRACTING. THE BANDS BELOW HIS KNEES ARE OF FINELY BRAIDED FERN-ROOT, AND ARE KNOWN AS 'UNUS'; OCCASIONALLY THEY ARE OF STRIPS OF RATTAN BOUND WITH BRASS WIRE. UNUS ARE UNIVERSALLY WORN BY THE MEN, AND THEY THINK THAT WITHOUT THEM A MAN LOOKS EXCEEDINGLY NAKED.

The tattoo-marks on the Kayan men are small in size, and confined to certain portions of the body. There are only four or five, and they are placed on the thighs either in front, below the groin, or on the outer surface, just below the hip-joint, and on the flexor surface of the forearm. The designs consist of extremely conventionalised representations of 'dogs,' 'scorpions,' and the 'head of a prawn;' these are the native names given to the different patterns; in none of them is it possible to recognise the animal after which it is named.

Professor Alfred C. Haddon, whose opinion commands all respect, has expressed to me the extremely ingenious explanation, that, notwithstanding the native names, all these patterns represent the head of a dog. To this I modestly and most humbly demur, and incline to the belief that it is rather the head of that animal which enters so largely into all their ceremonials, namely, the pig. Dogs, on the other hand, are treated by all Borneans uniformly with great contempt. It may be noted, furthermore, that this same pattern, whatever be its origin, enters into all Kayan decoration, whether of doors, of beams, of implements, of bead-work, or of graves.

The patterns are selected purely according to fancy, and, as far as I could ascertain, serve solely as personal embellishment. The only mark which is really a male distinction is placed on the back of the hands and fingers after a man has taken a head. The designs on the hands of these men are always very indistinct, owing to the constant exposure and rough treatment to which the tattooing is necessarily subjected before it is thoroughly healed; hence the lines become faint and merge into one another, so that the appearance of a head-hunter's hands reminds one forcibly of Edward Lear's nonsensical Jumblies, whose 'heads were green and their hands were blue, and they went to sea in a sieve.' I never saw a head-hunter's hands that were freshly tattooed, nor did I ever see the stamps wherewith these designs are marked out. I am, therefore, unable to give a description of these important marks further than that the backs of the hands appear to be covered with narrow parallel lines running transversely, and the knuckles and their interspaces are covered with triangles with base and apex alternating; on the joints of the fingers are oblong patches of solid black.

The tattooing on the men, except, of course, the badge of a head-hunter, is done at about the age of puberty. It is not at all a ceremony; the youth himself decides when it shall be done and selects the pattern. In many tribes allied to the Kayans, in the Dutch possessions in South Borneo, some of the men are far more elaborately tattooed than the Kayans and Kenyahs of Sarawak, and extend the tattooing to the chest and back, and even to the cheeks and neck; but these elaborately tattooed men are the exceptions and not the rule in their tribe, and the marks are by no means as characteristic as are the 'dog,' 'scorpion,' and 'prawn' of the Baram Kayans. The Dayaks, or, properly speaking, the Ibans (the name *Dayak* is a mere Malay name, meaning 'up-river people,' and never used by the natives themselves to whom it is applied) tattoo on the wrists, forearms, chest, neck, and thighs, but never in large designs. On the chest, and on the point of the shoulder, they bear many-pointed stars, with a spiral sometimes double and interlocking in the centre. On the throat I have often observed narrow zig-zag lines connecting two designs like the escapement wheel of a watch. The zig-zag lines, they said, represent chains, but why a chain should be appropriate for the neck they did not say. The stars on the chest and shoulder, some maintained, represent flowers; others said they were silver dollars. With the exception of the few links of chain on the front of the throat, they do not seem to aim at the representation of ornaments, such as necklaces, bracelets, anklets, etc. In addition to these marks on the chest, arms, and neck, a very common position for a small design is directly on the prominent end of the ulna at the wrist; almost every Iban has over this prominence a small star, or a wheel-like design, with radii extending beyond the circumference.

Far more elaborate, on the contrary, is the tattooing of Kayan women, which, in the case of married women, invariably covers the thighs, legs, forearms, hands, and feet.

On the arms, it extends from the second joint of the fingers, (whereon is a simple black patch about a half inch square,) to just a little below the bend of the elbow. The knuckles and intervening hollows are decorated with a row of solid black triangles with base and point alternating; on the back of the hand are four small ovals surrounded by five concentric ovals, the outer four merging into the contiguous series, so that the upper and lower arcs form merely wavy lines. This row of concentric ovals is enclosed in a border of five lines, following the margin of the back of the hand below the knuckles to the wrist.

TATTOO DESIGNS ON THE FOREARMS OF KAYAN AND KENYAH WOMEN COPIED FROM THE ARM OF A WOMAN IN TAMA BULAN'S HOUSEHOLD.

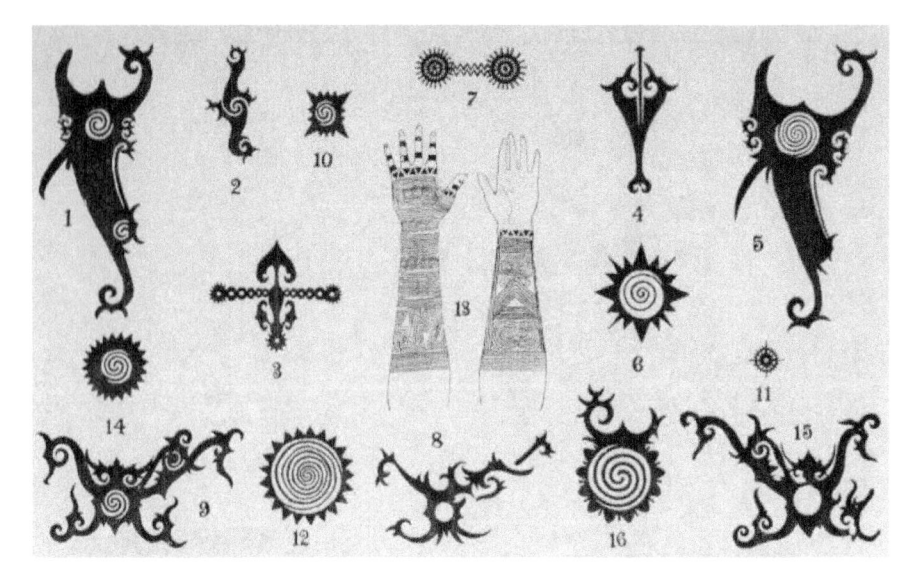

TATTOO DESIGNS USED BY IBANS OF THE REJANG AND BY KENYAHS OF THE BARAM.

- 1. IBAN. 'KALA,' THE SCORPION, – ON THE OUTSIDE OF THE THIGH.
- 2. " 'TAIA GASING,' THE COTTON SPINNER, – ON THE ULNAR SIDE OF THE WRIST, EXTENDING UP THE ARM.
- 3. " ON THE FRONT OF THE THROAT.
- 4. " ON THE FRONT OF THE THROAT.
- 5. " 'KALA,' THE SCORPION, – ON THE OUTSIDE OF THE THIGH.
- 6. " 'BUAH ANDU,' THE ANDU (?) FRUIT, – ON THE SHOULDER IN FRONT.
- 7. " 'TALI SABIT,' – ALONG THE RIBS.
- 8. KENYAH. 'ASU,' THE DOG, – ON THE FOREARM.
- 9. " 'KALA ASU,' THE SCORPION DOG, – ON THE FOREARM.
- 10. IBAN. 'BUAH ANDU,' – ON THE SHOULDER IN FRONT.
- 11. " 'LUKUT,' – ON THE POINT OF THE SHOULDER.
- 12. " 'TANDAN BUAH,' THE TANDAN (?) FRUIT, – ON THE CHEST.
- 13. KENYAH. ON THE BACK AND FRONT OF A WOMAN'S FOREARM.
- 14. IBAN. 'BUNGA TRONG,' THE TRONG (?) FLOWER, – ON THE SHOULDER.

- 15. KENYAH. 'KALA ASU,' – ON THE FOREARM OR THIGH.
- 16. IBAN. 'RINGGIT SALILANG,' – ON THE CHEST OR BREASTS.

On the back of the wrist is another row of four concentric ovals; above these, nine narrow lines and then two rows of five concentric ovals alternating with bands composed of five narrow lines. Above these, again, are intertwining zig-zags and scrolls composed of seven lines; this pattern, they told me, represents the root of the Tuba-plant, which is used in drugging, or poisoning, the water to get fish. The concentric ovals, so they say, are pictures of the moon. It is barely possible that an explanation of this frequent figure of the moon is to be found in a remark made to me by a tattooer, that when a woman died and passed to the next life, 'her tattooing becomes luminous like a firefly's light, and that without it she would wander in total darkness.' Above the Tuba pattern are eleven, sometimes more, finely waving lines completely encircling the arm, like rings. From these rings to the wrist, along both sides of the arm, is a narrow recurrent line making four laps on itself, and dividing the patterns on the flexor and extensor surfaces of the arm.

On the flexor surface of the arm, the pattern begins at the wrist with a row of triangles like those on the knuckles; then a band of narrow lines and two large concentric moons; above these, a large triangle whose sides and base are composed of seven narrow, parallel lines, – this represents the spring bow-piece, affixed to a canoe when shooting rapids; above this, two more large moons and then the band of rings around the arm.

These patterns vary to a slight extent in different households, but the main features are always present; the concentric ovals may be replaced by a spiral coil surrounded by radiating lines; or the twists and zig-zags of the Tuba-root may be arranged according to the artistic ability of the operator. The concentric moons are, however, considered a higher grade of work than the spiral coils.

The pattern on the thighs extends externally from the level of the hip-joint to the calf of the leg; it consists of four panels, each enclosed in a border of five delicate and parallel lines. At the top of these panels are conventionalised designs of 'scorpions,' of 'dogs,' or of the 'heads of prawns;' at least they closely resemble these patterns in the tattooing of the men. Beneath these, are small Tuba-root designs, and then a chain of interlocking diamonds, whereof the smaller and underlying diamonds have their vertical apices terminating in little hooks and curves; these, they assert, represent a creeping vine with hooked tendrils, like many of the palms and rattans. Round the calf is a series of rings, sixteen, more or less, in number, which completely encircle the leg like the rings on the forearm. Directly down the back of the thigh, from the fold of the gluteus muscle to the rings on the calf of the leg, a strip about an inch wide is left blank; this is an invariable feature, but they could give me no explicit explanation of its meaning. Dr. Hose expressed to me his belief that the natives considered this space to be necessary in order that the 'blood might run up and down.' On several occasions I tried to verify this interesting explanation, sedulously avoiding all leading questions, but always failed to elicit satisfactory answers. It would be remarkable should it prove that they knew anything about the circulation of the blood. As far as my observation goes, even the most experienced old Dayong, who, as an *haruspex*, must cut up, yearly, hundreds of pigs and fowls and examine their internal organs, has not the slightest accurate knowledge of the function of any organ, not even of the heart. By one tattooer I was assured that if this space were not left unmolested the leg would swell excessively and the tattooing prove a failure. It is not impossible that she had herein found the true reason for this 'safety valve,' as it were, of healthy skin. When a limb is girdled with tattooing, done under such septic conditions as always obtain in Borneo, the inflammation and swelling are very considerable; the skin becomes tense and non-elastic, and if there be no healthy area of elastic skin whereby to relieve tension, consequences might prove serious.

The markings on the feet are plain, broad stripes running from the bend of the ankle in front, over the dorsum of the foot, following the metatarsal bones to the toes; these stripes are interrupted once, dividing off the upper third over the instep. There is also an oblong patch of black on the second joint of each toe.

TATTOOING ON THE FOREARMS AND FEET OF A KENYAH WOMAN.

The persistence of the Tuba-root design in all of these patterns is, possibly, due to the fact that Tuba-fishing is considered more or less a feminine sport, although men participate in it and do the greater part of the work; nevertheless, it is the only sport wherein women join, and it is always a picnic and jollification.

The conjecture may be hazarded that the bands of rings close to the elbow and around the calf of the leg may possibly represent the 'Unus,' or rings of braided fern-root, worn by men and boys. The wavy lines look much like the impressions which these narrow braids make in the skin.

The tattooing of girls is begun when they are about four or five years old; the fingers and toes and knuckles are then decorated with the squares and the triangles, but here the process ceases until the girls become of marriageable age, when the tattooing of arms, and next of legs, is completed.

In connection with the operation of tattooing (which, by the way, they call 'Bityek,'—a disyllabic *Bit-yek*), there seems to be no particular lali or taboo; no objection to spectators was ever made either by the operator or by the patient; nor at being photographed was there shown any more than the usual reluctance.

As an indispensable preliminary, before the skin is touched, several beads must be given to the operator, who may not keep them all, but must hand over some to the 'Toh,'—the demons who are always lurking about to see that the rules of the house are obeyed. It is lali to draw human blood in a house unless the Toh be previously informed that it is for a lawful purpose. Some of the beads are, therefore, flung broadcast out of doors, for the Toh to gather up at their leisure. The girl is put on no special diet while undergoing the operation.

All tattooing is done by women, (be it remembered that I am here speaking only of the Kayans,) who, as far as I could ascertain, have no privileged position in the community, nor is any qualification demanded of them other than artistic taste and manual skill. The office is not hereditary, although it often happens that the profession descends from mother to daughter, merely because the daughter from an early age is employed as an assistant, and thereby acquires a familiarity with the process, and naturally inherits her mother's instruments.

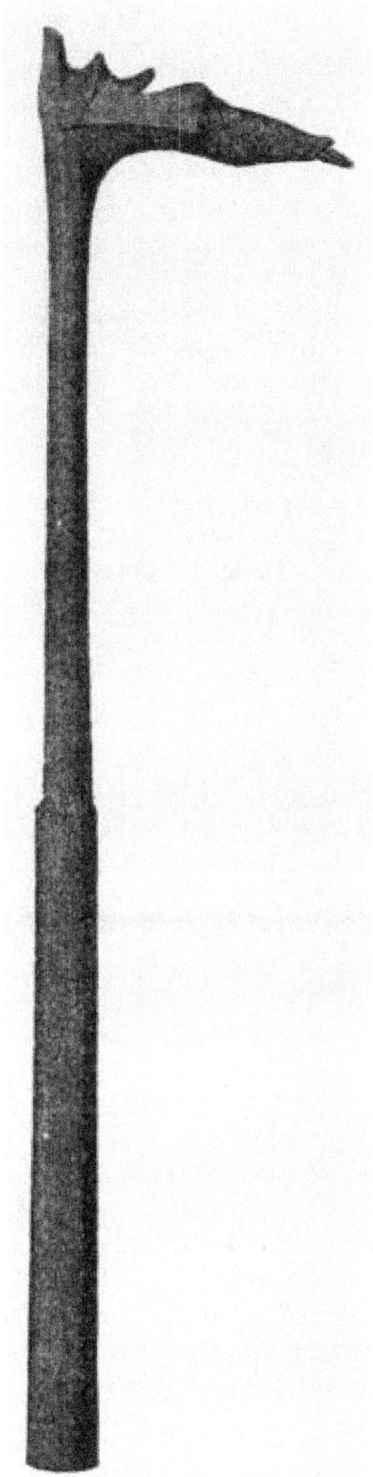

Kayan Tattooing Instrument. Two-thirds of the natural size.

The pattern to be tattooed is marked out on the skin by means of wooden stamps whereon the raised patterns have been carved out, leaving the designs in high relief; these stamps are inked and pressed on the skin, leaving a print which sufficiently guides the operator. For tattooing, three needles are bound tightly together, and inasmuch as it is considered advisable to force them obliquely into the skin, they are inserted slightly slantwise in the head of the wooden holder (shaped somewhat like a hammer), and enveloped in gutta-percha to about an eighth of an inch from their points, which holds them firmly in place and regulates the depth to which they may penetrate the skin. Not infrequently the handle and the head of the needle-holder are ornamented with carving.

The ink is made of the juice of sugar-cane, thickened with the soot of damar gum; it is kept in a bowl of soft wood, wherein the needles can be dipped without dulling the points; and finally the operator provides several pieces of soft bark-cloth for wiping away the blood, which flows profusely. All these instruments are usually kept in a cob-webby, sooty, blood-smeared box; but as heirlooms and tools they are of almost priceless value.

During the operation the girl sits or lies upon the floor; beside her squats the operator, with her toes pressing upon the skin to be tattooed; an assistant on the opposite side keeps the skin stretched. At the edge of the design marked out by the wooden stamp is placed a roll of soft bark-cloth, so thick that when the handle of the needle-holder rests upon it the needles exactly touch the skin. The needles, well dipped in the ink, carry enough fluid to tattoo lines several inches in length. Using the roll of cloth as a rest, the operator follows out the design and punctures the skin to a proper and uniform depth by means of quick taps with a small iron rod on that portion of the handle which rests on the roll. The assistant, following the track of the needles, wipes away superfluous ink and blood. (*Experto crede*, when I say that the pain of the Kayan operation, even for small designs, is very considerable; when endured for more than an hour, it becomes torture. Having also experienced for many consecutive hours the Japanese method, I can affirm that in comparison the Kayan verges on the inhuman.) A roll of bark-cloth or a stick is held by the victim, and, as an anæsthetic during the operation, clutched with desperate strength. (The photograph herewith given necessarily had to be taken in a very dark room. A magnifying glass will greatly assist an examination of the details.)

TATTOOING A KAYAN GIRL.

WHILE THE SKIN IS KEPT TENSE BY THE HANDS OF AN ASSISTANT AND BY THE FEET OF THE TATTOOER, THE DESIGN, WHICH HAS BEEN MARKED ON THE SKIN WITH INK-SMEARED WOODEN STAMPS, IS PRICKED IN BY TAPPING ON THE BACK OF THE NEEDLE-HOLDER WITH AN IRON OR A WOODEN BEATER.

Of course, the complete pattern on women is never finished at one sitting; it would involve more suffering than can be borne without, perhaps, serious shock; but the martyrdom is often endured for a couple of hours, and then, to fill in chance gaps and weak places, that which has been already pricked in, and is become an exquisitely tender welt, is mercilessly jabbed and hammered over again, not only once but even twice. The instant that the poor wretch of a girl is released from the hands, and toes, of her tormentor, she runs with the swiftness of agony to the river, there to soothe with the cool flowing water the frightful, burning ache. The absorption of so much foreign matter by the lymphatics often induces high fever; suppuration also not infrequently results from the septic manner in which the operation is performed; this naturally injures the sharpness of the lines. After one session, the tattooing is not resumed until the skin is entirely healed, unless an approaching marriage necessitates the utmost speed; should a woman have a child before her tattooing is completed, she is lastingly disgraced. The Kenyah women are tattooed only on the forearms and hands and on the dorsum of the foot, not on the legs or thighs.

Woe worth the behests of Bornean fashion! Tattooing is not the only torture that the Kayan or Kenyah damsel must endure who would fain be a belle; her ear-lobes must be pierced and stretched with weights until they hang down to her very bosom in long, slim loops of skin. One evening, in Tama Bulan's house, I was entertaining his daughter, Bulan, with the pictures in some illustrated papers that I had brought with me, and was trying my best (my fluency in Malay, at that time, was limited) to make them intelligible to her. As I have mentioned above, she was filled with boundless amazement at the slim and wasp-like waists of the women, and utterly failed to understand how any woman could endure the hourly suffering entailed by being horribly squeezed in by steel bands, which, I managed to tell her, were the secret of the extraordinary and unnatural shape. But while in the very act of gazing and marvelling at these pictures of what rational human beings will suffer in order to appear more beautiful, she was herself constantly relieving her poor, elongated ear-lobes of the several pounds weight of copper rings dangling and clinking on her shoulders, by sustaining in her hands, if only for a brief moment, these monstrous demands of Bornean fashion.

With a prophetic eye to future charms, they begin early. The ear-lobes are slit when a baby is two or three days old, and as soon as ever the cuts are sufficiently healed several small pewter rings are inserted, and gradually increased in number until their weight amounts to five or six ounces, and by the end of the first year the lobe has been lengthened three or four inches.

This gradual increase of weights is kept up with girls until the lobe stretches seven or eight inches. I have seen many a loop of skin, thus formed, sufficiently large and elastic to allow it to be slipped over the head.

It is by no means uncommon to see women with as many as three pounds of copper rings dangling in their ears; of course, this precludes all rapid motion unless the weights are supported by the hands. When they stoop over their work the rings are tossed behind on the back.

It often happens that the weights in the ears are increased injudiciously, and the thin band of skin gives way; it may be that the loop catches on a twig in the jungle or on some projection in the house, and, in a minute, all the long years of suffering have been in vain; immaculate beauty is for ever gone. To be sure, the ends may be spliced by instantly binding them fast together; but an ugly, tell-tale lump is the result, and nevermore are the two ears of a symmetrical, lovely length, and nevermore can they, like John Gilpin's bottles, 'keep the balance true' by bearing equal weights of copper rings. The patched lobe remains the weaker.

A KENYAH WOMAN WITH ELONGATED EAR-LOBES.

THE PROCESS OF ELONGATING THE EAR-LOBES IS BEGUN ON THE SECOND OR THIRD DAY AFTER BIRTH, BY MAKING IN THE LOBE A SMALL PERPENDICULAR SLIT, WHICH IS KEPT OPEN WITH A PLEDGET OF CLOTH OR A PLUG OF WOOD UNTIL THE WOUND HAS HEALED; THEN SEVERAL SMALL PEWTER OR COPPER RINGS ARE INSERTED AND GRADUALLY INCREASED IN SIZE AND NUMBER UNTIL THE LOBE AND THE SKIN OF THE NECK BELOW THE EAR BECOME SO STRETCHED THAT THE EAR-RINGS HANG FAR DOWN ON THE CHEST. SHOULD THE ORIGINAL SLIT NOT PROVE SUFFICIENTLY LARGE, OR SHOULD A GIRL WISH TO ENHANCE HER CHARMS BY AN ENLARGED EAR-LOBE, A SMALL, SPLIT CYLINDER OF

BAMBOO, HAVING THE EDGES OF THE SPLIT, SHARPENED LIKE KNIVES, IS CLAMPED UPON THE SKIN ABOVE THE FORMER SLIT, AND GRADUALLY CUTS THROUGH, THUS ENABLING THE STRETCHING PROCESS TO EXTEND HIGHER UP TO THE SKIN OF THE EAR AND THE CHEEK.

The women of the Berawan tribe, instead of weights, insert discs of wood three or four inches in diameter, often carved on both sides in delicate star-shaped patterns, and sometimes brightened by bits of colored glass or mirrors inlaid in the centre.

The Kayan and Kenyah men never stretch their ear-lobes to the same length as do the women; it is effeminate in a man to have his ears depend further than just to graze the shoulder. Men seldom wear more than one small copper ring, which is heavy enough merely to keep the loop taut.

The men of these same tribes, although they escape from extreme length of ears, must endure a second mutilation of this appendage. But this time it is in the upper part that a hole is punched, wherein, when they attain to full manhood and have been on a war expedition, there is inserted a tiger-cat's canine tooth decorated at the large end with a tuft of bead-work, or a silver cap, to keep it in place. Before they are entitled to this adornment, the hole, at least half an inch in diameter, is kept open by a simple wooden plug, which is generally worn, even by warriors, except on ceremonial occasions, and especially when in mourning for the dead.

These holes for the tiger-cat's tooth are not punched at the same time that the lobe is slit; the operation is not performed until the boy is about ten years old. The best time for it, so they claim, is in the evening; the wounds then have the benefit of the quiet, cool night, whereby the pain and chance of severe inflammation are notably lessened. A very opportune occasion is during a war expedition, when quietude and idleness are the rule, frequently for days, while the seers are finding the Omen Birds, and consulting them as to the success of the expedition. Young boys always accompany head-hunting raids, and serve in all menial capacities, such as, baling out the boats, collecting wood, starting the fires, etc. Inspired by the excitement of the hour, they are more than willing to undergo the pain of having their ears punched, in anticipation of the respect with which they will be regarded by their playmates when they return.

The operation is never performed unless the boy has had an auspicious dream the night before. It is auspicious to dream of bathing in clear, cold water, or of fruit trees laden with fruit, or of fish in large schools. It would be absolutely prohibitory of all thought of the operation were the lad to dream of fire or of eating anything hot, such as chillies or wild pepper. To make ready for the operation, the boy stands against a tree or post, so that the back of his ear stands out from his head with the firm support of the wood behind it; the hole is then punched out with a cylinder of bamboo of the proper half-inch size, which has been sharpened round the edge so that it makes a clean cut when driven by a smart blow from a billet of wood.

In the hole a plug of wood is at once inserted, and there remains until the wound is healed. The poor little chaps suffer horribly from the swelling and inflammation that always ensue. But have they not advanced the first step toward that happy day when they may be so blest as to kill a foe, and ever after entitled to wear a tiger-cat's tooth?

It was not until I saw the women of Tama Bulan's household dressed out in all their very best during the ceremonies of The Naming of the son and heir, that I noticed that they, too, had the upper part of the ear pierced for the insertion of a small tassel of beads. The hole is very small, and lies concealed in the fold of skin at the margin of the outer ear.

The Ibans do not stretch the ear-lobes more than an inch or two; but they make up for it by puncturing the edge of the outer ear in a series of small holes about an eighth of an inch apart, extending from the lobe all round the ear to where it joins with the skin of the head. In these diminutive holes they insert either a series of small white-metal rings or an elaborate ornament of open brass rings, either plain or strung with cowrie shells, and connected, opposite the opening whereby they are slipped into the holes in the ear, with a narrow band of brass, from which are suspended many small diamond-shaped pieces of the same metal, which clink and jingle and glitter. The rings at the top of the ear are about half an inch in diameter, but they increase gradually in size until at the lobe they are an inch or more. When an Iban is bedizened with these aural adornments, and has a red and yellow cloth wound around his head, and ten yards of Turkey red calico tied and twined about his waist, elegance of Iban costume can no further go.

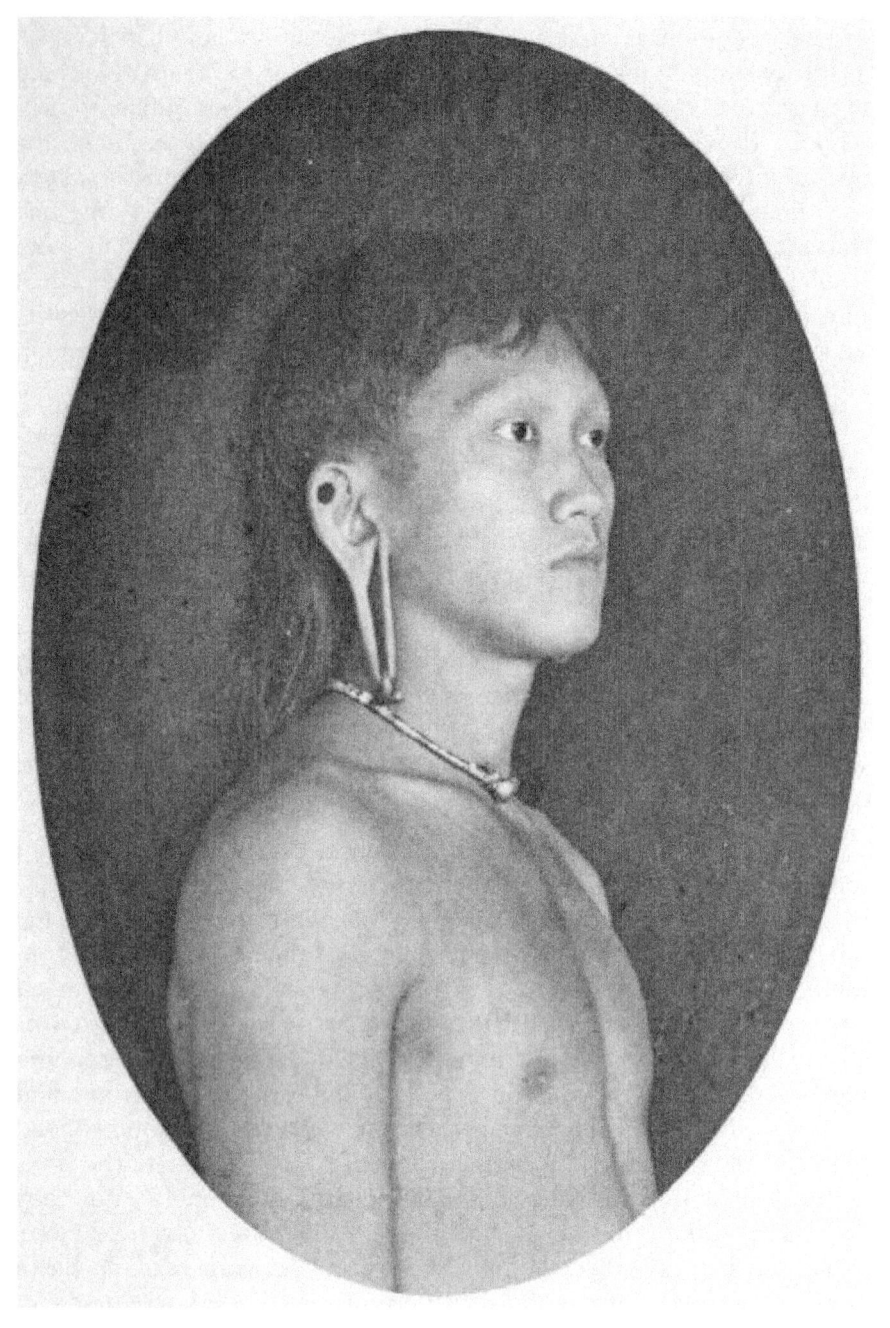

BATU, A KAYAN YOUTH OF THE BARAM DISTRICT.

HIS EAR-LOBE IS OF THE FASHIONABLE LENGTH DESIRED BY ALL THE KAYAN MEN. THE LARGE, ROUND HOLE IN THE

UPPER PART OF THE EAR IS FOR THE INSERTION OF A TIGER-CAT'S TOOTH, WHEN THE PRIVILEGE OF WEARING THAT BADGE HAS BEEN WON BY VALOUR ON A HEAD-HUNTING RAID.

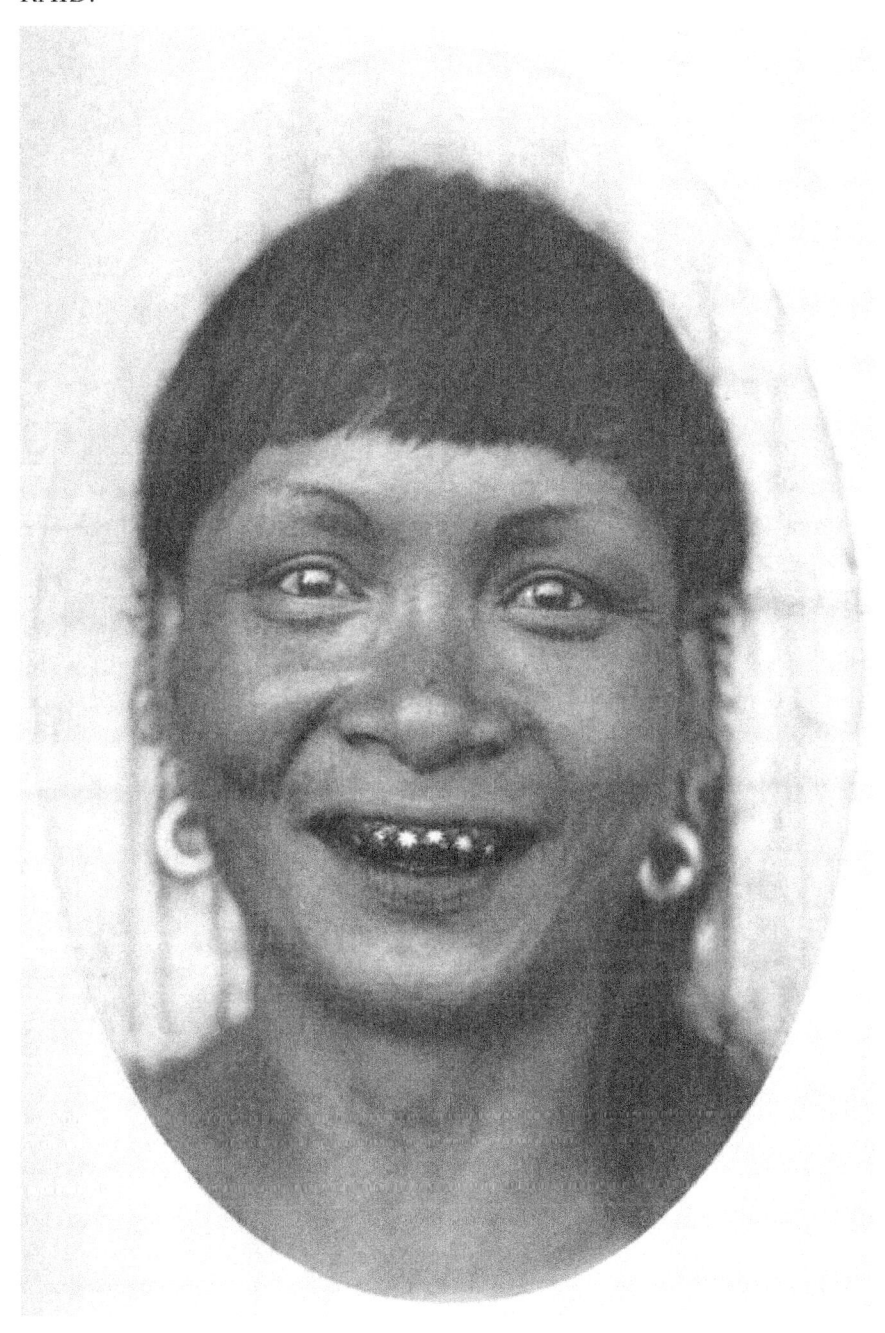

AN IBAN WITH FILED, STUDDED, AND BLACKENED TEETH.

THE TEETH ARE DRILLED THROUGH THE CENTRE, AND IN THE HOLES ARE INSERTED EITHER PLUGS OF BRASS WIRE OR BRASS-HEADED TACKS, WHEREOF THE HEADS HAVE BEEN CUT INTO STARS OR CRESCENTS. THE FOUR FRONT TEETH IN THE UPPER AND LOWER JAWS ARE FURTHERMORE FILED TO POINTS. THE FILING, DRILLING, AND BLACKENING KILL THE NERVES; THE GUMS RECEDE, AND AT A COMPARATIVELY EARLY AGE THE TEETH DECAY AND DROP OUT.

THE PHOTOGRAPH ALSO SHOWS ONE OF THE IBAN FASHIONS OF ORNAMENTING THE EARS WITH A SERIES OF SMALL PEWTER RINGS, ABOUT ONE-EIGHTH OF AN INCH APART ROUND THE MARGIN OF THE EAR.

In the way of improving nature, there is yet a third form of cosmetical adornment in which, it is safe to say, almost every tribe in Borneo indulges, namely, blackening the teeth. White teeth are universally considered frightful disfigurements, and he or she, who for a few days neglects to renew the stain, is sure to be jeered at by all companions with the scoffing remark that white teeth are no better than a dog's. I have had that reproach cast at me many a time by little children. The staining is effected with a paste made of a greyish-black shale rock, called 'Tunai,' powdered very fine and mixed with water and the ashes of a wood, which probably contains a considerable quantity of gallic or of tannic acid; two or three applications of this paste impart to the teeth a brilliant, shining black, which color remains for several days, and then must be renewed by fresh applications.

The Ibans use a mixture of the ashes of cocoanut husks and of a wood, known to them as 'Garang,' and the burnt juice of a green rattan. This mixture produces the same evenly tinted black as the Tunai stone.

Incomprehensible as it may seem, a row of regular, well-shaped teeth of inky jet is not devoid of charm; at a distance, I admit, the mouth looks cavernous, but near enough to distinguish the teeth at all, I venture to say it is attractive.

Now comes the fourth mandate of fashion, of an ineffably excruciating character:—

The Ibans, not content with blackening the teeth, actually drill holes through and through the faces of the six front teeth, and therein insert plugs of brass, whereof the outer end is elaborated into stars and crescents. Then they finish up by filing the teeth to sharp points! No dentist's chair can hold a more hideous torture than this. The drill,—usually no more delicate an instrument than the rounded end of a file,—bores directly through the sensitive pulp of the tooth, tearing and twisting a nerve so exquisitely sensitive that but to touch it starts the perspiration and seems the limit of human endurance; yet an Iban will lie serene and unquivering on the floor while his beauty is thus enhanced by some kind and tender-hearted friend. Of course, the tooth dies and becomes a mere shell, tanned inside and out by repeated applications of the astringent blackening; the gums recede, exposing the fangs of the teeth and sometimes portions of the alveolar process,—I need not add that the mouth of a middle-aged Iban is anything but attractive.

The brass plugs can be inserted or removed at will. When a young Iban lad whom I took with me as a servant to Singapore and Siam, noticed that the people in the streets stared at his bestudded teeth, he at once removed the brass studs and kept them carefully locked up in his private box.

For a fifth time Nature and the Borneans are at odds:—

Nature's beneficent provisions of eyelashes, eyebrows, beard, and moustache are all disdained, and plucked incontinently away. On the score of beauty, I draw the line at blackened teeth. The depilation of eyebrows and eyelashes is a backward step, and mars every face subjected to it, and is the cause, naturally enough, of much discomfort, if not of actual disease. At almost every house where we stopped we were called upon to treat cases of severe conjunctivitis, for which we could find no more reasonable cause than that it was due to the irritation caused by the depilation of eyelashes, coupled with bathing in muddy water. Furthermore, the absence of the slight shade given by the eyelashes in the glare of the sun seemed to me to be the cause of that anxious, distressed expression, or of a fierce and wild scowl, observable on so many faces. The moustache is very seldom allowed to grow, except on one side, and then only in a tuft at the corner of the mouth. The beard likewise is usually limited to a few straggling hairs on one side of the chin.

There is a certain tribe,—the Malanaus,—among whom the custom obtains of flattening the foreheads of female children; the practice is begun about the fifteenth day after birth, and continues for several months, until the bones of the skull begin to harden. The process is as follows: — On the forehead of the child a small padded board is held in place by means of cords, which pass through its ends and are attached to a band of cloth which passes round the back of the child's head. On the upper surface of the board the cords pass through a perforated coin, one from above downward and the other from below upward, so that by turning the coin the cords are twisted and the band shortened. By this means the pressure is exerted regularly by just so many turns of the coin each day. The compression is applied only during sleep, and, unless very carefully done, there is danger lest under too great pressure the skull be forced apart at the fontanelles. The Malanaus maintain that a forehead thus flattened imparts to the face a very beautiful and mild expression. Inasmuch as this compression is restricted to very early infancy, I am inclined to think that the skull resumes its shape. I did not observe any deformity of the foreheads in adults or even in the young girls.

MALANAU HEAD-COMPRESSION.

THE PADDED BOARD WHICH IS BOUND ON THE CHILD'S HEAD IS KEPT IN PLACE ONLY WHILE THE CHILD IS ASLEEP OR LYING QUIETLY IN ITS MOTHER'S LAP. THE PRESSURE EXERTED BY TWISTING THE CORD RUNNING OVER THE HEAD-BOARD IS NEVER VERY SEVERE, AND THE FLATTENING OF THE FOREHEAD IS BARELY PERCEPTIBLE IN AN ADULT.

THE OPEN BOX, CONTAINING FOUR SMALLER BOXES, IS THE 'BETEL' BOX, WHEREIN ARE KEPT LIME, WILD PEPPER LEAVES, GAMBIER, TOBACCO, CLOVES, AND BETEL NUTS, ALL NECESSARY ADJUVANTS TO THE CHEWING OF BETEL, A PRACTICE TO WHICH THE MALANAUS ARE ALMOST UNIVERSALLY ADDICTED.

None of the tribes mutilates the nose either with rings or sticks through the septum, or with studs through the alæ. Nor do they ornament themselves with scars, except as practised by the boys to show their fortitude. In this display of valour, they have adopted a species of moxa, — small pieces of tinder are placed along the forearm, set on fire, and allowed to burn out undisturbed by any sign whatever of pain. The straight line of scars bears an enduring testimony to the fortitude of the youth, and is infinitely precious in the eyes and to the heart of his dusky love.

What with browless and lashless eyes, inky teeth, brass plugs, looped ears, and blue legs, I am afraid I have given but a sorry picture of those whom I would fain have my readers regard with as much kindliness as my memory now holds for the originals. These freaks of fashion are, however, merely external; underneath I found honesty, hospitality, gentleness, and a child-like simplicity. The Kayans and Kenyans harmonise with their surroundings. The very word 'jungle' possesses an indefinable charm, — it is full of gay, exuberant life in insect and flower; but in its depth, side by side with these, lurks swift death. Deep seated in the heart of the joyous, child-like Borneans there reigns in their bosoms, true to their jungle home, an inextinguishable yearning for a head not their own. Nevertheless, I like them.

Permantong, or Lali – A Bornean Species of Taboo

During the days devoted to search for omens in reference to the sites of the rice-fields, and also again in reference to the planting, the Kayans refrain from their usual daily occupations, and neither leave their houses themselves nor allow strangers to enter. These days of seclusion are termed 'Permantong Padi,' or 'Lali Padi,' and correspond very closely to taboo elsewhere. Permantong is the word among the Kayans in the Baram district in the northwest of the island; but among the Kayans in the valley of the Kapuas River, in Dutch Borneo, it is 'Pantang;' both these forms are possibly derived from the Malay word 'Hantu,' — a Demon or evil Spirit, — with the prefix *per* and the affix *an*, both used to form derivative substantives; thus the Malay word in full would be 'per-hantu-an,' meaning *possessed by Spirits*, or, more freely, *bewitched*. 'Lali' is probably a pure Kayan word; its derivation I do not know. Between it and permantong I could discover no shade of difference in meaning.

The work of clearing off the jungle is tedious in the extreme, and, if after all the heavy labour, the crops should fail or be destroyed by monkeys, or by birds, or by a beetle called 'pangau,' or by blight, the whole household in their discouragement become convinced that they have committed some act to incur the displeasure of the Spirits; therefore, before this arduous work is begun, it is of prime importance to ascertain the exact temper of the Spirits, by observing the actions of certain birds, mammals, and reptiles, all of which are known to the Kayans as 'Amau,' and are supposed to be in the confidence of the unseen Powers. It needs but a close observation of bird, beast, and snake to detect the supernal favourable or unfavourable dispositions.

The experienced husbandmen of the household usually select a patch of jungle, which in their opinion will make a good rice-field if the Spirits be favourable; then each family does its share in clearing off the undergrowth.

IBANS FELLING A BUTTRESS TREE.

A TREE'S WIDE-SPREADING, BUTTRESS-LIKE ENLARGEMENTS AT THE FOOT NECESSITATE THE BUILDING OF A SCAFFOLD, WHEREFROM, IN THE FELLING, THE TRUNK MAY BE CUT THROUGH AT ITS SMALLEST DIAMETER. WHEN A TRACT OF JUNGLE IS TO BE FELLED. THE LARGEST TREES ARE CUT PARTLY THROUGH AND LEFT STANDING, SUPPORTED ONLY BY THE TREES AND BY THE INTERLACING VINES ROUND ABOUT; THE LARGEST TREES ON THE CONFINES OF THE TRACT ARE THEN FELLED, AND IN THEIR FALL START ALL THE OTHERS, AND, WITH A SOUND AS OF THUNDER, THE JUNGLE IS PROSTRATED.

During this preliminary stage, when the labour is not as severe as when heavy trees must be felled, the household is not as yet lali; nevertheless, every individual looks out most anxiously for any evil omens. If, on the way to the clearing, a snake called 'Nipa matei ekoh' (*Dead-tailed snake*) is encountered, which has a brilliant red head and a red-tipped tail, or should any one see a deer called 'Tela-au' (*Cervulus muntjac*), or a Civet cat (*Arctogale leucotis*) called 'Munin,' or a Rain bird called by the Kayans 'Pajan,' and by the Kenyahs 'Talajan' (*Platylophus coronatus*), they will relinquish the site, and, regardless of the work already done, abandon the place for ever. These four animals are most unfavourable omens when seen near the clearing, and wilfully to disregard their warnings, even at this early stage, not only compromises the abundance and quality of the crops, but also the health, or even the life, of the whole household. Should a man hear a downright warning and yet pay no attention to it, it is natural enough that during the ensuing year he should attribute to this disregard, whatever bad luck or even slight accident might befall him. If on the third day of work on the clearing, the whistle of the Talajan bird is heard near by, the omen is favourable; up to this time it is ill-omened, but now it indicates that the crops will be enormous, and that the rice-houses or granaries must be made of hard, enduring wood, to stand the weight of the rice harvest.

If, during three days, no evil omens have been observed, there is sufficient encouragement therein to proceed to the next stage of felling the heavy timber, and to incite the entire household to co-operate in the search for further requisite auguries.

All the families remain secluded in the long veranda, or in their small private rooms, and sit all day long quite still, smoking and talking; not a soul is allowed to leave the house, or, at most, to go further than the bank of the river, except two men designated as the 'Laki-Niho,' (*Hawk-men*,) whose duty it is to look for a hawk, called 'Niho.'

While these Hawk-men are engaged in this search, no one must call them by their true names; even an accidental infringement of this rule is punished by a fine of a few beads, or of a coarse china plate. It is the custom of some households for the Laki-Niho not to return to the house during the whole three days' search for omens; at such times they build in the jungle, near the clearing, a small hut, which they indicate to be permantong, by putting up beside it two poles, called 'ponkut,' whereon the bark is stripped into bunches of shavings at intervals down the pole. While living in this hut, members of their own household may communicate with them, if urgent necessity arises, but with strangers, who ought to know from the ponkut, the serious nature of the permantong, they will hold no communication whatever.

Should the hawk be seen on the first day of the search, but not on the two succeeding days, it is unfavourable; nevertheless, they would continue the preparation of the soil, with the expectation, however, of poor crops, which, if from no other cause, would be sure to follow the half-heartedness with which people work when discouraged at the very outset.

On the second day the search is kept up, and if the hawk be now seen, it is favourable, but not completely favourable; if they returned to the house, they would not probably refer to it, lest their chances for the morrow be thereby jeopardised. But should they fail to catch sight of the hawk on the third day, they would accept the omen of the second day, and be fairly well content; the search must be continued, however, until the last chance of the most favourable of omens is gone.

If on the third day's search, the hawk is again observed, the omen of the second day is rejected, and the omen of the third day is the only one accepted. A small pile of chips is at once set on fire, to inform the hawk, that a blessing is expected on their crops, and the Laki-Niho hurry back to the house to spread the good news. Every one in the house now lights a cigarette or waves a fire-brand, whereby a blessing is invoked on his or her particular rice-farm, and all eagerly watch for the hawk, to see whether or not he sails around without flapping his wings. Should he sail away out of sight without once flapping his wings all are delighted; it means that the clearing of the jungle may now continue prosperously, and that neither attack of enemies nor accident to the workers need be feared. Should the hawk flap his wings, it follows that some men, in felling the jungle, will be badly cut by their axes or perhaps crushed under falling trees. All instantly avert their eyes from the flapping hawk, lest the bird should recognise them in the fields and select them as victims. After they have made their wishes known to the hawk by means of the fire, there is a respite of a day or two in the permantong, and the people are allowed to go out of doors.

FIELD OF HILL RICE, CLEARED AND PLANTED BY IBANS IN THE BARAM DISTRICT.

After this short respite, the same two Laki-Niho again set out, this time in search of the Talajan bird; and again the people are housed. This search lasts three days also, and on the third day, if successful, they perform the same rite as before with fire and smoke. Next follows a three days' lookout for the Tela-au deer, which must be not only seen but heard; if it dart off the minute it is seen, without giving its gruff bark, it foretells a misfortune, but to an individual merely, not to the whole household; consequently, but very little attention comparatively is paid to it.

The tedious formalities are now nearly over, and there remain but two more animals to be observed, namely, the Munin and the Makong, (*Berenicornis comatus*, the white-headed Horn-bill;) these two, also, must utter some sound to show whether or not they are favourable. These are all the omens that must be consulted before the heavy timber can be felled and the rice planted. During each period of three days, all members of the household must remain within the house.

When the felled jungle is become dry, it is burned over, and as soon as the ground is cool they dibble in the grain. From the hour when the real labour of felling the jungle begins, until the seed-planting is finished, no stranger is allowed to enter the house or field; should inadvertence or necessity bring a neighbor within the lali district, he must pay a small offering to atone for the trespass. This offering is known as 'Usut,' and is ordinarily a few beads or something of iron, such as a spear-head, or an old knife. The usut is placed in a basket and hung up in the rice-field until it rusts away or disappears. To see that this usut is properly paid, is the duty of the women, who call the custom 'Toh Lali,' or Lali of the Spirits. (Once, when on our way down the river from Tama Bulan's, we stopped at a house, and, finding no one about, walked boldly up the bank, whereupon the head-man hurried down to meet us, and demanded, with considerable persistence, that we should give him a knife. Thinking he was hinting at a present, I searched in the canoe for one of my good hunting-knives. On receiving it, he incontinently thrust it into a basket and sent it off to the rice-fields to be hung up and to rust away. An old table-knife or any bit of old iron would have done as well, but my ignorance cost me a valuable knife, which I am sure was wasted on the Toh.)

The crop is now fairly started. The heaviest part of the task of keeping down the weeds falls to the women, who rise with the sun, and, as soon as the household is fairly awake, start off in rain or shine for the fields, in parties of six or eight, armed with their little, short-handled, lop-sided hoes. Usually they do not eat until they arrive at the scene of their labours; sometimes they halt at a pebbly 'karangan,' where dry wood is plenty, and there break their fast, but do not eat again until they return to the house in the evening.

Shortly before the rice is cut, a basket containing pieces of wood, roots, leaves, and strings of beads is carried to the field and left there for three days. This basket of offerings, or charms for the crop, is called the 'Tigga,' and after the rice is cut the basket and its contents are placed either on a shelf in the granaries or else on the platform just outside the door.

During the harvesting of the 'Parai Agit,' a small patch of rice planted first, and always harvested first, there is a lali of four days, known as the 'Lamali Parai,' (lali of the pregnant rice.) Of the Parai Agit no woman must eat; if she does eat of this rice, she will go mad. Reiterated questionings failed to disclose the origin of this belief, and even the reason for planting the Parai Agit itself.

When the rice is all harvested, the household is lali to strangers, and for eight days no one can go off on any expedition nor return to the house from an expedition. No sooner does this lali end, than another begins, while the rice is being stored in the granaries. But as soon as this harvesting is over, a general feast is prepared, and merriment of all sorts makes up for the weariness of the long day's work. The women don every stitch of their finery and every bead to their name; some even assume men's clothes, and carry shield, spear, and parang. In the evening, all join in a long procession round the house; guests are invited to participate in the festivities, and 'jest and youthful jollity' rule the hour; the brimming cup passes freely, and to the harmonious strains of the kaluri the women 'trip it as they go,' or leap in war-dances, in imitation of the men. As a half apology for all this 'heart-easing mirth,' they told me that this harvest at least was theirs, — they might not live to see another.

IBAN CAMPHOR-COLLECTORS SPLITTING UP A CAMPHOR TREE IN SEARCH OF CRYSTALS.

WHEN ALL THE OMENS HAVE BEEN AUSPICIOUS, THE CAMPHOR TREE IS FELLED AND THEN, DECKED OUT IN THEIR FINEST WAR CLOTHES, THE COLLECTORS EXAMINE WITH MINUTEST CARE EVERY CRACK AND CREVICE IN THE TRUNK OF THE TREE WHERE THE CRYSTALS MIGHT LURK. THERE IS NO PRODUCT OF THE JUNGLE ABOUT WHICH THERE IS SO MUCH MYSTERY AS ABOUT CAMPHOR, AND WHILE SEARCHING FOR IT THE COLLECTORS ARE HEDGED IN AT EVERY TURN BY PERMANTONG OR TABOO, AND MUST TALK IN A LANGUAGE USED ONLY DURING QUESTS FOR THE ELUSIVE CRYSTALS.

After this festival there follows another lali, known as the 'Lali Neboko;' it lasts for ten long days, and is apparently devoted by the women to the resumption of their proper sphere and duties; they make all sorts of cakes out of the new rice, and vie with each other in devising toothsome dishes for their lovers and husbands. During all this lali, no one is permitted to do a stroke of any work that resembles the cultivation of rice; a parang or a billiong, or any tool used in felling the jungle, is a strictly lali article; should any restless creature express a desire for active work, he is scoffed at and scorned as a spoil-sport and kill-joy.

During the Permantong Padi, the large wooden mortars, wherein the rice is husked, are enclosed in bamboo railings, to prevent human beings, and dogs also, from touching them. The store of rice will last but a short time should these mortars be touched by any hands other than those whose duty it is to use them. If a dog in search of food, or of a place to sleep, crawl into one of them, he is straightway caught, and his hair rubbed the wrong way with a cord, which they call a 'Tali Gamai.' During this rubbing, the owner of the mortar exorcises the evil Spirit by saying: 'I stroke this dog thus, because I do not wish my food to disappear on account of this dog. Let my food last until the next year's crop. One! Two! Three! Four!' The dog is sure to die, so they say, very soon after this ceremony. These large mortars are fastened to the floor, and when not in use are often used as seats, except during the Permantong Padi, when even the deep hollow in the centre is plugged up, to keep the dogs, which no railing can exclude, from licking it in their search for remnants of rice.

Besides the Permantong Padi, there are many minor permantongs in the daily life of the Kayans; for instance, in a Kayan house it is permantong to whistle after dark. To play the kaluri, or the nose-flute, is allowable, even though thereby the same sound as whistling is produced; whistling summons evil Spirits, and is sure to bring mischief into the house. Some Ibans aver that in old times it was strictly against all rule ever to whistle in the house, even in the daytime.

It is permantong, or lali, for a member of a dead man's household to give anything to be used in laying out the corpse; cloth or other things necessary for such purposes may be obtained from any other than a member of the same house. When in need of such things, the relatives and friends should ask for them when the patient is moribund, and not after death has put a seal on his lips, preventing him from making the request himself. When the corpse has been laid out for several days, no one, whether a member of the household or not, is willing to sell or give any thing to be placed upon the corpse; it may be placed, however, close by the corpse with perfect propriety, together with cigarettes, which carry messages to dead friends. Dr. Hose told me that on one occasion, while he was talking to Tama Bulan, in his long-house on the Pata River, a message was brought to the Chief from a very sick man, with the request for enough white cloth to make a 'Bah' or waist-cloth, wherein to die. Tama Bulan asked whether the message came from the man himself or from his relatives, and showed no inclination to give the cloth until he learned that the man was still alive; then he very willingly produced the number of fathoms desired. He explained afterward, that had the man been dead, and the request come from the relatives, he would not have given the Bah. Had he given it under these circumstances, it would have angered the Spirits, and they would have claimed the giver as the next victim.

When a man is sick and likely to die, no one in the house is allowed to open boxes, or any receptacles whatever, at night, except it be the small tobacco boxes of bamboo which all carry, or the ordinary baskets wherein they keep the sleeping-mats; breach of this law brings death into the room in which the offence was committed.

PUNAN CAMPHOR-COLLECTORS.

PUNANS TESTING THE PRODUCTIVENESS OF A CAMPHOR TREE BY SMELLING THE CHIPS CUT FROM THE TRUNK ABOUT

TEN FEET FROM THE GROUND. EXPERT COLLECTORS CAN TELL BY THE STRENGTH OF THE ODOR WHETHER OR NOT THE TREE IS RICH IN CRYSTALS.

It is lali to cook inside the house the flesh of deer, buffalo, wild cattle, tiger-cats, many of the smaller mammals, and the large lizard (*Veranus*,—sometimes as much as six feet long,) and only old and proved warriors may eat the flesh of deer; the timid disposition of the animal enters the souls of youths who are rash enough to eat of it.

Very similar to the search for omens in reference to the rice-fields is the observation of omens preliminary to the search for camphor crystals, (which are found in a tree known to botanists as the *Dryobalanops Camphora*.) Before setting out for the depths of the jungle where the camphor trees grow, the Kayans first look for a bird known to them as 'Isit'—a Spider hunter, (*Arachnothera longirostris* or *Anthreptes malaccencis*,) and should it be seen flying across their path, from right to left, the omen is not good, there will be poor luck in their search; if it be seen flying in the opposite way, there will be good luck. After they have seen the Spider hunter, they must next look for the common Red Hawk, whose flight must be also from left to right; if its flight be from right to left, their search will be fruitless, or else some heavy calamity will happen to them, and they had far better return home at once. When both these Omen bearers have been seen flying favourably, the Pajan, or Rain Bird, and the Tela-au, or Barking Deer, must be either seen or heard on the right-hand side of the trail; but even when all these omens have been favourably observed, the camphor searchers are not yet free to pursue their quest. For a final omen, they seek for a certain snake, 'Batang limu,' (*Simotes octolineatus*,) and the most strenuous efforts must be made to kill it; should it escape, they may as well return home; they will find no camphor, even though all the other omens have been auspicious.

As soon as they have decided upon the tributary stream, near whose banks they are to direct their search, a rattan is stretched across its mouth, as Jamma explained to me, and as is set forth on page 148 above; on this rattan are hung wooden images and models of parangs, billiongs, spears, and the wooden wedges used in splitting up the trunks of the felled camphor trees; this gives notice to other camphor hunters, or to passing strangers, that the stream is closed and all trespassing forbidden. When they have selected the camphor tree, which they intend to cut down, they build their hut near it, and then, after the first strokes of the axe, if they hear the note of an Omen bird, they give up work for the rest of the day, and sit idle in their hut. But if all omens are favourable, and they find that the tree is likely to prove rich in camphor, they plant near their hut a stake, whereof the outer surface has been cut into curled shavings and tufts down the sides and at the top. (I suggest as possible that these shavings represent the curling tongues of flame which communicate with the unseen Powers.) When the Kayans are collecting camphor, they are under no restrictions as to food, nor are they forbidden to speak to people whom they may meet, although they will not allow strangers to enter their hut. With many other tribes, all communication with strangers is strictly forbidden; the Sibops, for instance, when asked, by people whom they meet, the usual question: — 'Where are you going?' maintain a stony silence.

When the camphor tree has been felled, the trunk is cut into small pieces, and during this process the searchers are clad in their most showy war-clothes and armed with parang and spear. It is in the crevices of the fibre of the wood that the crystals are found, (a peculiarity of the Borneo camphor,) and the searchers seem to regard the tree as a fallen foe, who can be made to yield his hidden treasure only at the point of sword and spear.

The search for the crystals is tedious work; each piece of wood must be split with the greatest care and examined with minuteness. No camphor is found beyond twenty feet from the root, and trees productive of camphor crystals are always hollow; it is, therefore, probable that no crystals are found unless the tree has been in some way injured. Besides the crystals, there is always an abundance of oil, useful as an embrocation; and there is also usually a quantity of soft camphor, called 'Kapor Bata,' not yet crystallised; yellow, resinous crystals are of no value. The blossoms of the tree have a strong smell of camphor, and near its roots is usually found a peculiar luminous fungus.

Many tribes when on an expedition for camphor must not talk among themselves in their own language about their quest, but must use 'camphor language.' The Malanau tribes are herein very strict, the crystals will immediately dissolve if any language be used other than the camphor language. The Malanau word for *to return* is 'muli,' but when in the presence of a camphor tree they say 'beteku;' *to hide* in the Malanau language, is 'palim,' but when on a camphor hunt they say 'krian.' Similarly, all common names for implements and for food are changed. One would expect to find an interesting remnant of an ancient language in this camphor dialect, but it is very doubtful if there be any such remnant there. This curious custom prevails throughout Borneo, and in the Malay Peninsula also; possibly, it was introduced by the Malays to preclude all outside interference in the trading transactions between the natives and themselves.

KAYAN CAMPHOR-COLLECTORS SELLING THEIR STORE OF CRYSTALS TO CHINESE TRADERS.

THE PRICE GIVEN FOR CAMPHOR DEPENDS LARGELY UPON THE SIZE AND PURITY OF THE CRYSTALS; YELLOW AND SOFT CRYSTALS ARE OF LITTLE VALUE. THE BOY ON THE LEFT IS HOLDING IN HIS HAND SEVERAL ROLLS OF COPPER CENTS TIED UP IN PACKETS OF FIFTY.

Among some tribes, when engaged in camphor collecting, the names of Chiefs and of influential men must never be mentioned; should any one violate this rule, the trees are always found camphorless.

Wives dare not touch a comb while their husbands are away collecting this valuable gum; the fibres of the tree will duly reveal abundant spaces where camphor ought to be found; but if a comb has been touched at home, these spaces will prove empty and resemble the spaces between the teeth of a comb.

Husbands are able to discover, by certain knots in the tree, when their wives are unfaithful; and in former days, many women are said to have been killed by jealous husbands on evidence no better than these knots.

The leathery sheath of the leaf-stalk of the Penang palm is used as a plate for food, and it must not be washed during the whole time of an expedition for camphor, for fear that the camphor will dissolve and disappear from the crevices of the tree.

No one is allowed to bathe except at daylight and at nightfall; no song is sung; no deer of any species should be eaten at these times; the collectors are, however, allowed to hunt for smaller game with the blow-pipe.

(The finest camphor is that which is found in large, transparent crystals, about three-quarters of an inch long; this often brings in the up-country bazaars as much as forty or fifty dollars a pound. The chief camphor workers are the Punans, who are either hired as guides and helpers by the Kayans, Kenyahs, Sibops, or Ibans, or else they collect the camphor themselves and barter it with the other natives, who in turn sell it to the Chinese.)

With almost every tribe the name for camphor-hunting is 'Paji.'

The Punans

When we parted company with the somewhat unpeaceful Peace-party at Tama Aping Buling's, as previously narrated, we set out by ourselves to visit a settlement of Punans, which had been for some months past in the jungle a short distance from the head-waters of the Dapoi. The sense of freedom and relief from the responsibility of that host of warlike peace-makers could not fail to add to our enjoyment of this lovely river; but, even apart from this private, personal emotion, nothing can be imagined more thoroughly and charmingly tropical than the scenery, shifting and changing at every stroke of the paddle, on which we now entered. The sky was cloudless, the temperature delightful; great trees, slanting far over the river, interlocked their branches overhead, and, in perfect sun-flecked shade, we pursued our slow way over the curling, bubbling, and babbling water, with our men lazily poling or paddling the canoes. Little blue, green, and red king-fishers darted across our bows, hither and thither, from the tangled undergrowth on the banks; from huge, distorted branches covered with delicate little bright-green ferns, dangled long, sweeping vines, which had caught in their coils clumps of stag's-horn fern and gay orchids, thus adorning our pathway with hanging-baskets of Nature's own handicraft; large, startled fruit-pigeons glided swiftly under the archway of boughs, stirring the leaves with the wind from their swift wings; and from the depths of the ever-dripping jungle resounded the hoarse croak of the horn-bill or there was wafted the plaintive, melodious call of the Wawa monkey. Except for these sounds and the gurgling of the water, all nature was absolutely hushed, and the odor of damp, rich earth and warm leaves was heavy, like the atmosphere in an orchid-house in winter.

The banks of the Dapoi are somewhat thickly populated, and we halted at several houses, where we made ourselves most welcome by largesses to the women of strips of bright yellow or of gay red cloth, for frontlets, and to the men we gave handfuls of Java tobacco. From the female heart, as grateful as, in this instance, it was vain, our gifts received an immediate appreciation; when we took our departure, the river-bank looked like nothing so much as a bed of marigolds and poppies in fullest bloom.

TAMA BALAN DENG, A CHIEF OF THE SIBOP TRIBE. HIS THREE DAUGHTERS, AND TWO SONS.

PIPES AND OTHER REQUISITES TO TOBACCO SMOKING.

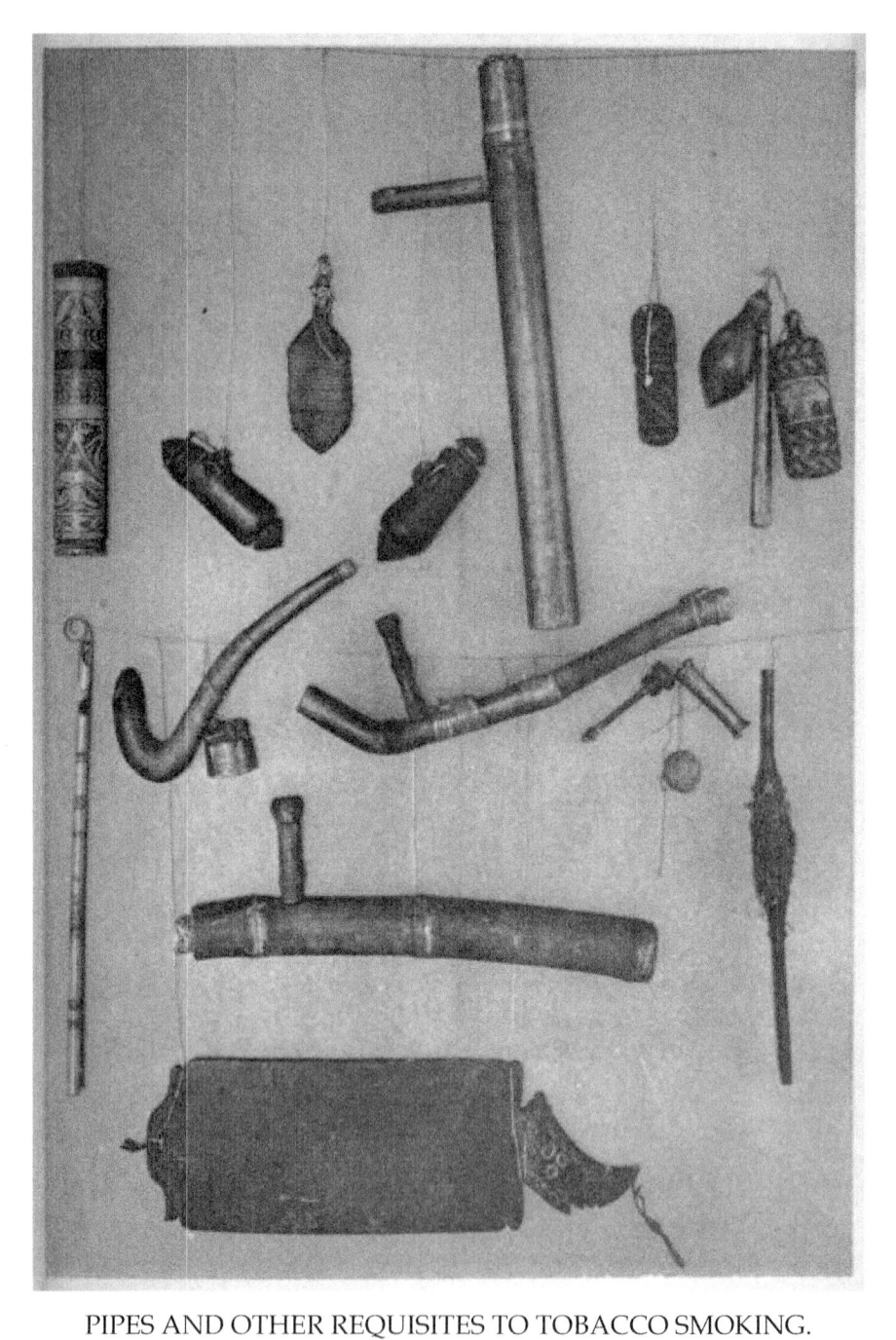

ON THE LEFT, IN THE UPPER HALF OF THE PHOTOGRAPH, IS A CARVED, BAMBOO TOBACCO BOX, USED BY THE KAYANS TO

HOLD BOTH TOBACCO AND ROLLS OF BANANA LEAF, WHEREOF CIGARETTES ARE MADE. NEXT TO IT IS A PAIR OF WOODEN TOBACCO BOXES, PROBABLY MADE BY A KELABIT. ABOVE THEM IS A POUCH OF PLAITED RATTAN. THE THREE LONG SECTIONS OF BAMBOO, WITH SLIM BOWLS INSERTED AT RIGHT ANGLES, AND ALSO THE BENT ROOT WITH A SMALL BOX ATTACHED, ARE PIPES USED BY THE SIBOP TRIBE. ON A RIGHT IS A PLUG OF PALM LEAVES, FASTENED IN A CLEFT STICK, WHICH IS INSERTED IN THE STEM OF A PIPE TO STRAIN THE SMOKE AND TO KEEP THE ASHES OF TOBACCO FROM BEING DRAWN INTO THE MOUTH. NEXT TO IT IS A FIRE-SYRINGE, USED BY THE SARIBAS IBANS, CONSISTING OF A BRASS CYLINDER LINED WITH LEAD, AND A TIGHTLY FITTING, WOODEN PISTON; ON THE TIP OF THE PISTON IS PLACED A SMALL PIECE OF TINDER MADE FROM A MOSSY LICHEN, AND BY DRIVING THE PISTON VIOLENTLY INTO THE CYLINDER AND RAPIDLY WITHDRAWING IT, THE SUDDEN COMPRESSION AND EXHAUSTION OF THE AIR IGNITE THE TINDER. THE OPERATION REQUIRES GREAT DEXTERITY. ABOVE ARE TWO SMALL TOBACCO BOXES, ONE COVERED WITH BEAD-WORK, THE OTHER WITH PLAITED FERN-FIBRE; TO THE LATTER ARE ATTACHED A WHET STONE AND A GOURD TO HOLD A SUPPLY OF PITH BUTTS FOR THE BLOW-PIPE DARTS. IN THE LEFT LOWER HALF IS A STRAIGHT BAMBOO PIPE, USED BY MADANGS. AT THE BOTTOM OF THE PICTURE IS A BOARD, WHEREON CIGARETTES ARE ROLLED AND TOBACCO IS CUT INTO THIN STRIPS.

(From *The Furness-Hose Collection*, Philadelphia.)

At dusk we arrived at Tama Balan Deng's,—a village of Sibops recently moved over from the Rejang. The Chief gave up his own room to us, and, hospitable soul, without hinting it to us, quietly and silently moved his family into an adjoining temporary hut; for his house was only partially completed. We found here that tobacco was smoked by the men much more frequently in pipes—a rare custom in this part of Borneo—than in cigarettes. These home-made pipes differ so widely from any I have ever seen or heard of, that possibly they are worth a word of description:—The stem is a piece of bamboo more than an inch in diameter, into which is set a straight, slim bowl, which can hold only a small wad of tobacco. In the stem they insert a plug of shredded palm leaves, or of shavings of wood, bound on a stick; and then take the end of the stem into their mouths, and having first got the tobacco well alight by a few gentle puffs, they give a powerful suck, whereby the wad of glowing tobacco is drawn down through the bowl into the stem, but is prevented from reaching the mouth by the plug of palm leaves. Their name for a tobacco-pipe is 'S'puk,' which seems to be an imitation of the sound of the check given by the plug of palm leaves to the wad of tobacco under the vigorous suck.

Very few of the inmates of the house had ever before seen white people; and we had a crowd of gaping spectators constantly about us. During our first night, almost all the inmates crowded into our room, as I said above, where they remained, positively the whole night through, watching us, exchanging observations on our personal appearance, and lost in wonder at our clothes, our marvellous paleness, the colour of our eyes and of our hair. We opened our eyes at daylight, in time to catch sight of the women in the group creeping out, almost on all fours. This creeping, crouching, feminine mode of walking obtains among almost all the tribes; when women pass a group of men on the veranda, they must crouch down as low as they can; or even when they have themselves been of the group and wish to leave it, they must creep away, not rising higher than a squatting position until they are at a distance. Thus it was, on this present morning; when they withdrew from this inquisitive vigil they crouched until they were outside the room.

Tama Balan's was the last house on the Dapoi, and as we continued up the pleasant stream we seemed to have left all Borneo behind us. Suddenly we caught sight of a young Punan girl standing in a canoe near the shore, and so earnestly engrossed in stamping grated tapioca root through a piece of matting to strain it, that she never noticed our approach. When at last she looked up and caught sight of our canoes, and the inconceivable white beings in them, in a flash she snatched up her mat and basket of tapioca, and darted into the jungle, like a startled fawn. She was such a pretty picture, as she stood in her canoe, absorbed in her work, that I told one of our men to find her and lure her back with promises of rich presents, if she would allow me to take a picture of her. She was quickly found, and brought back somewhat reluctantly; never before had she seen white folk, and what idea the making of a picture conveyed to her poor, little, bewildered brain, cannot be fathomed. In reminiscence, it must have seemed to her a hideous dream; she was told to go on with her work, while a horrible monster, with a face as pale as ashes, and incomprehensibly clad, stood off at a distance, and placed on three long sticks an awful object, that expanded and contracted, hid his face in a black cloth, looked at her with an awful eye for a moment, gave her a big piece of yellow cloth and a handful of tobacco, and then with his black object and long sticks was off again in a canoe;—such, at least, was her utterly bewildered and dazed expression, as she stood motionless in her canoe, holding in her hands the yellow cloth and the tobacco, her only proofs that she was not dreaming, and glancing from them to us alternately as we disappeared rapidly round the turn of the river, vanishing into empty space from which we had as suddenly and mysteriously emerged. No Punan mind could doubt that she had been visited in a trance by supernatural Spirits.

PUNAN HUTS NEAR THE HEAD WATERS OF THE DAPOI.

THESE LEAFY SCREENS, THE MOST SUBSTANTIAL HABITATIONS WHICH THE PUNANS EVER BUILD, ARE DESERTED AS SOON AS THE TAPIOCA OR OTHER JUNGLE PRODUCT, ON WHICH THE PEOPLE LIVE, IS EXHAUSTED IN THAT LOCALITY. THE PUNANS DO NOT PLANT RICE, NOR DO THEY CULTIVATE ANY CROPS, BUT LIVE SOLELY ON WHAT THEY FIND GROWING WILD IN THE JUNGLE.

PUNAN GIRL STRAINING GRATED TAPIOCA.

THE TUBERS ARE FIRST FINELY GRATED AND THEN, DILUTED WITH WATER, PLACED IN A MAT, AND BY A VIGOROUS TREADING THE FINE PARTICLES ARE STRAINED THROUGH AND COLLECTED IN THE BOTTOM OF THE BOAT OR OTHER RECEPTACLE USED FOR THE PURPOSE.

Not long after this, the river grew so shallow that we deserted the boats, and walked for miles and miles, so it seemed, up the bed of the stream.

At last, as we were nearing our destination, we halted for rest and refreshment, at a rice-field hut; and here there strolled in upon us one of the Punans themselves from the settlement; he had been out with his blow-pipe after small game. He made no attempt to conceal his speechless wonderment at white people, and silently gazed at us in open-eyed and open-mouthed astonishment. When our Sibop guide, whom we had brought from Tama Aping's, as an interpreter, asked him whether he had ever before seen white men, he replied, with awestruck earnestness, 'Never anything like them have I seen! Surely they must be the Fathers of all People!' Ever after he referred to us or addressed us as his 'fathers.'

Not long after resuming our march, our guide suddenly turned off from the river-bed into the open jungle, — that is, jungle in which there is but little undergrowth, except thorny palms and rattans. It is the ideal forest primeval, where old and majestic trees form in every direction vast, illimitable, solemn vistas. On a sudden, our guide asked us to halt and keep perfectly silent, while he went on ahead to give notice to the Punans that some peaceful, friendly visitors were approaching. Unless this notice were given, he declared that the people would scatter at the first sound of our approach, and we should find nothing but empty huts. When he returned, he guided us down a slight hill and over a stream, and through a dense hedge of tall plants of wild tapioca. We emerged into more open ground, and were all at once in the Punan village. The huts could be hardly distinguished from the surrounding grasses and palms, so low and fragile were they. The walls were merely boughs and twigs interlaced, and against them leaned broad palm leaves; the roofs were a loose thatch of leaves and boughs, but could not be more waterproof than the natural roof of leaves overhead. The 'village' comprised only four huts, and in not one of them could I stand upright.

Outside the huts, when we approached, there seemed to be only a few old women. Although our friendly intentions had been announced, the younger folks had hidden in the huts, so as to observe us from a safe distance through the chinks in the leafy walls. There were only two men in the village when we arrived; all the others were away hunting with blow-pipes, or after camphor, gutta-percha, rattans, or other products of the jungle, which from time to time they trade off with their more civilized neighbors, the Sibops and Berawans, for cloth, tobacco, salt, etc. Three old women, however, at once greeted us, and, coming up boldly, insisted on touching all of us, passing their hands over our arms and our backs, and talking volubly all the while in a plaintive and much injured tone of voice. It was quite depressing. I was sure that we had unconsciously wounded their tenderest and holiest feelings, and that they were reproaching us for wandering near their 'sacred bower' and molesting their 'ancient solitary reign;' but, before long, I was immensely relieved by finding that a tone of petulant but resigned remonstrance was the common and invariable intonation of each and all. Little by little all fear was dismissed, and we were soon surrounded by a merry, but sad-voiced, crowd of boys and girls, young women and old; even babies in arms,—I should say, babies in slings on their mothers' backs,—were pressed forward, not merely to look at us and to touch us, but to be touched by us. Gentle, simple-hearted creatures, they believed that merely to stroke us or to be stroked by us, brought them blessings; this then, we found, was the meaning of the feeble stroking and caressing touches that greeted us from the old women. Our interpreter told me, that what I had imagined were reproaches, was a continuous plaintive murmur of how good and kind it was of the wonderful white people to come so far just to see them and bring them blessings. They examined and admired everything we had with us or on us; our coats, our hats, our shoes, the buttons and button-holes on our clothes,—these excited their profound wonder.

A book of photographs, which I had taken during a former visit to the Baram, was looked at over and over again; they never wearied of it, and their clucks of admiration were constant while they explained to one another the meaning of the pictures. After they fully understood that these miraculous pictures had been made by my camera, they became absolutely without fear of having their pictures taken,—indeed, in their simple hearts, they had somehow come to believe that thereby bodily ailments would be cured. In the photograph of a group of women and children, on the opposite page, in the corner on the right, there sits a poor, unhappy mother, whose unfortunate little baby is so hopelessly and enormously hydrocephalic that it could never leave the basket which she holds in her lap. She begged me for medicine to cure it, but when I told her that there is none that would do it any good, she piteously begged to be allowed to sit in the front line, so that the little patient might derive the full benefit of the picture-making. Just beyond her stands another devoted mother, who, in order to bring the powerful curative effect of the camera to bear on the alleviation of the severe sufferings of her little boy, is holding her hand on the abdominal locality, where little children most frequently have pains. On her right, and again in the front row, are women afflicted with goitre, which they, too, hoped would be cured by the picture-making.

HUNTING FOR SMALL GAME WITH THE SUMPIT.

THESE MEN ARE NOT PUNANS, BUT LEPPU ANNANS OF THE TINJAR RIVER; THE MANNER OF HOLDING THE SUMPIT IS, HOWEVER, THE SAME IN ALL TRIBES. THE JOINT OF BAMBOO, HANGING AT THE BELT, IS THE QUIVER FOR POISONED DARTS; IT IS USUALLY LINED WITH FUR, TO PROTECT THE DELICATE POINTS OF THE DARTS. THE POISON SEEMS TO ACT VERY SLOWLY ON BIRDS; UNLESS THE WOUND FROM THE DART CRIPPLES THE FLIGHT OR ENTERS A VITAL PART, THE GAME ESCAPES THE HUNTER. FOR KILLING SMALL BIRDS, CLAY PELLETS ARE QUITE AS EFFECTIVE AS DARTS.

WOMEN AND CHILDREN OF THE PUNAN SETTLEMENT NEAR THE HEAD WATERS OF THE DAPOI.

BECAUSE THEY SAW IN THE PHOTOGRAPHS WHICH I SHOWED THEM ONLY HEALTHY-LOOKING PEOPLE, THEY BELIEVED THAT THEREFORE PICTURE-MAKING MUST BE A PANACEA FOR ALL AILMENTS.

The Punans are nomads, never building permanent houses, nor remaining long in one locality. Of all the tribes they are, perhaps, the most mild and gentle; they are not head-hunters, and care no more for a collection of human heads than for that of any other animal, and, therefore, never go on a raid. They know the country more thoroughly than any other natives, and are always sought by the Sibops, Kayans, Kenyahs, and Ibans as guides in expeditions after camphor, gutta-percha, and bees-wax. They live solely on the products of the jungle, esculent roots and plants, such as caladium, wild tapioca, a species of canna, the tender, uncurled fronds of ferns, and the heart of several species of palm.

The men are extremely skilful with the blow-pipe and in the construction of snares and traps. When they are not surfeited with small birds, they are completely happy with roast or boiled monkey, and as for the small Bornean porcupine,—it is a delicacy never to be rejected. For some reason, which I could never discover, they will not kill a python. Salt, tobacco, and rice are downright luxuries. They cultivate no fields, owing to their nomadic life; consequently, the Punan fathers and husbands and sons work hard to obtain from the jungle, far and near, those articles for which they themselves have no use, such as camphor, bees-wax, etc., which they can barter with Malay and Chinese traders. Most valuable of all these articles is rhinoceros horn; in fact, the killing of a single rhinoceros places the wealth of a Punan village almost 'beyond the dreams of avarice;' there is no scrap or portion of the animal that is not prized; the flesh is coveted food; the horn, nails, hair, skin, and even the contents of the stomach, are traded at the highest rate of exchange to the Chinese, who use them all for medicinal purposes.

It falls to the lot of the women to prepare the tapioca root for food, an operation which takes the place of the monotonous pounding and threshing of rice in other tribes.

These roots, which look much like sweet potatoes, are first scraped or grated on a piece of the stalk of a rough, scaly palm, and the coarse pulp is then washed and strained by stamping it through a mat while water is constantly poured over it; this washed and strained pulp is then collected in wooden troughs and allowed to settle. The sediment is a thick, white paste, which when boiled makes a very palatable farinaceous diet. The paste may be also dried and preserved for future use. The roots of the *Caladium esculentum* are either boiled like potatoes or mashed and made into a sort of gruel. We partook of all the toothsome dishes of the Punans except boiled fern-fronds and monkey; neither happened to be in the Punan larder at the time. I must candidly admit that to me the sight of the preparation of tapioca is not appetizing. In the first place, the hands which hold the tubers while they are being scraped are none too icy clean, they often dabble in the pulp just after they have been successfully busy in alleviating a neglected or troublesome coiffure. In the next place, the finely scraped pulp is taken to a stream and deposited in a mat which rests in a trough, or in a large wooden bowl, on a little platform over the stream. The operator then jumps into the mash and executes therein a lively dance, while, from time to time, a small boy dips up water from the stream and splashes it over the legs of the dancer, to wash down the particles that may have been spattered up, and also to moisten the mash. Strange to say, the paste, when strained, is of the most pure and dazzling whiteness.

To be sure, this operation is no worse than wine-making; but then we very seldom see the must foaming round 'the white feet of laughing girls;' whereas we cannot pass a day, where tapioca is the standing diet, without seeing our dinner mashed by girlish feet by no means white, — or clean.

SIBOP GIRLS IN THE HOUSE OF TAMA BALAN DENG GRATING TUBERS OF TAPIOCA.

THIS IS THE FIRST STAGE IN THE PREPARATION OF TAPIOCA; AFTER THE ROOTS HAVE BEEN FINELY GRATED BY RUBBING THEM ON PIECES OF ROUGH, SCALY PALM-STEM, THE MASH IS STRAINED THROUGH A CLOSELY WOVEN MAT.

PUNAN WOMEN STRAINING GRATED TAPIOCA ROOTS.

THE GRATED TAPIOCA IS THEN PLACED ON A MAT IN A WOODEN TROUGH, WHICH IS SUPPORTED ON A PLATFORM OVER A STREAM, AND BY EXECUTING ON THE PULP A LIVELY DANCE, THE FEET, NONE TOO IMMACULATE, OF THE WOMEN PRESS OUT THE FINE WHITE PASTE, WHICH IS WASHED THROUGH THE MAT BY CONSTANT ADDITIONS OF WATER DIPPED UP AND POURED INTO THE MASH BY A SMALL BOY WITH A LARGE PALM-LEAF LADLE. THE PASTE SINKS TO THE BOTTOM OF THE TROUGH AND THE WATER IS DRAINED OFF.

Our men built for us a temporary hut, which, in comparison with any of the Punan huts, was a palace; unfortunately, it had one serious defect; its location seemed to be over an extremely popular thoroughfare of stinging ants,—those veritable little devils. Just as we were about to turn in for the night, a broad procession of thousands of them, every single one with its vicious little tail turned defiantly up, began a diabolical march across our floor of bark. The natives, however, immediately built a small fire directly in their path, which at once caused, first, a stampede of the vanguard, and then all the rest turned tail, and, still in quadruple or sextuple file, retreated somewhat more rapidly than they had advanced, and, at last, all disappeared under the leaves on the ground outside. Next to land-leeches, they are the most pestiferous and noxious insects in the jungle. They do not wait to be attacked, but are instantly aggressive when a victim comes within their ken; and they know to a nicety where the skin is most sensitive. Their bite is quite as severe as the sting of a wasp or of a hornet.

The Punans are pure jungle-folk, and know very little about canoeing or swimming. When we asked to be taken to some place where we could bathe, we were led about a mile away to a delightful, deep, sandy-bottomed pool; but our guide thither could not be persuaded to enter the water, and warned us repeatedly to be careful, as the water was very deep, — it was hardly up to our waists. When we ducked under, a native bystander shouted in genuine terror that one of the 'white fathers' was drowned.

To test their skill in marksmanship with the blow-pipe, we fastened a potato about an inch and a half in diameter on a pole, and from a distance of fifty paces they stuck in it six darts out of ten. For small birds, they seldom use darts, which cost some trouble to make; little pellets of clay are equally effective; poisoned darts are reserved for monkeys and larger game. They assert that with a properly prepared dart they can kill even the formidable rhinoceros. For such large game, the point is weighted with a little triangular head of bamboo or of tin, which carries more poison, and becomes detached in the wound.

When we bade farewell, we gladdened every Punan heart by distributing all that remained of our gay cloth and good tobacco; the cloth was quite sufficient for every woman and child in the village to meet the tolerant demands of fashion in the way of apparel; and as for the tobacco, — I longed to know what prodigious stories they would rehearse, as they sat round their fires in the evening, of the marvellous appearance and mysterious actions of the 'White Fathers.' But my heart was woeful for that little mother as, day by day, she would discover that the 'picture-making' had brought no healing balm to her poor, hydrocephalic boy.

There is one product of the Punan country which I think deserves a note: it is that luxury so dear to the Chinese palate, the edible nests built by swallows, or swifts, in certain limestone caves. In the Niah hills, near the coast, these caves have been the breeding-places of these birds from time immemorial, and in supplying the market with their nests the Punans have been for many a year employed by Chinese traders, and the estimate is well within bounds that several hundred tons of nests have been there gathered by this tribe.

Within the caves of Mt. Subis,—one of the Niah hills,—there is a small settlement of Punans who, during the building season, collect nests. There are three harvests of nests, then the season closes, and the swallows are allowed to rebuild undisturbed and rear their brood.

When I visited the village of Niah and the caves in Mt. Subis, the season was closed, but it had been so very successful and had kept all the natives so busy that those, whose duty it was to attend to the rice crop, had neglected it; consequently, the people of Niah,—a mixed tribe of Malanaus and Punans,—were actually suffering from a rice famine; boats had been sent to neighbouring villages to purchase rice, but they had been away for thirty days or more, and almost every pound in the village had been consumed, except a goodly store in the secure granaries of a stingy, avaricious old head-man, Orang Kaya Perkassa by name, who demanded such an unconscionably exorbitant price for it that even to starving men it was almost prohibitory.

PUNAN WOMAN CARRYING HER BABY IN A SLING MADE OF RATTAN.

THIS MODE OF CARRYING CHILDREN ENABLES THE MOTHER TO HAVE BOTH HER HANDS FREE, AND THE SOMEWHAT CRAMPED POSITION OF THE CHILD KEEPS IT OUT OF MISCHIEF. ON THESE SLINGS ARE USUALLY HUNG SHELLS OF LAND SNAILS, CURIOUS KNOTS OF WOOD, MALFORMED BOAR TUSKS, OR SEVERAL LARGE BEADS, ALL OF WHICH ARE EXCEEDINGLY EFFECTIVE IN WARDING OFF THE EVIL SPIRITS, WHOSE OBJECT IT IS TO HARASS SMALL CHILDREN.

And thereby hangs a tale. A strange old fellow was this Orang Kaya Perkassa, tottering on the brink of the grave, and, possibly for this very reason, saturated with superstition. I took the opportunity, when he happened to pay me a visit, to beg him graciously to grant me the privilege of taking his picture. He refused point-blank and with unusual vehemence; but at last he so far relented that he professed his willingness to submit to the hazardous operation, if he might be allowed to return to his house and procure such charms as would safeguard his person and counteract the baleful effects of the picture-making. Of course, I readily acquiesced, and in a few minutes he reappeared with a ponderous bundle of infallible charms, (they may be seen in his photograph, girdling his waist,) which were oddly shaped pebbles, malformed boars' tusks, strange knots of wood, etc., (I was not permitted to see them, but from my knowledge of Bornean charms, I cannot be far astray.) As soon as the exposure was over, in an imperative tone he demanded a picture of myself, saying, 'Since the Tuan now has my picture, it is in his power to do all manner of harm to me, unless I have one of him to keep me safe.' Before I had time to tell him that I really had no picture of myself with me, several of the natives who had accompanied me on the trip besought me most urgently to refuse his request, insisting that should this wicked old man once get hold of my likeness he would work most powerful charms with it, and I should inevitably die within the month.

It appeared that Orang Kaya Perkassa had recently suffered, under his own roof, an extraordinary piece of ill-luck; a Malay had there run amuck, and, after slashing several of the inmates very severely with his parang, had fled to a hut on the river-bank, where he had been surrounded and finally speared to death. This, of course, involved no end of bad luck to the Orang Kaya's house; wherefore to exorcise the evil Spirits a great feast had been held, poles elaborately decorated with carved faces were erected to frighten away demons; and, finally, the blood of slaughtered pigs and chickens, together with pieces of their flesh, was sprinkled over both cooked and uncooked rice, which, combined with salt and native ginger, was enclosed in small packages, and solemnly placed in a miniature boat and set adrift on the river, to the end that it might bear out to sea all the ill-luck of the household, and waft it where it could do no one any harm.

After I had finished photographing the Orang Kaya in my own quarters, I left him busy talking to some of his friends, and, with my camera, strolled casually toward his house. After having taken a picture of the 'demon frighteners' erected near his dwelling, my attention was attracted to a collection, on his veranda, of uncouth, worm-eaten, water-worn, wooden idols, openly displayed on a shelf and draped with extremely dirty bits of coloured cloth. I had just finished photographing them, when the Orang Kaya himself suddenly hobbled up the notched log, and was at my elbow. He was exceedingly angry, I am sorry to say, at my boldness in taking a picture of them during his absence, and I did my very best to soothe him, and apologized humbly for my intrusion by urging my ignorance. I succeeded at last in appeasing him, and had just calmed him into a fairly peaceable frame of mind, when, unwittingly and most unluckily, I undid all that I had done, by innocently offering to buy one of the worm-eaten figures. Never shall I forget the violent, vehement, towering rage into which he fell, nor the flood of Malay which my proposal called forth. 'How dare Tuan ask such a thing?' he almost shrieked, his wrinkled and cross-wrinkled features working with rage. 'Shall I sell for money my gods of good fortune! Those are gods, *gods*, I tell you! they are not wood! they are my honored guests, my dearest friends! from the broad sea they came to me! and they will bring me blessings if their livers are not enraged by having a picture made of them. Never would I have suffered it had I been here; the people in the house should have stopped it! Surely, surely more misfortunes will now fall on me!'

He then stamped into his room and slammed the door. The evil my camera had done must be thwarted. Accordingly, from that sunset till dawn, and even into broad daylight, every gong, big and little, in the Orang Kaya's house was kept hot with beating. All through the weary vigils of that night we heard this incessant din. 'The good that's done we may compute, but not the ill prevented;' therefore, who can say what success attended this fervent zeal? That it was not successful, the Orang Kaya himself probably believed. For certain it is that he sickened and died within three or four weeks. His death was really due, I believe, to old age, hastened by an unbridled temper and a life of avarice, so strong that, as I have mentioned, he was willing his neighbors and even his own household should die of starvation if only he could add to his wealth.

His people, I learned afterward, attributed his death to my camera, but I rather imagine that by this time they have found out that my camera really brought them an unmixed blessing in disguise.

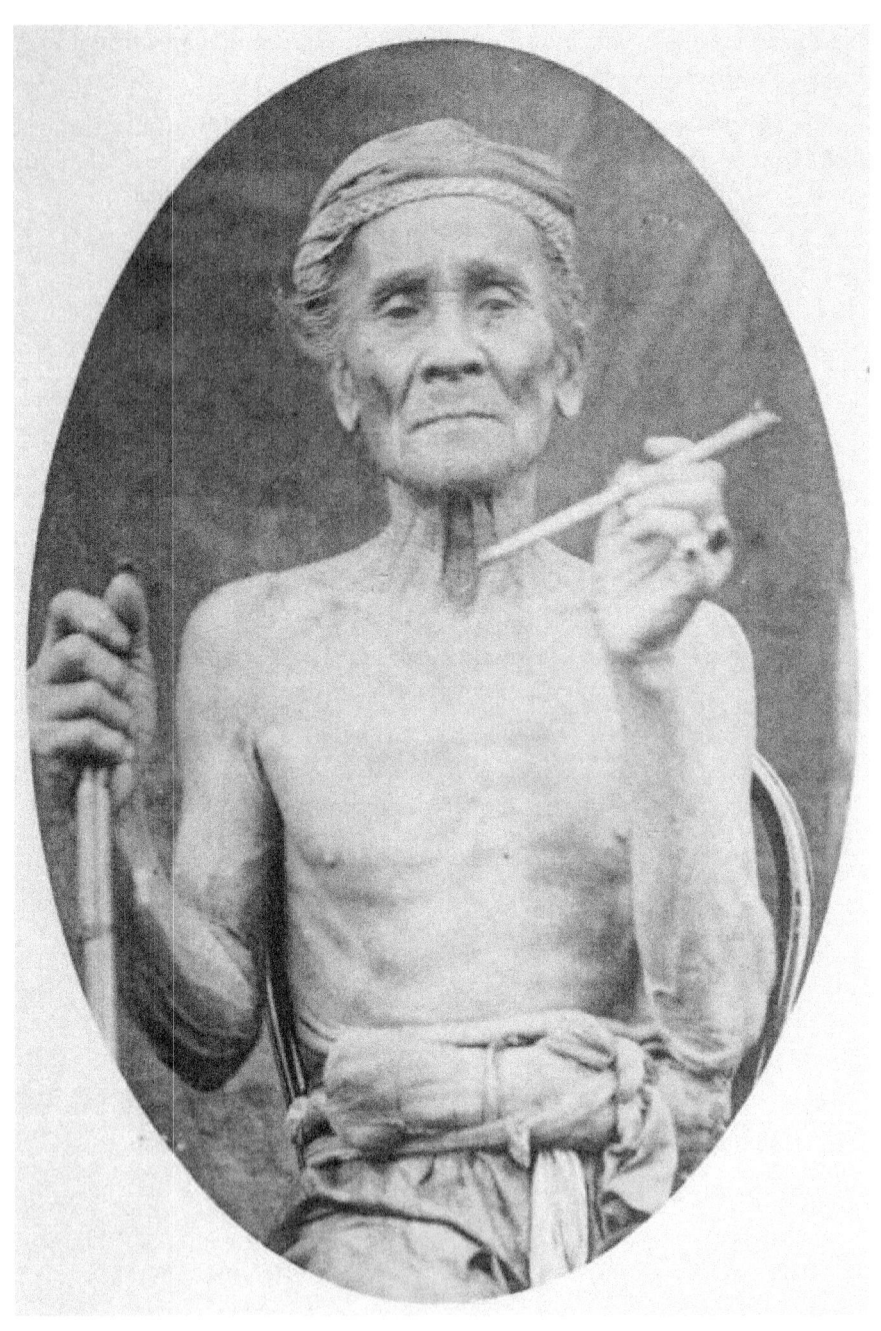

ORANG-KAYA PERKASSA, HEAD-MAN IN THE MALANAU
VILLAGE AT NIAH.

ROUND HIS WAIST IS TIED A BUNDLE OF HIGHLY POTENT CHARMS, WORN ESPECIALLY FOR THIS OCCASION, TO COUNTERACT THE EVIL EFFECTS OF HAVING HIS PHOTOGRAPH TAKEN. IN HIS LEFT HAND HE IS HOLDING A NATIVE-MADE CIGARETTE OF THE USUAL, GENEROUS SIZE. THE CHARMS WERE, HOWEVER, IMPOTENT; A MONTH AFTER THE PHOTOGRAPH WAS TAKEN HE DIED.

THE HOUSEHOLD GODS OF ORANG-KAYA PERKASSA.

THESE WATER-WORN, WOODEN IMAGES WERE WASHED UP ON THE BEACH AT THE MOUTH OF THE NIAH RIVER; THE ORANG-KAYA, PERCEIVING AT ONCE THAT THEY HAD COME, OF THEIR OWN FREE WILL, TO BRING HIM GOOD FORTUNE, ESTABLISHED THEM IN A PLACE OF HONOUR IN THE VERANDA OF HIS HOUSE, AND ADORNED THEM WITH SUITABLE RAIMENT.

THE FEATHERED WAR-COAT HANGING TO THE LEFT OF THE IMAGES WAS WORN BY THE ORANG-KAYA AT THE TIME OF THE FEAST, WITH ITS ATTENDANT SACRIFICE OF PIGS, WHICH WAS HELD TO COUNTERACT THE EVIL ENTAILED BY THE VIOLENT AND SUDDEN DEATH OF A MEMBER OF THE HOUSEHOLD WHO RAN AMUCK. THE BLOOD-SMEARED COAT IS HUNG NEAR THE GODS, TO ASSURE THEM THAT EVERY RITE HAD BEEN PERFORMED TO PRESERVE THEIR DIGNITY.

Mt. Subis is only about fifteen hundred feet high, and the entrance to the birds'-nest cave on the mountain side is some little distance from the base, and can be gained only by a very tortuous and narrow path round the ledges and projections of slippery limestone.

Not far from the main cave is a smaller one, known as the 'Traders' cave,' wherein is a village of twenty or thirty huts, for the accommodation of the Chinese traders who come to pay for the nests that have been collected. It is a village of houses without roofs; within the cave there is no fear of the sun smiting by day nor the moon by night, nor of rain from clouds; consequently, the houses are merely walls and floors, and pretty wobbly walls and floors in addition. The roof of the cave, frescoed with green mould and lichen, is fifty or sixty feet overhead, with irregular projections of limestone, but free from stalactites. No swallows build here, the cave is too light and shallow.

The Punans' cave, beyond, is of majestic size; just within the entrance the floor dips abruptly to a deep valley, and the roof curves upward in a vast dome; hence, from the level of the valley to the roof is at least six hundred feet. Insensate, indeed, must he be who is not filled with speechless awe as he turns from the brilliant sunshine and enters this illimitable abode of silence and of night. It seemed the veritable entrance to the Inferno; and as the light from the opening struck the massive projections here and there, and cast long, blacker shadows, it became a landscape in the moon, while the appalling, death-like stillness seemed to presage a frightful cataclysm in nature. Underfoot is a deep carpet,—fully three feet deep,—of what seemed tan-bark, but which proved to be a fine, dry, odorless guano, composed mostly of the wing-covers of insects, of a dark-brown color; the jagged sides and roof, and here and there boulders projecting through the covering of the floor, were covered with a deep-green mould or lichen, except where the white limestone gleamed out in patches and seemed almost phosphorescent. The extent beyond, in the utter darkness, seemed illimitable.

Our presence and the echoing of our voices soon startled the swallows, and forth they emerged, in myriads on myriads, from the darkness, and circled round us and above us, and about the mouth of the cave like swarming bees; the whirr of their wings and their twittering sounded like waves on a pebbly beach.

On a flat ledge at one side, near the entrance, was a line of fifteen or twenty of the platform dwellings of the Punans, even more fragile and tumble-down than the huts in the 'Traders' cave.' At the time of our visit, the huts were deserted, giving an air of even greater desolation.

The nests are obtained by lashing long, stout poles, end to end, and then supporting them with guy-ropes of rattan until they reach to the very top of the cave. Up these poles the agile Punans climb hand over hand and foot over foot, walking up them like monkeys; when at the top, they scrape down the nests within reach, by means of a long pole bearing a hoe-like blade, and with a home-made wax candle fastened to it to show where the nests are. An assistant below gathers the nests as they fall. There are two varieties of nest, the black and the white; the latter sell for two thousand Mexican dollars a picul, (one hundred and twenty-three pounds,) the black nests bring only a hundred dollars for the same weight. Unfortunately, the Niah caves are 'black nest' caves; but the nests are so very abundant that the export revenue tax assessed on them by the Sarawak Government amounts to thousands of dollars in a year.

The Punans, however, are not the owners of the poles in the caves, but, on account of their skill in climbing, are hired by a Malay or Chinaman, who pays so much a season to the Government for all the nests gathered in an area prescribed by the length of the detaching-pole. The Punans do not use the nests as food, and have learned their value and the best times and methods of harvesting them only since Chinese and Malay traders have come to Niah. The caves, however, have been inhabited by the Punans for very many years. We found tobacco growing wild not far from the mouth, and we were told that it is to be found in considerable quantities all about this locality. The Punans know it well and gather it, but maintain that it is none of their planting, and that it has been known to them and used by them as long as they can remember.

THE BIRDS'-NEST CAVES AT NIAH.

THE LINES INTERSECTING THE PHOTOGRAPH DIAGONALLY FROM RIGHT TO LEFT ARE GUY ROPES OF RATTAN, SUPPORTING THE POLES WHEREON THE COLLECTORS CLIMB TO REACH THE NESTS. THE PHOTOGRAPH WAS TAKEN FROM THE CREST OF AN ELEVATION, ABOUT FIFTY YARDS WITHIN THE MOUTH OF THE CAVE, WHENCE A VIEW COULD BE OBTAINED ACROSS A DEEP VALLEY TO THE SUMMIT OF ANOTHER HILL. THE GROUND WITHIN THE CAVE WAS COVERED WITH A FINE, DRY GUANO, ABOUT THREE FEET IN DEPTH AND OF A DARK-BROWN COLOUR, APPARENTLY COMPOSED MAINLY OF THE REMAINS OF BEETLES.

PUNAN HUTS WITHIN THE BIRDS'-NEST CAVES.

WITH THE ROOF OF THE CAVE OVERHEAD, THERE IS NO NEED OF ROOFS TO THE HOUSES; CONSEQUENTLY, THIS IS A VILLAGE OF HOUSES WITHOUT HOUSE-TOPS.

As to the relationship of the Punans to the other tribes of the interior, Aban Deng, of the clan of Long Wats, (who in turn are closely allied to the Kayans, Kenyahs, and Sibops,) gave us the following account:—'An old Chief living far in the interior highlands of Borneo, left, at his death, two sons, one of whom was energetic and laboured in the rice-clearings, while the other was incorrigibly lazy. With such different temperaments, the affairs of their common household soon became much disordered, and they agreed to separate, each one choosing the families that were to follow them, and thereafter all were to live as they pleased. The lazy brother and his adherents, who preferred hunting and roaming, betook themselves to the jungle, never built houses nor cultivated rice; their descendants are the Punans of to-day. The industrious brother, named Plian, and his adherents cleared the hills of jungle, planted rice, and built strong houses; from them are descended the Sibops and Long Wats. The Punans, after many years of wandering, determined to begin the cultivation of rice; two of their Chiefs collected them in a fertile valley near the base of "Bukit Bulan," or the Mountain of the Moon, that high mountain in the centre of Kalamantan, (Borneo,) and they all set to work clearing off the jungle, while the Chiefs stood in a group and gave directions on all sides. The Punans, utterly unversed, however, in the cultivation of land, set fire in many places at once to the jungle when it was felled, and their leaders, thus surrounded by a circle of fire, perished in the flames. Dispirited and discouraged at the loss of their leaders, they once more scattered, and have ever since wandered in small bands throughout the jungle, depending on their blow-pipe, and snares, and the fruits of the forest, for their sustenance.'

When a Punan of the common class dies, his body is stretched out simply in a little hut of boughs and leaves, with no further burial. The corpse of a head-man or of one of his family is, on the other hand, wrapped in a coarse mat or a sheet of bark-cloth, and, doubled up in a squatting position, is forced into one of the baskets they use for carrying loads on their backs. It is then placed on a platform of poles, and over it a flimsy shelter of leaves.

PUNANS CAMPED FOR THE NIGHT.

A LARGE, FLAT BUTTRESS ROOT OF A TAPANG TREE FORMS THE BACKGROUND ON THE RIGHT. THE STICKS CUT INTO CURLED SHAVINGS ARE THE CHARMS INVARIABLY PUT UP TO WARD OFF EVIL SPIRITS. THE HEAD-MAN OF THE PARTY IS HONOURED WITH THE PROTECTION OF A ROOF OF PALM LEAVES, BUT HIS FOLLOWERS SLEEP EITHER ON THE GROUND

OR ON PALM-LEAF MATS, WITH NO OTHER COVERING THAN THE 'CLOISTERED BOUGHS' OVERHEAD.

Were the choice of a residence in a Bornean tribe forced on me, I should not hesitate long in casting my lot with the Punans. They have never a thought of the morrow; no cares; no responsibilities; no possessions; no enemies, for they desire nothing that other people have, not even clothes; money is dross; and home is where they rest their blow-pipes and hang up their parangs. Night can never find them homeless; home is wherever the setting sun finds them; does rain threaten, a few poles and a few leaves make a house; let the night be clear, and a soft bed of leaves in a nook between the great flat roots of a Tapang tree is luxury itself; for 'where youth with unstuffed brain [never was a Punan brain 'stuffed'] doth couch his limbs, there golden sleep doth reign.'

And, finally, in the happy land of the Punan there is no dressing and undressing morning and evening.

Tuba-Fishing

There are two varieties of Tuba[15] known to the natives, and used by them to poison fish in streams; these two varieties are called by them 'Tuba Berábut,'—a shrub, and 'Tuba Ja Jaran,'—a creeper; Tuba Berábut is more generally used, and is known to Botany as *Derris elliptica*. The poison is extracted from the bark of the creeper, and from the tubers and roots of the shrub. It seems to kill the fish by suffocation, and does not injure them for food; and as they do not die at once, but rise to the surface of the water, and dart hither and thither to evade the poison, there is not a little sport in spearing them or scooping them up in nets; at any rate, a Tuba-fishing is made a great occasion by all the tribes, and furnishes almost as fruitful a topic of conversation as a war expedition. To none of the tribes is the sport more attractive than to the Kenyahs, who live in the mountainous districts of the interior of the island.

The streams usually selected for this form of fishing, are the tributaries of the larger rivers,—mountain streams as clear and cool as crystal, flowing over pebbly beds. High over-arching trees, draped and festooned with ferns, orchids, and vines, ward off the heat of the sun and tone down its glare to that emerald, translucent green of damp, dense tropical forests. The swish and tinkle of the water as it rushes over the rapids above and below the deep pools which the fish frequent, and the musical calls of the Wawa monkeys, alone break the stillness, until the arrival of the merry, happy party of fishers from a Kenyah long-house. The women are bedecked in their finery of gay

---

[15] Allow me to call attention to the fact, whereof the significance I am hardly competent to judge, that in the Mohammedan Paradise 'the most remarkable tree is called Tûba, or the tree of happiness,' which among its manifold blessings, 'will supply the blessed with food.' Sale's *Koran. Preliminary Discourse*, p. 68, ed. London, 1857.

head-gear and bright bead-work necklaces. The young, unmarried damsels prove to be the life of the party, and are endlessly chaffing their lovers; the sidelong glances from beneath palm-leaf hats are as arch and coquettish as any ever cast from behind a spangled fan. Fun and innocent frolic rule supreme as the canoes race and jostle with each other round sharp turns where the stream runs swift, or over the turbulent rapids. The women catch the excitement of the fierce, desperate paddling; they stand up to the work, their jet-black hair streams over their shoulders, their tawny bodies sway with the boat as they dash from their paddles the 'tender, curving lines of creamy spray.' The men shout in triumph or laugh in defeat; and even the old crones cackle and urge on the youths to the sport. The scene is idyllic; there is nothing to revolt, everything to charm. Careless, untamed life amid a tropical jungle is to be seen at its very fairest on one of these Tuba-fishings among the Kenyahs.

The best time for the sport is during the dry season, when the rivers are low and the stones, left bare on the wide banks of the river, supply material for the dams, where the fish may be 'rounded up.' A dam is built of loose stones, either straight across the river, or else in a wedge-shape with the point up-stream, thus forcing the fish close to the bank on each side, where the chase is to end. When it has been built about eighteen inches high, a platform of rattans, with little fences at the sides, is placed in the centre of the dam or wherever the fish will be apt to congregate. The up-river end of this platform rests on the bottom of the stream, and the down-river end is about on a level with the surface of the water. In their mad endeavour to escape the suffocating poison, the fish make futile attempts to leap the dam, but by the force of the stream and their own exertions they land on the platform, where an active watcher deals death to them with a stick.

SCENE ON A LEVEL STRETCH OF RIVER IN THE CENTRAL-HIGHLANDS.

The day before the expedition, all who wish to have a share in the fish must contribute a due proportion of Tuba root, which is gathered in the jungle and scorched over a fire to make it more virulent. After the Tuba has been gathered and the day appointed for the fishing, then so much as even to breathe the name of Tuba is forbidden; if reference must be made to it, then it is to be called 'pakat Abong;' Abong is a strong-smelling root something like Tuba, and pakat means *to agree upon*; thus, 'pakat Abong' means *what we have agreed to call Abong*. This concealment of the truth deceives all the bats, birds, and insects, which are always keen to report to the fish all the sayings and doings of men, and, as Tuba has not been mentioned, no warning can be given. On one occasion, after a Tuba-fishing had been planned for the morrow, one of our party noticed a man with a bundle of roots, which he recognised as Tuba, and, following the usual Bornean custom of asking a question when at loss for a subject of conversation, inquired what was in the bundle. The reply was 'pakat Abong.' 'Indeed,' said the questioner, 'I thought it looked like Tuba.' At this mention of the fatal word, woe-begone looks passed round and every countenance fell, whereupon the Chief explained: 'We Kenyahs call that root Abong when we wish to use its white juice, and those animals which live in the water [avoiding the word *fish*] we call "Daun" [*leaves*] which float down stream; did we not do so, when we want to stupefy them with this juice, those good-for-nothing, prying beetles called "Balli sunggong," or some other friends of the *leaves* such as the bats, or some kind of bird, would instantly carry the news of our intentions, and then where would be the use of all of our preparations? The *leaves* would quickly disperse, and we should have to return from our pleasant excursion empty-handed and hungry. They might even invoke their powerful charm-working *leaf*,—the bony Balira,—to call down heavy rains and make the streams rushing torrents, and then good-bye to all our sport. But calling things by their wrong names, we fool these *leaves that float down stream*, and have a good day's sport out of them.'

The 'Balira,' a fish full of bones and worthless as food, is supposed to be the Dayong of the fish. The legend runs that the fishes, aware that there was none among them who would devote himself to working charms, determined to elect a Dayong. No fish could be found to accept the office until, finally, the Balira offered his services on condition that every fish should give him one of his bones. They all agreed, with the result that now the Balira is choke full of bones, and a very skilful worker of charms to counteract the plans of mankind.

The boats assemble about a quarter of a mile above where the dam has been built in the river. On the bank, logs are placed, whereon the Tuba roots are pounded to a pulp, which is then swashed round and squeezed out in some of the smaller canoes, which have been half filled with water. The men pound, keeping time with their blows; and again and again the pulp is washed in the canoes until every drop of the sticky, white juice has been extracted. Then whitish clay or lime is mixed with the poison, to make it sink and spread through the water. Sometimes as much as two or three hundred weight of roots are pounded up for one fishing, the amount, of course, depending on the size of the stream. But before any poison is cast in, a certain quantity must be set aside for the Spirits. One of the party, therefore, goes a little further up the stream to some insignificant pool which has been left on the pebbly bank, (wherein—alas! for poor human nature,—any one could see with half an eye that there was no fish,) and, pouring in the Tuba juice, he calls out:—'O Spirits of the Rocks! of the Wood! of the Smooth, Flat Stones! of the Karangans! of the Earth! and of the Leaves! here in this pool is your share of the numberless fish! Spoil not our sport by any interference!'

After this generous sacrifice has been made to the superior Powers, all the boats assemble round the canoes containing the poison, which are then suddenly tipped over, and the milk-white paste sinks to the bottom and contaminates all the water. One man in a small canoe goes in advance of all the rest, and the first fish that rises to the surface is caught in a scoop-net and thrown out on the bank; at the same instant the man again shouts to the Spirits that this fish is for them, and that they ought not grudge the small share that will probably fall to the lot of the party. This pious duty having been performed, the fun at once grows fast and furious. With shouts and splashes and jeers and laughter, all the canoes plunge into the chase after the fish which rise to the surface. As every where under the cope of heaven, here, too, the funny man is on hand, and laughs uproariously at his own fun after he has excitedly given false directions as to where the largest fish are coming up, and mocking those who miss their game; boats get entangled, but an occasional upset creates no ill feeling; the occupants are soon back in their places, and engrossed with spearing and scooping up the fish. The very old and the very young are stationed on the bank to catch the small fish or to drive the larger ones from their hiding-places under the overhanging roots and branches.

FLAT PALM-LEAF HAT WORN BY WOMEN.

THE CENTRAL ORNAMENT IS COMPOSED OF YELLOW AND BLACK BEADS. THE SMALL, WHITE DECORATIONS, IN GROUPS OF THREE, ARE PORCELAIN SHIRT-BUTTONS, THE FIRST EVIDENCE OF THE ADVANCEMENT OF CIVILIZATION, INTRODUCED BY 'TRADE'S UNFEELING TRAIN' AS SUBSTITUTES FOR COWRIE SHELLS.

So the whole party slowly drift down-stream, heaping their boats with the stupefied game until they reach the dam, where the man stationed on the rattan platform, or 'Bering,' has had a busy time of it, too; not only has he had to see to it that no fish escape, but he has also to keep a very keen look-out for his own safety; many of the fish have sharp, poisonous spines, which, if he be not careful, make ugly and excruciatingly painful wounds in his feet.

When all the fish possible have been caught, the party disembark, and fires are lit beneath green-wood platforms whereon the fish are spread after having been split and salted for future use. The plumpest and largest are always cooked and eaten on the spot by the keen-set fishermen, who revel, even to gorging, in the dainty change from their monotonous daily fare of boiled rice and dried salted fish.

With canoes, and hampers, and bodies filled, as the low descending sun sends shafts of amber light down the long reaches of the river, the fishers again embark, and lazily dip their paddles in the glowing water as the current drifts them on their homeward way. The red-letter day is over, but the joy of it remains for ever in the laughing gossip round the evening hearth.

A KENYAH GRAVE.

Index

- Aban, — the prefix to a name, 27, 68
- Aban Avit, 68
- Aban Avit's veranda, 70, 72, 84
- Aban Jau's house, 145
- Aban Liah, 150
- Aban Liah's final illness, 168
- Abun, the Chief at Long Lama, 87
- Admiration denoted by clucks, 132
- Adorn, 37
- Affection among the Borneans, 176
- Amau, — Omen birds and mammals, 206
- Ambuscade, a Bornean, 108
- Amok at Tama Aping Buling's, 170
- Apoi, 37
- Appreciation of photographs, 161
- Appreciation of foreign songs, 37
- Arrack, drinking of, at naming ceremony, 55
- Attainment of paradise, 79
- Attempt to deceive the Omen birds, 39

- Bállo, — the prefix to a name, 27
- Bamboo, burning a strip of, to determine the giving of a name, 54
- Bamboo, ceremonial use of ashes of, 54, 55
- Bamboo drinking-cups, 139, 140
- Bananas, salt, and ginger root given at a Naming, 46, 55
- Batu, 98
- Beads, Lukut sekála, 153
- Beads, imitation of valuable, 153
- Belief in future life, 78
- Benefits from skulls hung in veranda, 74

- Berawans,—Disposal of the dead, 174
- 'Bintang sikópa', 78
- Bird's-nest caves, 234, 238
- Blackening the teeth, 200
- Blari, 37
- Blood, indifference to sight of, 78
- Blood of a fowl, inspection of, 63
- Blow-pipes, the making of, 146
- Blow-pipes among the Punans, 232
- Borrowing a head, 113
- Breaking a taboo, 148
- Bulan, daughter of Tama Bulan, 40
- Bulun matai, Fields of the Dead, 76
- Burial in jars, 174
- Burial of a Chief, 175
- Burial custom in the Naga Hills of Assam, 180
- Burial of Punans, 242

- Calling the name to revive a dying person, 63
- Camphor collecting, 217
- Camphor collecting, pre-empting a river, 148
- Camphor language, 217
- Camphor, reluctance to mention, 24
- Cases for war-coats, 14
- Casting off the taboos of mourning, 118
- Caves, bird's nest, 234
- Ceremonial fire, 49
- Ceremonies at the naming of a Chief's son, 23
- Ceremonies on the return from a war expedition, 116
- Changing name after sickness, 23
- Chanting of returning warriors, 117
- Charm to divert evil Spirits at the Lelak house, 130
- Charms for abundant crops, 211
- Charms worked with portraits of a person, 237
- Children initiated as warriors, 118
- Cigarette-making, 41
- Clucking to denote admiration, 132
- Communication between Omen birds and man, 209
- Conjunctivitis, 37
- Conveying thanks to Omen birds, 101
- Cord of life,—Tebuku urip,—Naming Ceremony, 45
- Corpse, presents to a, 213

- Costume of Berawan women while mourning, 174
- Costume of Kayans and Kenyahs, 30
- Council Negri, 29
- Council of war, 94
- Crops, charms for abundant, 211
- Cupping to relieve headache, 62
- Curled shavings on sticks, 217
- Cursing a house, 171

- Daily routine of household, 19
- Dancing performed by women of the Lelak household, 132
- Dayong, the, in case of illness, 19
- Dayong's attempt to recall a departing soul, 63
- Dead bodies not carried through usual doorways, 65
- Dead father's name not mentioned, 24
- Death posts, 85
- Decorated house posts, 87
- Decorating grave of dead Chief, 121
- Deer may not be cooked in the house, 91
- Deng, 37
- Depilation of eyebrows and eyelashes, 203
- Designs tattooed on the legs and arms of Kayan and Kenyah women, 247
- Determining a name by burning a loop of bamboo, 54
- Disposal of the dead, — Berawans, 174
- Dogs, 14
- Dreams, auspicious and prohibitory, to perforating the ears, 198
- Drinking arrack at a Naming, 55
- Drinking-cups, bamboo, 139, 140
- Drinking a toast, 137
- Dulit, Mount, 180

- Ear-lobes, elongated, 194
- Ear ornaments, 196
- Ears, perforation of, 198
- Early training of a Head-hunter, 67
- Eating of the flesh of deer, 213
- 'Eat slowly', 103
- Edible bird's-nests, 234, 241
- Education in indifference to sight of blood, 78
- Eternal life in the jungle, 81

- Etiquette in regard to weapons, 69
- Etiquette in entering a house, 166
- Evening chat with Aban Avit, 72
- Evil omens in pig's liver at Aban Liah's feast, 157
- Evil omen in pig's liver at Tama Aping Buling's, 168
- Evil Spirits exorcised by fire, 39
- Evil Spirits exorcised at the Naming ceremony, 44, 52
- Evil Spirits exorcised by spitting, 39
- Evil Spirits exorcised when a dog touches a rice-mortar, 212
- Evil Spirits warded off by gong-beating, 45
- Eyelashes and eyebrows depilated, 203
- Exhortation to the sacrificial pig at Aban Liah's, 156
- Exorcism of Evil Spirits, 39, 44, 52

- Facsimile of valuable beads, 153
- Family rooms (*Lamin*), 15
- Fat pork feast at Naming ceremony, 57
- Fear of making life-like images or pictures, 69
- Feast at Tama Aping Buling's, 169
- Feast after return of war party, 123
- Feast, injunction at beginning of, 59
- Feasting of a war party, 103
- Female tattooers, 192
- Fields of the dead, 76
- Fine for violating a permantong, 19
- Fire, a means of communicating with Omen birds, 9, 101
- Fire, ceremonial, 48
- Fire-drill, 48
- Fireplaces, 9
- Fire-saw, 48
- Fish not spoken of before a Tuba fishing, 24, 247
- Flattening heads, 203
- Food, 17
- Food of Punans, 228
- Freeing women from mourning restrictions, 119
- Future life, Belief in a, 78

- Game of tag in the water, 22
- Gathering edible bird's-nests, 241
- Gau, 37
- Ghost's clutch, 67

- Ginger root, salt, and bananas given at Naming ceremony, 46, 55
- Gong-beating to counteract effects of photography, 238
- Gong-beating to ward off evil Spirits, 45
- Government's pig at the feast at Tama Aping Buling's, 167
- Grave, decoration of a Chief's, 121
- Greeting, absence of signs of, 177
- Grippe in Borneo, 35
- Grippe at Tama Bulan's, 62
- Guest chambers in Lelak house, 133

- Handling of skulls, 82
- Harvest festival, 211
- Hawk-men, — *Laki Niho*, 206
- Head, borrowing a, 113
- Head-flattening, 203
- Head-hunter, early training of a, 67
- Head-hunters, mark of successful, 185
- Head-hunting, Origin of, 74
- Head-hunting, punishment for, 87
- Horn-bill, Image of, hung with cigarettes, 42
- Hose, Dr. Charles, invitation to people of Batang Kayan, 141
- House-building, 6, 7, 9
- House-building, sacrifice, 7
- House-posts, decorated, 69
- Humble attitude of women, 220
- Husking rice, 12

- Iban ear ornaments, 198
- Iban tattooing, 247
- Ill luck consigned to miniature boat, 237
- Images, fear of making life-like, 69
- Image of horn-bill hung with cigarettes, 42
- Images made to work evil as they decay, 119
- Importance of a name, 27
- Indemnity, — *Usut*, 146, 209
- Indifference to sight of blood, 78
- Inflammation of the eyes, 37
- Influence of skulls hung in the veranda, 82
- Initiation of children as warriors, 118
- Injunction at beginning of feast, 59
- Ink for tattooing, 194

- Inspection of pig's liver at Aban Liah's feast, 156
- Inspection of spattering of blood from a fowl, 63
- Instruction in the art of defence, 95
- Invocation of the sacred pig at a Naming, 53
- Invocation to the Spirits before a Tuba fishing, 250
- Iron given for infringement of permantong, 209
- Isit, the Omen-bird, 217

- Jamma, 143
- Jamma's curse on Tama Aping Buling's house, 171
- Jamma's feigned death, 170
- Jawa, 150, 166
- Jawa, Violation of rules of, 165
- Jawa, or peace-making, 127
- Joke, a Bornean, 164
- Journey to Tama Bulan's, 34
- Juman, 86
- Jungle, the, 81

- Kaluri, kaludi, or kaleeri (musical instrument), 11
- Kaluri among Naga tribes, 11
- Kayan songs, 104
- Kayan war dances, 132
- Kayans and Kenyahs, 30
- Kayans and Kenyahs, Costume of, 30
- Kenyah lunar calendar, 42
- Kayu urip, — *Tree of life*, 45
- Killing of Tinggi the murderer, 86
- Kilup breaks the rules of Jawa, 165
- Kissing, the Bornean custom, 21
- Kromong, a musical instrument, 143
- Kükenthal, Dr. Willy, 136

- Lack of affection, 176
- Laid Jok Orang, 137
- Laki La, 66
- Laki Niho, — *Hawk-men*, 206
- Laki Oi, Kayan Prometheus, 48
- Laki Pesong, — the Fire-saw, 48
- Lali, or permantong, 206
- Lali of the pregnant rice, 211
- Lali imposed on unnamed child, 44

- Lali of mourning removed, 121
- Lamin, or family rooms, 15
- Language of camphor collectors, 217
- Laram—meaning cool—idiomatic use of, 52
- Legend about origin of head-hunting, 74
- Lelak clan or tribe, 130
- Lelak, guest chamber, 133
- Leppu Anans, a small clan or tribe, 160
- Leput,—*blow-pipes*—Manufacture of, 146
- Leron clan, Jawa ceremonies, 153
- Lijow, Tama Bulan's son, 55
- Lishun, 37
- Love tokens before a war expedition, 95
- Lueng's death at Tama Bulan's, 62
- Lukut Sekála, valuable beads, 153
- Lunar calendar, 42

- Ma Obat, 109
- Madong, 98
- Manin,—meaning warm—idiomatic use of, 52
- Manufacture of Sumpits or blow-pipes, 148
- Mark of successful Head-hunter, 185
- Marksmanship with the blow-pipe, 232
- Maternal advice before a war expedition, 98
- Meals, 17
- Medicine, Rhinoceros used as, 231
- Method of burial among the Berawans, 174
- Method of tattooing, 192
- Methods of resuscitating a fainting woman, 62
- Miniature boat to carry away ill-luck, 237
- Moon, Phases of, 42
- Mosquitoes, 32
- Mourning for a dead Chief, 174
- Mourning, restrictions of, removed, 118
- Mourning, restrictions of, removed from women, 119
- Mount Dulit, 180
- Musa—the Fire-saw, 48
- Music of the kalui, 13
- Music of the kromong, 145
- Mutilation of the ears, 196

- Naga Hills, burial customs in, 180

- Nalika,—the Fire-drill, 48
- Name, determination of, 54
- Name of dead father not mentioned, 24
- Name, Reluctance in telling, 23
- Name, Importance of, 27
- Names of tattoo designs, 185
- Names, Paraphrases of, 27
- Names of relatives not mentioned, 24
- Naming ceremonies, 23
- Naming ceremonies, fat pork feast, 57
- Naming ceremonies, exhortation of sacred pig, 53
- Naming a Kenyah child, 44
- New Fire, 48
- Niah village and bird's-nest caves, 234
- Night before a war expedition, 44
- Nicknames of very young children, 94
- Nipa palms, 32

- Oaths on a tiger's tooth, 169
- Object of a hunt not mentioned, 24
- Objection to having idols photographed, 238
- Observation of Omens before clearing of the jungle, 209
- Occupations of the Punans, 228
- Omen animals, 206
- Omen birds and mammals—amau, 206
- Omen birds, attempts to deceive, 39
- Omen birds, communication between man and the, 209
- Omen birds conveying thanks to, 9, 101
- Omen bird,—Isit, 217
- Omens in pig's liver, 56
- Omens in pig's liver at Aban Liah's feast, 157
- Omens in pig's liver at Tama Aping Buling's feast, 168
- Omen birds of house-building, 9
- Operation of wet-cupping, 62
- Orang Kaya Perkassa, 234
- Oratory, 94, 158
- Ordeal of a feast of raw pork, 57
- Origin of head-hunting, 74
- Origin of Punans, Legend, 242
- Ornaments worn in the ears, 196
- Ornamentation of the teeth, 200

- 'Pakat Abong', 247
- Paradise, attainment of, 79
- Parangs, taken off on entering a veranda, 69
- Paraphrases of names, 27
- Peace-making, or Jawa, 127
- Perforation of the ears, 196
- Permantong or Lali, 206
- Permantong before house-building, 9
- Permantong, breaking of a, 148
- Permantong during sickness, 19
- Permantong during camphor collecting, 217
- Permantong, fine for violation of, 19
- Permantong of a room, 19
- Permantong in a Kayan house, 213
- Permantong, infringement of, 209
- Personal embellishment, 183
- Pestles used in husking rice, 13
- Phases of the moon, 42
- Photographing the Punans, 227
- Photographing idols, objection to, 238
- Photography, evil effects of, 45
- Photography, superstitions in regard to, 237
- Pictures of animals always conventionalised, 69
- Pig's liver, Omens consulted in, 56
- Pipes, tobacco, 220
- Planting the corner-post of a house, 7
- Platforms on the veranda, 12
- Plugs of brass in the teeth, 200
- Portrait of a woman taken by Dr. Kükenthal, 136
- Posts recording head-hunts, 6, 85
- Pre-empting a river for camphor collecting, 148
- Prefixes of names, Meaning of, 68
- Preliminary to speech-making, 158
- Preparation for war expedition, 94
- Presents to guests at Naming ceremony, 68
- Presents to a corpse, 213
- Presents sent to tribes on Batang Kayan River, 141
- Primitive customs revived in all ceremonies, 116
- Pronouncing a name for the first time at a Naming, 55
- Propitiation of Spirits before tattooing, 192
- Propriety in broaching a subject for discussion, 94
- Punans, 218

- Punans,—burial customs, 242
- Punans' bill of fare, 228
- Punans' fear of water, 232
- Punans' method of preparing tapioca, 231
- Punans, relationship to Long Wats, 242
- Punans, story of their origin, 242
- Punans, Village of, 226
- Punans, Village of, in bird's-nest caves, 245
- Punishment for head-hunting, 90
- Purification after unlucky journey, 39
- 'Put,'—a blow-pipe, Manufacture of, 146

- Rack on which parangs are hung, 69
- Raw pork feast, 57
- Reasons for obtaining heads, 82
- Recalling the soul of a dying person, 63, 64
- Relationship of Punans to Long Wats, 242
- Religion of the Borneans, Negative, 81
- Reluctance to mention the name of the object of a search, 24
- Retaliation for the killing of Tinggi, 90
- Return of a war expedition, 116
- Return to earth of Spirits of the dead, 175
- Rhinoceros used as medicine, 231
- Rice husking, 13
- Rice mortars, 13
- Rice mortars protected during the Permantong Padi, 212
- Rivers pre-empted for camphor collecting, 148
- River scenery, 32
- Rivers tabooed, sign of, 217
- Rules of Tama Bulan's house, 29
- Running amuck, 170

- Sacrifice of slave girl—house-building, 7
- Sacrifice of slave girl at burial of a Chief, 175
- Sacrifice of slave for education of boys, 78
- Sacrifice of pig on arrival of a Peace party, 162
- Salt, ginger root, and bananas given at a Naming, 46, 55
- Second day's ceremony of Naming, 48
- Serious consequences to us on account of Lueng's death, 65
- Shaving the hair after mourning, 118
- Shavings, curled, on sticks, 217
- Shy Punan maiden, 224

- Sign of permantong of a river, 217
- Sign of permantong in case of sickness, 19
- Singing among the Kayans, 104
- Skulls, the handling of, 82
- Skulls, influence of, hung in veranda, 82
- Skulls in Aban Avit's veranda, 72
- Slaves, sacrifice of, 78, 175
- Sleeping-closets, 16
- Smearing face and body with soot as sign of mourning, 174
- 'Snappang,' the name for a gun, 86
- Soap, 21
- Songs, appreciation of foreign, 37
- Speech-making, 94
- Speech-making at Aban Liah's, 158
- Spitting to banish evil Spirits, 39
- Spitting on the hair cut off after mourning, 119
- Sprinkling with water at a Naming, 52
- Start of a war party, 100
- Sticks cut into curled shavings, 217
- Stinging ants, 232
- Stretching the lobes of the ears, 194
- Substitution of names, 26, 27, 68, 247
- Summit of Mount Dulit, 180
- Sumpits, — *blow-pipes* — Manufacture of, 146
- Superstition with regard to photography, 237

- Table manners, 17
- Taboo or permantong, 206
- Taboo, the breaking of, 148
- Tag in the water, Game of, 22
- 'Tama', 27
- Tama Aping Buling's house, 162
- Tama Balan Deng's house, 171
- Tama Bulan, 27, 30
- Tama Bulan's son, 41
- Tama Bulan's farewell to the Peace party, 141
- Tama Liri's house, 134
- Tama Talun, 37
- Tapioca, Method of preparation, 231
- Tattoo designs, names of, 185
- Tattooers, female, 192
- Tattooing, propitiation of spirits before, 192

- Tattooing of Kayan men, 183
- Tattooing of Kayan and Kenyah women, 186
- Tattooing needle and ink, 194
- 'Tebok bulu,' — *bamboo cup*, 139
- 'Tebuku Tali' (note), 45
- 'Tebuku urip,' — *cord of life*, 45
- Teeth, Ornamentation of, 200
- Terluat, 37
- Tiger skin regarded with awe, 169
- Tiger skin used in uttering a curse, 171
- Tiger's tooth, oath sworn on, 169
- 'Tigga' — charms for the crops, 211
- Timidity of Punans, 226
- Tina — a prefix to a name, 27
- Tinggi, a murderer, 86
- Toasts, the Bornean custom of giving, 136
- Tobacco growing wild, 242
- Tobacco pipes, 220
- 'Toh Lali', 209
- Tokong, the father of head-hunting, 74
- Tone of voice of Punans, 227
- Tree of life, — Kaya Urip — Naming ceremony, 45
- Tuba berábut, and Tuba ja jaran, 247
- Tuba-fishing, 247
- Tuba-fishing, fish not mentioned before, 24, 247
- Tuba-fishing, invocation of spirits, 250

- Unfavourable sign in pig's liver at Aban Liah's feast, 157
- Unnamed children, 27, 44
- Unselfish love not a trait of the Borneans, 176
- 'Usut,' The rite of giving, 146, 209

- Valuable beads, — Lukut Sekála, 153
- Verandas of Kayan and Kenyah houses, 9
- Violation of the rules of 'Jawa', 165

- Wailing for the dead, 65, 174
- War-coats, cases for, 14
- War dances, 132
- War expedition, 85
- War expedition, ceremonies on return of, 116
- War expedition, preparation for, 94

- War party, the feasting of a, 103
- Water, use of, in Naming ceremony, 52
- Wawa monkey sacred to some families, 68
- Weapons, etiquette in regard to, 69
- Wet cupping, 62
- Why the Balira is a bony fish, 249
- Wild tobacco, 242
- Wit of Borneans, 164
- Women dressing as men, 211
- Women, humble attitude of, 220
- Wooden discs as ear-ornaments, 196
- Words of invitation to a feast, 103

THE END

Printed in Great Britain
by Amazon